Remittance as Belonging

Remittance as Belonging

· ·

Global Migration, Transnationalism, and the Quest for Home

HASAN MAHMUD

Rutgers University Press

New Brunswick, Camden, and Newark, New Jersey

London and Oxford

Rutgers University Press is a department of Rutgers, The State University of New Jersey, one of the leading public research universities in the nation. By publishing worldwide, it furthers the University's mission of dedication to excellence in teaching, scholarship, research, and clinical care.

Library of Congress Cataloging-in-Publication Data

Names: Mahmud, Hasan, author.
Title: Remittance as belonging : global migration, transnationalism, and
    the quest for home / Hasan Mahmud.
Description: New Brunswick, New Jersey : Rutgers University Press, [2025] |
    Includes bibliographical references and index.
Identifiers: LCCN 2024003469 | ISBN 9781978840409 (paperback) |
    ISBN 9781978840416 (cloth) | ISBN 9781978840423 (epub) | ISBN 9781978840430 (pdf)
Subjects: LCSH: Emigration and immigration—Economic aspects. | Emigrant
    remittances—Social aspects. | Immigrants—Economic conditions. | Immigrants—
    Social conditions. | Transnationalism. | Belonging (Social psychology)
Classification: LCC JV6217 .M34 2025 | DDC 305.9/06912—dc23/eng/20240329
LC record available at https://lccn.loc.gov/2024003469

A British Cataloging-in-Publication record for this book is available from the British Library.

References to internet websites (URLs) were accurate at the time of writing. Neither the author nor Rutgers University Press is responsible for URLs that may have expired or changed since the manuscript was prepared.

∞ The paper used in this publication meets the requirements of the American National Standard for Information Sciences—Permanence of Paper for Printed Library Materials, ANSI Z39.48-1992.

rutgersuniversitypress.org

For my mother, Azizunnahar, who brought me to this world,
my wife, Sumiya Fatima Mahmud, who stood by me throughout this
project, and our daughter, Afreen Fatima Mahmud, who inspires me to
look forward.

Contents

Contents

Remittance as Belonging

Introduction

●●●●●●●●●●●●●●●●●●●●●●●

The Migrant, the Family,
and Money

On a Saturday evening in July 2013, I saw Rahman[1] smoking a cigarette in front of *Deshi*[2] in "Little Bangladesh"[3] in Los Angeles. He had an unpleasant look on his face, which was unusual for him. Usually, at this time of day, Rahman would finish his nine-hour shift at a downtown hotel and return to Deshi for dinner and *adda* (casual chat)[4] with his friends. While his tiredness would show on his face and in his movements, it was always clear that he was happy to have completed work for the day and come back home to Deshi. Like many Bangladeshi immigrants engaged in low-paying, blue-collar and service sector jobs, Rahman found respite at Deshi from his grueling daily schedule. Smoking a cigarette outside the door after an early dinner with desi food and friends would be his happiest moment in the day. He would spend a couple of hours chatting, watching Bangla TV programs on a large flat-screen TV hanging on the restaurant wall, and reading Bangla newspapers, which were casually spread on the tables, before crashing on his meager bedding in the room he shared with three roommates.

For over a year, I had observed his routine and so his unusual manner caught my attention. At my prodding, he told me:

> My mother has asked for $400 in addition to what I regularly send her every month. She wants to buy a gold necklace as a wedding present for my sister's daughter. This is because she gave an expensive wedding gift to my elder brother's daughter a few months ago. I don't like this. I think I don't have the

1

same responsibility as an uncle for my sister's daughter as I have for my brother's daughter [referring to the patriarchal and patrilocal family customs that create gendered conceptions of rights and privileges]. But my mother wants to be equally generous to both of her granddaughters. This is putting an extra burden on me.

I nodded my head to show sympathy with his annoyance and understanding of the cultural rationale. Rahman then took me to an empty corner of the parking lot nearby where we sat under a small tree for about an hour while he opened his heart to me. He shared stories about how much money he sent home on various occasions, money that in many cases he would not have sent without feeling pressured by his mother and other close relatives. He explained that he wanted to save money to support his mother and siblings once they arrived in the United States as immigrants with his sponsorship,[5] but that his family in Bangladesh kept asking for more and more money. Rahman explained that they had the common misconception of vast affluence throughout the United States where, they believed, people earned huge salaries and "spent money like it is water."[6] His failure to make them understand his difficulties as an immigrant was painful for him but, ironically, he was also partially responsible as he had never disabused them of their misconceptions. Rahman had never told them about his grueling work for a very modest salary, the cramped living conditions in the dilapidated room he shared with friends, his frustration with a lack of job advancement, and so forth. As we talked, he used the logic of not having told them about his actual American lifestyle as a means to justify their naivety and then forgive their constant requests for more money. He hoped they would be equally understanding of him after they migrated to the United States. So, our adda started with Rahman's annoyance with his family and ended with his compassion for them and hope for their reciprocity.

A year later, I was sitting with Mian in a coffee bar outside Shinjuku West Gate, a bustling place in Tokyo. I first met Mian in 2008 while I was working toward my master's degree at Sophia University in Tokyo. By this time, he had completed his studies in a *nihon gakko* (Japanese language school) and a *senmon gakko* (vocational school) and subsequently started work at a Japanese electronics factory. Hearing that I had returned to Tokyo, he invited me to a popular Indian restaurant to celebrate his getting a job.

I noticed Mian was more confident now than he had been as a hesitant and doubtful Bangladeshi student who had been uncertain about his future and exhausted from working multiple part-time jobs in addition to his studies. Having a professional job in a Japanese factory allowed him to convert his student visa to a professional visa and might even lead to permanent residence in Japan.[7] Moreover, it gave him a steady income and much needed free time after his regular work hours. So, Mian was cheerful during our visit. He told me that he had moved out of his cousin's apartment to a studio apartment of his own near the factory where he worked. He also talked about his plan to buy a car, which surprised me: I had not heard of a single Bangladeshi man buying a car in Tokyo. Mian also told me he planned to get married and had begun renovating his house in Dhaka to make it more habitable, with more space, appliances, and a new look: "I send more than a half of my monthly salary to my father in Bangladesh every month. Besides, I have borrowed a large sum of money to reconstruct our old house. As the only son, I will inherit it and will need to renovate it someday. I am sending money to my father to refurbish it now so that he and my mother can live in it in comfort and feel happy about having a modern house."

Mian's parents lived in a single-story brick house on the outskirts of Dhaka, which his father had built with his retirement fund. Now it was Mian's turn to renovate and expand the house. The timing was particularly important because of his plan to get married. As he elaborated, a person living abroad for several years should have a new house with modern appliances in Bangladesh to corroborate his success.[8] Mian also told me that his father was paying installments on a plush apartment for him in a prestigious housing project in Dhaka. And since Bangladeshi parents tend to take pride in their children's success, Mian anticipated that his expenditure on renovating their old house and amassing wealth in Bangladesh would make his parents happy. His sense of having accomplished something worthwhile was evident in his behavior. We spent about two hours at the coffee shop, during which time I mostly listened to Mian's stories about his future plans and the hardships he had faced completing his education and getting a job. When we were about to leave, Mian asked me to meet him frequently on weekends while I stayed in Tokyo. Such an invitation stressed his upward mobility into the professional class: he no longer had to work weekends like most of his compatriots in Tokyo. I gladly accepted his invitation.

This book tells the stories of migrants' lived experiences to examine why they send remittances. Popular theories in academia and public discourse offer simplistic explanations for remittance that focus on migrants' attempts to either maximize their own self-interest or sacrifice their own interest for the welfare of their immediate family and relatives. However, the opening vignettes show that remittance is far more complex and involves relationships between the migrant and the remittance recipient in culturally specific ways. Like Rahman and Mian, the migrants I met in Tokyo and Los Angeles shared their stories of remittance that involve their own personal economic interests as well as their concerns for the well-being of their families, relatives, and sometimes even neighbors. While remittance is obviously an economic transaction, it does not happen in a marketplace between strangers like more common economic transactions. Instead, remittance occurs primarily among family in the most intimate and loving relationships, with great emotional and social consequences. This book attends to these socioeconomic and relational dimensions of migrant remittance and offers a novel understanding of remittance patterns and practices in terms of migrants' social belonging.

Research Background

This book is based on my ethnographic fieldwork among Bangladeshi migrants in Japan and the United States. Since 2002, Bangladesh has been one of the top ten recipient countries of migrant remittance, a practice with which I am personally familiar. According to the Bangladesh Bank,[9] the total amount of remittance Bangladesh received in 2022–23[10] was $21.61 billion, making it the second-largest source of foreign currency earnings after the ready-made garments industry. The largest portion of remittance to Bangladesh comes from the earnings of temporary workers in Gulf countries in the Middle East (51 percent), followed by those in Southeast Asia. In 2022–23, the highest amount of remittance was $3.765 billion (17.4 percent of the total) from the Kingdom of Saudi Arabia, followed by $3.03 billion (14.03 percent of the total) from the United Arab Emirates (UAE), and $1.33 billion (7.09 percent of the total) from Kuwait. Another source of remittance is the Bangladeshi diaspora in developed countries, including the United Kingdom, the United States, Australia, and Italy. In 2022–23, Bangladesh received $3.52 billion (16.29 percent of the total) from the United States, $2.08 billion (9.62 percent of the total) from the United Kingdom, and $1.185 billion (5.48 percent) from Italy. Other destinations include Qatar ($1.45 billion, or 6.72 percent), Malaysia ($1.125 billion, or 5.20 percent), Oman, Bahrain, Libya, Singapore, Greece, and South Korea.

Most Bangladeshi migrants are male workers who go abroad for short periods and return after their employment contract ends. Being a Muslim-majority country, Bangladesh has restrictions on migration by women.[11] As a consequence, only about 150,000 women left Bangladesh as temporary migrant workers from 1991 to 2010. Recently, Bangladesh has reformed its migration policy to encourage women's migration, resulting in a sixfold increase in the number of women migrant workers from 19,094 in 2007 to 121,925 in 2017.[12] Another flow of Bangladeshi migration are single males who are young, educated, middle-class, and from urban areas. This wave originated in the wake of the first phase of the Gulf War and increased during the last two decades to countries in Southern Europe, namely Italy, Spain, Portugal, Greece, and Cyprus.[13] Finally, a few thousand Bangladeshi students go abroad every year for higher education, many of whom take employment and settle in their destination after graduation. According to UNESCO, 33,139 Bangladeshis enrolled in universities abroad in 2016. Australia, the United Kingdom, the United States, Japan, and Cyprus are the top five destinations for Bangladeshi students. The U.S. Embassy in Bangladesh reported that a total of 13,563 Bangladeshi students went to the United States for higher education in 2022–2023 academic year.[14]

My study involved a year of ethnographic fieldwork in Tokyo, including two months in the summer of 2012 and ten months from October 2013 to July 2014. In addition to participating in community events and daily interactions with migrants, I conducted 42 unstructured and in-depth interviews and a questionnaire with a purposive sample of 120 Bangladeshi male migrants: while nearly all (except a few married to Japanese women) were single in Japan, some were already married with a wife in Bangladesh; about a fourth of my informants were highly educated and professionals, some of whom had their wife and children with them in Japan. Thus, my interviewees included professional migrants, temporary migrant workers who entered Japan as language students, and long-term migrants who were visa overstayers and later acquired legal status by marrying Japanese women. In a megacity of over thirteen million people, Bangladeshis were nearly invisible due to their very small number. Yet, they had a distinguishable presence in the small pockets of immigrants in Tokyo. Bangladeshis owned a good number of *halal* shops[15] in Shin-Okubo (Korea Town), Ikebukuro, Akihabara, Akabane, and few other areas with notable migrant populations. They were also visible in the mosques in Tokyo and other areas. To find potential interviewees, I frequented these places and utilized my networks of friends and acquaintances made during my prior stay as a student in Tokyo. I also used the snowball sampling method to recruit interviewees.

My study in Los Angeles involved two years of ethnographic fieldwork between 2011 and 2013 and a follow-up visit of three months in the summer of 2016. I conducted 45 in-depth interviews with first-generation male immigrants and a used a questionnaire with 200 migrants that had similar questions to those on the Tokyo questionnaire. My fieldwork centered in the Bangladeshi neighborhood known as Little Bangladesh near Downtown Los Angeles. I identified research participants at various locations in the community, including four ethnic stores and two mosques, as well as made contact with people at community gatherings and social occasions like the Bangladesh Day Parade and the Bangla New Year celebration. I directly contacted my informants in addition to using referrals from friends and community leaders. I recruited interviewees from all possible subgroups of immigrants, including professionals and casual workers, single people and those with families, the documented and undocumented, recently migrated and long-term residents, and those living in the ethnic neighborhood and those living outside it.

In this study, I look at the relational and emotional aspects of remittance from a male perspective. In a notably exceptional study among older male and female Bangladeshi migrants in the United Kingdom, Gardner[16] explores the embodied events in migration that involve a range of emotional experiences, including the pain of separation, regret, disappointment, a strong sense of grief, and pride, excitement, contentment, and acceptance. Most other studies on similar relational and emotional issues such as feelings of belonging, displacement, and dislocation focus mainly on female migrants as caregivers or transnational mothers.[17] The studies on remittance from a gendered perspective present the female migrant as affective and emotional toward family and relatives, and male migrants as enacting the hegemonic gender role of breadwinner. But scholars increasingly recognize the need for emphasizing the dynamics of hegemonic masculinity.[18] As Pande[19] observes, Bangladeshi migrants often go beyond performing the role of breadwinner by reasserting "normative expectations about masculinity as the ability to aspire towards a better life and take risks." My focus on the male migrant perspective offers important insight into how their sense of self and belonging shape and are shaped by their remittance, thereby contributing to the emergent literature on the emotional and relational dimensions of migrant transnationalism.

This book explores Bangladeshi migrant remittance practices in terms of migrants' sense of belonging to their origin families and communities as well as demonstrates how the context of reception in the destination country shapes their social belonging and has consequences for their remittance. To this end, I found participants who represent all types of Bangladeshi migrants, including temporary and long-term, target-earners and settlers, working-class and professional, single migrants and those with families, and those who are part of new or older migration flows. I found that Bangladeshi migration to Japan and to the United States embodies most, if not all, of these traits. Bangladeshis in Japan were predominantly young, single, male migrants intent to earn as much as possible and send remittances home.[20] Except for a few hundred Bangladeshis entering Japan for higher education with government scholarships, most migrated to Japan with the help of their families in Bangladesh who were likewise motivated by higher income opportunities. They represent the classic economic migrants sent abroad by their families for a short period to earn and send money home. According to Japan's Ministry of Justice, in 2016, there were 12,374 Bangladeshi nationals among the total population of registered foreigners in Japan. Like most temporary migrations in which the destination state plays a decisive role,[21] Bangladeshi migration is heavily regulated by Japan,[22] which strictly limits opportunities to permanent settlement. This, coupled with other forms of social marginalization, encourages them to leave Japan and return to Bangladesh[23] or re-migrate to another country.[24] As a consequence, these migrants maintained close connections with their families and relatives in Bangladesh and strengthened those ties through frequent contact and remittance.

By contrast, Bangladeshi migrants in the United States often settle permanently, with subsequent chain migration of immediate relatives and their families.[25] These migrants constitute the second-largest Bangladeshi diaspora, which is also the fastest-growing Bangladeshi expatriate population in the world, and Los Angeles (LA) is one of the major destinations. In 2014, during my fieldwork, the Bangladeshi Consul General in LA estimated that the total number of Bangladeshis was somewhere between 20,000 and 30,000 (80,000 in California),[26] where they have established Little Bangladesh, an ethnic community within the Koreatown neighborhood. The first Bangladeshi business, a restaurant and ethnic store, was established in Koreatown in 1993. By 2020, there were eight Bangladeshi restaurants and ethnic stores, two afterschool prep centers, and three video and mobile phone stores in Little Bangladesh, and about 200 liquor stores and gas stations owned by Bangladeshis in greater Los Angeles.

Whereas Bangladeshi migrants in Tokyo see their stay in Japan as temporary and their return home to Bangladesh inevitable, those in LA perceive of the United States as their ultimate home for permanent settlement. This contrast is evident in the development and growth of the Bangladeshi community in LA and the gradual decline of its counterpart in Tokyo. Beginning with a few hundred Bangladeshis in LA in the late 1980s, the community had grown to over 50,000 by 2020. By contrast, the number of Bangladeshis in Japan dwindled from over 50,000[27] in the early 1990s to about 12,000 by 2016. Migration scholars have long recognized Japan's overall resistance to accepting foreigners in large numbers and allowing them permanent settlement, whereas the United States defines itself as a country of immigration. This difference in the destination states' orientation toward immigrants has affected Bangladeshi migrants in several ways.

First, Bangladeshi migration to Japan depends heavily on co-ethnic networks, leading to chain migration from a few areas in Bangladesh, whereas Bangladeshis in the United States come from across Bangladesh and are often the first persons in their families and neighborhoods to migrate. Second, most Bangladeshis enter Japan as tourists and overstay their visas or enter under the pretext of being college students and then engage in income-earning activities illegally.[28] By contrast, nearly all U.S. Bangladeshis either enter the country as permanent residents legally eligible to work full time or enter with the actual intent to study and then find employment after graduating from universities.[29] The liminal legality would push most Bangladeshis in Tokyo to the bottom of the labor market in unskilled and part-time jobs, whereas the legal status of those in LA would enable them to find both unskilled and professional work. Third, nearly all Bangladeshis migrate to Japan alone, regardless of their marital status, and return to Bangladesh to raise families, whereas their counterparts in LA bring their families and settle in the United States permanently.

I observe that the overall remittance patterns among Bangladeshi migrants in Japan remain high for the duration of their stay, while remittance among those in LA takes a U-shaped curve, with a general decline in the amount and frequency of remittance over time but then, for some migrants, an increase later in life. Given these two migrant groups' shared cultural background, the differences in remittance patterns between those in Japan and the United States are likely the result of variations in their experiences in the destination countries and their transnational engagements with family. Since migrants define their remittance as money they send home, I ask: How do these migrants perceive their home in Bangladesh while living abroad? Do they want to make their home in the destination country? If so, what resources and constraints do they find along the way? Ultimately, how does their success and failure in establishing a home in their destination shape their remittance practices? As I describe in this book, the resources and constraints my respondents find in these two national contexts affect their perception of self and social belonging, which, in turn, are reflected in their remittance.

Remittance as Belonging

Remittance is the money migrants send home from abroad. This book explores remittance in terms of migrant "belonging"—their sense of connectedness to a home from which they construct their identities.[30] Unlike popular images of the lone traveler, migrants move abroad as essential members of families and communities and maintain their sense of belonging within those social structures through transnational practices including remittance. The strength (or weakness) of this bond is reflected in the wide variation in remittance practices, which are influenced by the temporal dimensions of their migration (temporary/permanent),[31] government policies in the destination countries (open/restrictive),[32] the nature of families and households (patriarchal/matriarchal, extended/nuclear, joint/single parents, etc.),[33] overall normative structures in their society (traditional-collectivistic/modern-individualistic),[34] and the nature of migration itself (voluntary/forced).[35]

Remittance necessarily involves spatial separation across borders when migrants go abroad and leave their families behind. Yet, as I show in this book, migrants who bring their families with them to the destination country, thereby dissolving the spatial distance, still send remittances to their origin communities, especially if they do not feel "at home" in their new destination.[36] Likewise, migrants may settle abroad with their families and other relatives, thus creating a sense of belonging in their new destination that can lead to declining remittances.[37] However, they may resume sending remittances if their family and social relationships in the new home disaggregate to the point they no longer feel at home and recognize a need to reconnect with their roots in their origin communities.[38] Remittance behavior is not always linear or determined by spatial relations because, as I will show, spatial separation does not generate remittance in the absence of social relationships. In fact, relational distance inhibits remittance behavior. This book presents a detailed account of and a new approach to the emergence, growth, decay, and revival of remittance practices, which are largely determined by changes in migrants' sense of belonging to home.

By looking at attachment to the family—and by extension the origin community—this book takes us beyond the commonly touted rationality and sociocultural factors to understand migrants' perceptions of self and social belonging. Based on ethnographic fieldwork and interviews with Bangladeshi migrants in Tokyo and Los Angeles, it explores migrant perspectives on and recognition of how their sense of belonging is expressed in remittance. I offer an interpretive analytical framework that combines migrant agency and the social structures that constrain practices like remittance to advance ideas about effectively dealing with the long-standing problem of structure–agency dualism in social analysis.

More than a decade ago, I would visit money transferring agents in Tokyo to send money home to my parents and would meet other Bangladeshi migrants doing the same. The year I went to Japan with the Japanese government's scholarship for higher education, my father retired with a family to provide for and my two younger siblings still in school. I would have a few hundred dollars left from my monthly stipend, some of which I would send to support my father. I would also occasionally send small amounts of money to buy gifts for relatives and friends and, at times, send money to a few charitable causes. When I moved to Los Angeles, I continued to send small amounts of remittance home. I never thought about why I was sending remittances, I just knew that financially supporting the family was the normal thing to do. Much like in Tokyo, I would meet other migrants sending remittances and learned about their experiences earning and sending money, which confirmed my conviction that sending remittances was the right thing to do. However, as I began studying remittance in my sociology graduate program, I noticed that the many stories I heard from migrants, as well as my own experiences, did not fit with the scholarship. Academic literature about remittance prioritizes the migrant's economic considerations by defining remittance as motivated by either self-interest or altruism. As the dominant New Economics of Labor Migration (NELM) perspective[39] stipulates, migrant remittance is self-interested and the migrant sends money to purchase and maintain assets for themself, to expand social networks that are potentially useful to them once they return home, or to secure their place in the family. At the same time, this perspective defines migrant remittance as altruistic when migrants send money to spend on family needs, signifying that the migrant is sacrificing their personal interests. Thus, scholars adopting the NELM perspective ask: Do migrants send remittances to maximize their own personal economic gains or do migrants send remittances to alleviate the economic hardships of their families and relatives? Dyadic questions like these inevitably conceal the nuance of migrants' lived experiences with unintended and, at times, unpleasant consequences for understanding both migrants and their families.

For instance, the vignette at the beginning of this section reveals Rahman's deep understanding of his relationship to his family in Bangladesh and his own perception of his responsibilities to them. Since he does not gain materially from his generosity and sacrifice, his remittance appears motivated by altruism and characterized by love and compassion, embodied in the intimate relationship between a mother and son. However, this obscures the physical and emotional struggles Rahman experiences earning a living and managing his relationship with his family, on one hand, and the social pressures that confine him to sending remittances against his will, on the other. In contrast, the second story reveals Mian's sense of accomplishment and desire for social recognition for his successful migration and demonstration of his material wealth via an important social event like marriage. The personal and economic gains accomplished through his remittance clearly show Mian's self-interest. However, this overlooks Mian's altruism, which enables his parents to feel a sense of pride in their successful son and newly built house. Solely highlighting an individual's internal motivations as constrained to pursuing either self-interest or altruism fails to accurately describe the experiences of remittance. This approach also fails to analytically distinguish between self-interest and altruism.[40] At the core of this problem lies the challenge of incorporating contradictory motivations for both altruism and self-interest as determinants of migrant remittance, as is evident in the cases of Rahman and Mian. In fact, scholars have demonstrated that an ontological assumption that migrants are essentially rational (i.e., self-interested) fails to capture altruism in its true sense and renders all motives as forms of self-interest.[41]

The opening vignettes, as well as my own experience, illustrate that migrants primarily send remittances to their family and relatives, which is also supported by empirical studies from around the world. Therefore, I examine migrant remittance in the context of family instead of the context of an abstract marketplace where migrants presumably interact as rational individuals. We find that migrants engage in remittance as fathers, mothers, sons, daughters, brothers, sisters, uncles, aunts, grandparents, grandchildren, and so forth.[42] Recognizing the specific responsibilities and obligations associated with migrants' social and familial roles is key to understanding the personal and economic motivations of their remittance. In fact, first and foremost, migrants are concerned with understanding what is expected of them by family and society regarding remittance rather than with maximizing their self-interest. Performing this social expectation well and according to once's role in the family and society motivates migrant remittance. This is also because, as many scholars observe, migrants often judge each other by whether and how much money they send home as a measure of being "good sons"[43] and "good daughters."[44] I found similar judgements among my interlocuters in both Japan and the United States whereby migrants would take pride in how well they supported their family and relatives financially. Many informants were hesitant to talk about remittance that they sent to their personal savings accounts, and it took considerable effort on my part to hear from them about disagreement and conflict between them and their families over their remittance. That is, migrant stories about remittance demonstrate that they are well aware of—if not entirely guided by—the social expectations associated with their roles in the family and community in addition to their own economic considerations. This suggests that migrants do not act as rational individuals (i.e., *homo economicus*) in their remittance practices but make decisions within a social context characterized by a moral economy.[45] Here I adopt Thompson's[46] conception of moral economy to understand how customary and sociocultural factors define the boundaries of legitimate economic behavior, contrary to the idea of economic rationality guiding individual behaviors in terms of self-interest.

I posit that migrants act as members of social groups that belong to a home and are constrained by a shared set of norms and values enacted through existing social institutions. The migrants engage in acts of remitting within these cultural constraints and social relations that shape their behaviors. As such, the reasons for sending remittances cannot be fully understood by examining the intentions of the remitters perceived as rational individuals motivated solely by their economic interests. Hence, this book situates migrants' personal stories about their remittance within these sociocultural contexts and explores a moral economy between migrants and remittance recipients—in particular, family and relatives.

Conceptualizing Migrant Remittance

The limitations in the dominant NELM perspective are well established in the literature, which demonstrates that migrants neither act as rational economic beings nor are motivated by mere self-interest or altruism. Scholars have increasingly moved beyond economic approaches toward ethnographic studies to identify a range of motives for sending remittances: as a coping strategy to manage their integration into two (or more) settings,[47] deliverance of care for elderly relatives in origin families,[48] construction of gendered identities as filial daughters,[49] a means to escape social death by fostering familial belonging and sustaining social status,[50] a way to realize upward social mobility in their origin communities,[51] a way to maintain membership in the home community by contributing to social welfare in their countries of origin,[52] and so forth. Similarly, I recognize factors beyond economic interest that motivate migrant remittance by highlighting how belonging corresponds with remittance. Capturing the lived experiences of migrants and the nuances of their interactions with remittance recipients, my approach prioritizes sociocultural factors (e.g., norms, values, class, citizenship, interactions within and between ethnic groups) wherein a moral economy prevails over individual agency. For instance, Paerregaard observes how Peruvian migrants emphasize the well-being of their immediate family and relatives and view their remittance as a means to ensure it, which Paerregaard defines as a moral objective as opposed to a rational/economic objective.[53]

The turn to sociocultural motivations, however, overlooks an important part of the migrant experience, as the opening stories show. Rahman, in the first story, would be viewed as a good son by providing financial support to his mother and relatives. But this conceals Rahman's negative experience conforming to the norm of giving and his valid explanation about why the norm did not apply to the specific request for remittance. It also demonstrates how migrants like Rahman do not act as cultural dupes and mechanically conform to culture. Instead, migrants actively interpret the norms and values guiding their relationships with recipients of their remittance. This observation raises important empirical questions: If migrants do not uncritically comply with culture, what factors influence them to either follow a norm or not? What do migrants' lived responses to remittance norms tell us about their sense of self and their relationship with remittance recipients? By engaging such questions, this book explores migrant agency, which has received inadequate attention in academic and public discourses about the practice of remittance.[54]

It is important to note that agency is central to the dominant economic approach[55] to remittance, which defines agency in terms of the biological needs and tensions of the single human body and the rational economic behavior of the "head of the household"—implicitly assumed to be a man—that receives remittances.[56] Two shortcomings arise: first, this approach conceptualizes individuals as mere biological creatures constrained by biological motives alone; and second, it ignores the implications of social factors like gender and class in household organization.[57] Social-cultural approaches, by contrast, conceive of the migrant and the remittance recipients as embedded in social and cultural contexts characterized by class, gender, nationality, age, and various other sociocultural factors that influence how individuals acts. Yet, the social-cultural approach also minimizes and, at times, overlooks migrant agency, as Rahman's story illustrates. Both economic and sociocultural approaches to remittance begin with opposing ontological assumptions about the individual migrant as either rationally or socio-culturally oriented. However, as I point out above, migrants are neither characteristically utility-maximizing individuals looking for personal material gain, nor are they cultural dupes who mechanically follow social norms. Rather, they engage in day-to-day practices with their own perspective shaped by their position in specific social-cultural contexts, including family systems.[58] I recognize two common elements in the economic and sociocultural approaches: both assume that migrants and remittance recipients encounter each other as separate entities in their remitting practices and that there are preexisting connections between the migrants and their families. What I observed in the field contradicts the first assumption. As I will show, migrants remain intimately connected with their immediate families and relatives despite vast geographical distance, suggesting that migrants do not see themselves as separate from their recipients. That is, migrants' relational closeness to the family supplants their physical separation, further supporting the idea that physical separation is counterbalanced by continuous relational bonding. In fact, migrants demonstrate profound concern for the well-being of their families and relatives while simultaneously attending to the consequences of their actions for themselves and others they care about, as we saw in the opening stories.

This book presents migrants' perspectives about their remittance and explores their sense of self, belonging to home, and what they accomplish through remittance. I offer an empirical case of migrant agency by demonstrating how individual migrants make remittance decisions within the limits of their sociocultural contexts, such as legal status, their position in the job market, and the presence of co-ethnic networks and community. I adopt a structure/agency framework for understanding remittance, which involves modeling social actions in relation to their social structures, such as practice theory (Bourdieu, 1998), structuration (Giddens, 1984), and morphogenetics (Archer, 1995). This approach takes routinized practices as the locus and social structures as the outcome of collective practices. Within this broad framework, I adopt Lacroix's conception of migrants as "actors torn between different social status"[59] to highlight the situated dimensions of actor agency. I incorporate the centrality of migrant families characterizing both the NELM and sociocultural approaches. However, my approach goes beyond the NELM perspective in recognizing the continuous relation between migrants and their families instead of arbitrarily assuming separation. Additionally, my approach overcomes the problem of idealizing (i.e., assuming as natural, or given) family relations across borders by subjecting intra-family relations and other transnational ties and interactions (including remittance) to empirical investigation. I show how migrant remittance reflects their belonging to family and relatives in the origin country and thereby examine how such belonging helps us to understand migrant remittance.

Remittance, or the Money Migrants Send Home

I adopt the official definition of migrant remittance as "the money migrants send home." The head of the World Bank's Global Knowledge Partnership on Migration and Development and a leading economist on migration and remittance, Dilip Ratha, states: "when migrants send home part of their earnings in the form of either cash or goods to support their families, these transfers are known as workers' or migrant remittance."[60] My informants echo this conceptualization of remittance. In fact, all the migrants I talked to during my fieldwork defined their remittance as money for the daily upkeep of their family (*hat-khoroch* or *bazzar-khoroch* in colloquial Bangla), financial help, loan repayment, and so forth for family they left behind in Bangladesh. Surveys on remittance in Bangladesh also document that this is how people define remittance.[61] Empirical research from around the world also confirms that the family at home in the origin country is the primary recipient of remittance, a fact acknowledged in the United Nations' declaration of June 16 as Family Remittance Day.

I prefer the concept of home to that of "migrant household" or "migrant family" as the recipient of migrant remittance in my analysis. The concept of migrant household (including a household head—typically the father—siblings, and their spouses and children), central in the NELM perspective, misses the importance of sociocultural factors by offering a static and essentialized conception of home. Hence, many remittance studies adopt the concept of migrant family as members living across borders in two or more different countries.[62] For instance, Abrego[63] treats the families of Salvadoran immigrants in the United States, which includes immigrant parents, their children, and caregiving relatives in both the United States and El Salvador, whereas in other studies the family extends to include distant kin[64] and sometimes unrelated members (e.g., neighbors) from the origin community.[65] These studies recognize the family boundary in terms of social norms of obligation, dependency, inheritance, and belonging. Owing to social and cultural differences in these norms, the family boundary differs considerably across nations, a difference that becomes explicit in the legal definitions of family in the immigration law of various destination countries.[66] This leaves the boundary of the migrant family open and thereby renders the concept empirically elusive. Additionally, this concept of the migrant family fails to incorporate important attributes that the migrants attach to home. As I observed in my fieldwork, family separation leads to remittance only so long as the migrants feel belonging to the home in the origin country (i.e., when migrants identify with parents, siblings, and their close relatives and kin), and family unification does not stop sending remittances in the absence of belonging to home in the new destination country (e.g., when migrants experience marginalization). Thus, home is more than the family; it is the container or reservoir of the family together with other sensorial and place-based objects that allows individuals to feel "at home." My interlocutors frequently used the Bangla terms *bari* and *paribar,* which mean home and family respectively, whereby the former refers to physical structures hosting the family and the latter to the relatives constituting the family. That is, migrants' conception of home is simultaneously locative and relational. Therefore, we must consider both the people and sensorial objects and places that constitute a migrant's home to adequately understand why they send remittances there.

Given that migrants live in different countries with varying sociocultural and legal definitions of family, we need a generalizable definition of home applicable to migrants living in diverse national contexts. I propose that a way forward is to look at how the migrants themselves define home while talking about their remittance. Regardless of origin and destination, all migrants I met said they sent remittances "home," which offers a good starting point. So, what does home mean?

I notice an inseparable tether between migrants' sense of self and their concept of home. By and large, when migrants referred to home, they were talking about who they are and vice versa: my informants would introduce themselves to me with their names followed by their home, including both the material/physical things situated at a location and the people living in them. For instance, Mian told me that he was from Mirpur, a place on the outskirts of Dhaka city where he lived with his parents in a one-story house. This customary practice among Bangladeshis of introducing oneself in terms of original family relations and residential location is indicative of how critically important migrants' conception of home is to their self-perception. Thus, an understanding of the migrants' sense of self is necessary for understanding their perception of home. This connection will be examined to understand why migrants send remittances home.

Migrant Self

Contrary to the notion of a relatively static, essentially self-interested or social-ized "self" implicit in economic and social-cultural approaches, I adopt a con-ception of self that is "inextricably bound to forms of externality and materiality."[67] This conception of self has two dimensions: (1) self as a dynamic, reflexive, symbolic, and mediating agent, and (2) an object or container of the personality and identity of the person.[68] This understanding echoes Stuart Hall's conception of identity constituting "being" and "becoming,"[69] whereby the for-mer refers to the agentive self and the latter an object. Migration destabilizes an individual's perception of self by decentering them from their home, both in terms of location and the community of people who constitute home. This becomes evident when we examine the ways in which migrants describe them-selves in relation to places and people. Other empirical studies of migrants con-firm this relational perception of the self.[70] Thus, when migrants talked to me about the homes to which they sent remittances, they were simultaneously talk-ing about themselves. Based on these findings, I argue that along with references to family and relatives, talk about places, landscapes, and the material structures and objects of home also narratively construct who migrants understand them-selves to be. Thus, migrant conceptions of self are externalized through their dis-courses of home, so much so that the two concepts are inseparably intertwined.

Migrant Home

To empirically distinguish the concept of home as it emerged from the migrants I met, I find Chapman's[71] tripartite understanding useful. Chapman distin-guishes among three notions of home: 1) as a material and physical entity that includes location, structure, decoration, furnishing, and amenity; 2) as a rela-tional entity that includes family, neighbors, friends, and broader community; and 3) as font for deriving identity and belonging, including cultural identity, collective sense of social permanence, and security. Here, I observe the third meaning of home emerging from migrants' narratives about their remittance practices. Crucially, the significance of the material and relational dimensions of home depend on the degree to which migrants derive their identity and belong-ing from it. For example, once migrants permanently settle with their family in a new home in the destination country, they may no longer need to look back to their previous home in the origin country to identify who they are.

As I noticed in my conversations with other migrants, the concept of home involves a temporal dimension, as expressed in their references to their real home (in the present) and their aspired home (in the future).[72] Of these two, migrants emphasize more frequently the home they aspire to build with bet-ter quality material components and enhanced well-being for the family. This fact is documented empirically in studies looking at migrant remittance used for both conspicuous consumption[73] and investment.[74] Thus, the home to which migrants send remittances is not only already present at a particular location, it is also in the act of homemaking[75] that involves a process that Wise[76] calls "territorialization"—the active construction of home through conquering a space as one's own. In the case of remittance, migrants send money for the maintenance of their current home and to improve it both materially (e.g., infrastructural development) and qualitatively (e.g., enhancing the living standard of family members). Because migrants identify with their home, they experience an improved sense of self with its enhancement. This highlights how migrants understand remittance as an act of financially providing for a home to which they belong and not as an act of either self-interest or self-sacrifice. Therefore, I pay particular attention to what places and people migrants include in their conception of home and why, as well as how these might change over time.

Belonging to Home

In this book, I use belonging to refer to migrants' aspirations for and strategies to maintain membership to home. As I noted earlier, a preexisting intimate relationship between migrants and remittance recipients is a necessary condition for remittance. Harper and Zubida argue that "sending money and ceasing to send it or changing remittance practices has meaning. If sending connotes attachment, as the transnational literature implies, then not sending or changing patterns must also denote something."[77] For them, stopping remittance indicates a break in the migrants' sense of belonging to home in the origin country. Migrants send remittances so long as they feel a sense of belonging and stop sending remittances once they no longer feel that belonging. Therefore, I approach remittance as a reflection of migrants' sense of belonging to home, which includes the origin family and community in the country from which they hail.

The idea of place or location is important in understanding migrants' sense of belonging to home across borders. As I noted earlier, the concept of home is more expansive than a migrant's family, and it is located in "a larger geographic place where one belongs, such as one's community, village, city, and country."[78] Terms like "homeland" and "hometown" also reveal the broader spatiality of home for migrants. Thus, a migrant's home is place-bound.[79] However, it is not only a place that one comes from, but also a place that one inhabits. The migrants I met frequently talked about their home in both the origin and destination country. That is, migrants' conception of home rejects our commonsensical understanding of a single home in a particular country. Besides identifying with their ancestral home in the origin country, they establish another home in their destination country, which they inhabit and where they organize their daily lives. For home is where one derives identity and with which one realizes social belonging—through favorable outcomes when people feel a social connectedness—a basic human motivation.[80] Therefore, my study looks at migrants' perspectives about their homes in both their destination and origin communities to understand their belonging.

Based on my conceptualization of remittance as an expression of migrant belonging, I argue that the current flows of remittance from migrants in a particular destination country to their origin country are indicative of migrants' belonging. Empirical studies support this idea of remittance as an expression of belonging. For instance, Thai observes that Vietnamese immigrants in the United States send remittances to their origin family and relatives in Vietnam because they see a profoundly positive impact on the living standards of their families and remittance offers the remitters a degree of social recognition as successful migrants, which is often inaccessible to them in the United States.[81] That is, these immigrants maintain belonging to their home in Vietnam and derive a better sense of identity by improving the living standard of their families and gaining positive social recognition as a result. However, such transnational practice is not permanent since neither the immigrants' economic precarity in the United States nor their ability to turn to the origin community for social recognition is permanent. In reality, the sense of belonging to the home in the United States often improves through better incorporation of the family;[82] simultaneously, connections to the origin community may eventually dissipate due to, for example, the dissolution of the parental family and/or immigration of relatives and kin, leading to an erosion of immigrants' sense of cross-border belonging and ensuring remittance decay, as has been established elsewhere.[83] This assimilationist viewpoint on the likely integration into the destination state and eventual weakening of belonging to the origin state, however, is also challenged by recent studies examining migrants' collective remittances[84] and religious charity.[85] Therefore, I retain the idea that migrants simultaneously belong to the home in both the origin and destination countries.[86] Recent studies on remittance decay also identify and locate home at multiple places from which migrants realize belonging and send remittances.[87] Contrary to the assimilationist idea of settling in the destination country, migrants are iteratively establishing home and maintaining belonging to multiple countries in contemporary sociopolitical contexts characterized by racialization and marginalization of immigrants in Western countries.[88]

In sum, I conceptualize remittance as an expression of migrants' sense of belonging to home and study belonging as a means to understand why people send remittances and what they accomplish out of this transnational act. In doing so, I conceive of the remitter (the migrant) as someone who belongs to a home that includes family and relatives and which is co-located at multiple scales (e.g., family, kin, neighborhood, and the nation) in both the origin and destination countries. By looking at the plural and multifaceted conception of belonging, I offer an empirically grounded analysis of how such belonging transforms within and beyond the family to broader scales of community and nation, which is reflected in variations in remittance.

Analyzing Remittance as Belonging

The stories I gathered in my fieldwork embody migrants' emotional and nostalgic attachments to home and emotional aspirations for a better future. Contrary to the NELM supposition that distinguishes migrants and remittance recipients as separate entities who engage in remittance based on their separate interests, I suggest the migrant belongs to the home and family unit to which he sends remittances. This conceptual shift requires an examination of remittance as an economic act shaped by the economic motivations of remitters, as well as by the sociocultural factors that bind remitters with remittance recipients. Together, these two groups constitute "the home." Therefore, I looked at moral aspects, including ideas about deservingness, and examined how some of these aspects can be taken up by institutions (i.e., government organizations creating policies that promote or discourage remittance). Here, I borrow from Thompson's analytical concept of moral economy to understand remittance as a socioculturally motivated economic act.[89] Thompson argues that the sphere of production and economic exchange cannot be detached from the social world or from the moral conceptions that partially precede such relations and simultaneously give them meaning. Although Thompson[90] used the idea of moral economy to understand why the poor revolted against authority, later scholars recognize its application in various fields including welfare, humanitarianism, and civil society.[91] What I take from this approach is how a shared sense of social belonging allowed the poor rioters among the English working class to lay claim to fair treatment in terms of their common customs, traditions, and law. I concur with Brette's call to expand the use of the moral economy to cover any set of moral assumptions that underlie and structure how everyday economic relations are negotiated between different social classes within historical contexts.[92]

Contrary to the conventional knowledge suggesting a separation between the spheres of emotion and reason, sociologist Viviana Zelizer shows how the two often intersect in economic transactions like remittance.[93] What I find methodologically important in Zelizer's approach is her assertion that monetary transfers and social relations "coexist in a wide variety of contexts and relationships, each relationship marked by a distinctive form of payment."[94] In fact, social relations put individuals under various moral obligations that are central to ensuring exchanges—for example, between parents and their adult children,[95] which supports my decision to apply the idea of moral economy to studying remittances. As Rahman and Mian, and stories from other migrants throughout this book, show, customs and traditions relating to family responsibility as well as the expectations recipients have from the migrants vary widely and lead to divergent understandings among family members about who is deserving of remittance and who is not.[96] Thus, I examine the meanings migrants attach to their remittance to recognize the underlying relationships between remitters and recipients, as well as the moral aspects (i.e., social norms, values, customs, and traditions) that bind them together. In addition, I look at how variations in contextual factors (i.e., immigration regime, labor market, migrant organizations and networks, and history of immigration/migration) can correspond to changes in the meaning of remittance. By doing so, I identify the relational and normative structures that bind migrants and remittance recipients and how those structures change with subsequent changes in remittance. For example, I show that parental expectations of remittance tend to diminish once their sons abroad start their own families with wife and children, because the change from a single migrant to one who has the responsibility of family transforms the meaning of remittance from obligatory support to less-compulsory transactions like gifts.[97]

The materiality of remittance and its economic implications are clear, but remittance is also emotional[98] and relational,[99] which I study by examining the meanings migrants attach to their remittance. This, however, risks cultural determinism whereby individuals uncritically follow norms and values in their actions. While belonging to the same origin society characterized by a set of customs, norms and values, migrants often differ from their remittance recipients in interpreting those guidelines, as the opening vignettes indicate. For instance, my informants in Japan and the United States live in societies characterized by individualism in which individuals are primarily responsible to the immediate family. However, their origin community expects support not only for immediate family members but also close relatives, as Rahman's story shows. Living in two different societies with varying norms about family roles inevitably causes role conflict in migrants' interactions with their origin family, leading to confusion, tension, and at times unpleasant fallouts. Therefore, I use Carling's idea of a remittance script,[100] which highlights an individual's ability to choose one from among many competing norms that best suits their perceptions of remittance within the constraints and privileges of their particular social role. That is, a remittance script involves multiple meanings, allowing individuals to conform to a meaning of their own choosing while distancing themselves from other meanings, which empirically means that different actors might use dissimilar scripts in the same remittance transaction. Like the migrants in my study, other scholars also recognize migrants' ability to use different interpretations of remittance scripts and act accordingly.[101]

Both the public and academic discourses on migrant remittance view it as the sum of money going from migrants in the destination country to their home in the origin country. I find the notion of remittance scripts useful in understanding how various social and cultural factors, such as a family role, can lead individuals to choose a certain course of action—for instance, spending for an immediate family member's education instead of for an extravagant marriage ceremony of a niece—in addition to breaking up the aggregate flows of migrant remittance. I also find it effective in recognizing how transformations within the family (i.e., evolving into a family of procreation out of the family of origin) correspond to changes in the migrant's role and associated obligations. However, the concept of a remittance script overlooks how social and cultural factors might shape the motivation to remit that precedes any decision to send remittances. We must study the remitters and the recipients beyond the micro context of their act within the home by situating them in the larger cross-border context. Here, the transnationalism perspective offers an effective way through.

The transnationalism perspective[102] recognizes how migrants stand against repressive global capital and the nation-state in their pursuit of economic success through relatively uninterrupted cross-border activities, including remittance. The scholarly community has popularized this perspective in studying how larger sociocultural contexts shape migrant remittance.[103] This perspective recognizes how migrants move circularly between their countries of origin and destination, often developing economic as well as social, cultural, and political ties across national borders. For instance, Werbner[104] observed that Pakistani migrants in Manchester not only reproduced their origin culture and social relations in the host society but also reconnected with those they had left behind in Pakistan through remittance. Similarly, Gardner's[105] ethnographic study among Bangladeshis in the United Kingdom and Thai's[106] ethnographic study among Vietnamese immigrants in the United States demonstrate how migrants' concern about their status—lost in downward mobility in the destination country and expected to revive in the origin country—can motivate them to send remittances.

While placing the remitters in a transnational context, I take note of the risk of idealizing migrants' cross-border connections by overlooking the possibility of their acculturation, including integration into the destination society that may eventually reduce their attachment to their origin communities.[107] Given that transnationalism involves migrants' interactions with their families and relatives in the country of origin, how does transnationalism affect migrants' sense of self and place (i.e., belonging) within the family and society? Moreover, as sovereign nation-states exercise authority over international borders, do state policies affect migrants' belonging to home and their transnational practices, including remittance?

In sum, I explore migrant's belonging to home by looking at the relationships between migrants and remittance recipients and examine how changes in the migrant's perception of self and sense of belonging shape their remittance. My analysis situates the migrants in the context of reception in the destination country (including immigration laws, the local labor market, and community support), which shapes migrant decisions to permanently settle abroad or return to the home country. As I will show, the ability to bring their families to the destination country substantially reduces migrants' propensity to send remittances, as they no longer look back to the home/origin country. If migrants cannot settle in the destination country by bringing their family, they often eventually return to the home country, which organically dissolves remittance practices.[108] This suggests that migrants send remittances home—which is not a distinct entity, but one to which the migrant belongs.

Organization of the Book

In this book, I present migrants' own stories about their remittance. In these stories I recognize how the migrants identify with the recipients of their remittance—the family and relatives in the origin country. Like any ordinary individual, their actions demonstrate their intentionality as well as the social and cultural factors in the origin and destination countries that constrain that intentionality. I capture the socially embedded intentionally of the migrants in a theoretical framework by adopting a structure-agency approach from existing literature in relevant disciplines. The empirical chapters show how I examine migrant remittances in terms of their social belonging. I accomplish this task by organizing my book as follows:

Chapters 1 and 2 involve stories from Bangladeshi migrants in Tokyo. Following my theoretical frameworks, I explore the social and cultural factors constraining these migrants from decision-making until their return home. Much like temporary migration from Bangladesh to other destination countries, the family plays the most critical role in sending a member to Japan by taking advantage of the immigration policies of Japan. Contrary to popular ideas about migration as a matter of the individual and their families, chapter 1 demonstrates that the destination state plays an important regulatory role that significantly constrains the actions of migrants. Thus, while migrants are able to circumvent immigration control in Japan by various means and prolong their stay to maximize their economic benefit, they cannot bring their families with them and they ultimately leave Japan. Various social and cultural barriers join with the formal immigration regime to dissuade them from settling permanently. Chapter 2 discusses these migrants' remittance with particular focus on their inability to make a home in Japan by permanently settling with family. It highlights the reasons migrants share about why they send remittances, which include social customs and norms and values enacted through membership in the family and origin community. It shows how the lack of opportunities to establish a home in Japan leads migrants to look back to Bangladesh or to another country of immigration. While a small number of Bangladeshis in Japan qualify for immigration in immigrant-receiving countries, most, including those with Japanese permanent residency, return to Bangladesh to establish their home and raise a family. It concludes by explaining the high propensity to send remittances among Bangladeshis in Japan due to perception of belonging to home in their origin country.

Chapters 3 and 4 report the stories from Bangladeshi immigrants in Los Angeles. Like their counterparts in Japan, these migrants also receive substantial support from their family and relatives in managing their immigration through programs launched by the destination state. In both the Diversity Visa Lottery program and higher education channels to entering the United States, the family mobilizes necessary finances and relevant information for the migrants. Yet unlike in Japan, these migrants experience a more favorable reception in the United States: per immigration policy, the United States encourages them to settle permanently, offers several benefits and supports to get them started, and allows them to establish their home by inviting family and close relatives. As a consequence, these immigrants see their migration as permanently relocating to the United States. The emergence and gradual development of the ethnic neighborhood in Los Angeles called Little Bangladesh is proof of the United States' favorable reception. Yet, as chapter 4 shows, establishing home and finding belonging remain elusive as these migrants proceed through their life stages. Those in the working-class experience status loss due to their migration and face several economic and social barriers to upward social mobility in the United States. To compensate, most of these immigrants look back to their origin country and send remittances to generate economic profit and enhance social status. Hence, U-shaped patterns of remittance among these immigrants, with initial large and frequent amounts for family support until the entire family relocates to the United States, a decline in remittance due to family unification and the disintegration of the origin family, and finally a rise in remittance for economic and social gain in the origin country. Those in the professional class also experience increasing isolation and lack of belonging due to their family disintegration and diminishing social ties after retirement. Consequently, they become interested in reconnecting with their distant relatives and neighbors in the origin community by sending remittances.

Chapter 5 investigates the migrant family and explores how a family's sense of belonging transforms with the natural progress of its lifecycle. It particularly notes the changes in migrants' roles from dependent, young, and unmarried to becoming the main breadwinner for the family after migration. It also recognizes how the eventual disintegration of the origin family into several families headed by siblings leads to subsequent role transformation, with significant impact on the migrants' perception of home and belonging. While role transformations within the family are natural, they can also cause tension, dissatisfaction, feeling ignored or left behind, and many other negative emotions that further widen the emergent rifts in relationships among family members and relatives. The erosions of existing relationships and subsequent development of new relationships show strengthening and weakening in migrants' sense of belonging with consequent ups and downs in their remittance.

The book concludes by summarizing the findings showing how migrants' social belonging helps us understand their remittance. It demonstrates that looking at remittance by placing it within the migrant's biography and the sociocultural context that embeds migrants and remittance recipients offers a better approach to understand remittance practices. By looking at migrants' belonging to home, the conclusion shows how my study advances our understanding of migrant remittance by moving beyond individualistic and structural deterministic views. It ends by discussing how globalization offers increasing opportunity for individuals and families to have a better life in a world characterized by wealth and globalization, but also constraints.

1

A Rush to the East

●●●●●●●●●●●●●●●●●●●●●●●

Bangladeshi Migration
to Japan

Jamal, a Bangladeshi migrant in his mid-forties with permanent residency in Japan, told me,

> It was around 1985/86 when Bangladeshis would get transit visas and port-entry visas in Japan. Some people in Bangladesh would tell unemployed individuals that "If you pay me some money, I will take you you abroad. There are lots of income opportunities there. Go and get some income there so that you can establish yourself here." That was how some brokers acted at that time. But they were usually located in a few local towns. This did not include most of the rural areas like ours. Young individuals from middle-class families, such as the mediocre student who could not succeed in education, used this opportunity.

He then smiled, which I understood as him implicitly saying that he was one of those mediocre young students. As he pointed out, international migration had been a livelihood strategy for individuals from middle-class backgrounds in certain regions in Bangladesh.[1] Difficultly in finding adequate income opportunities at home, on one hand, and the perceived availability of greater income opportunities abroad, on the other, motivated young male Bangladeshis to migrate. It is important to note that Jamal did not think that opportunities for achieving success through proper education were absent in Bangladesh. Rather, it was his failure to get enough education that prompted him to try his luck abroad. Like many other potential migrants, Jamal saw the port-entry visa (which in fact was a visa-on-arrival for tourists from a few selected countries including Bangladesh) policy in Japan as an opportunity to realize his career goals, which were unachievable in Bangladesh.

In this story, we find Jamal to be a rational individual with an understanding of his own place in the origin society and the opportunities and challenges to succeed in life at home and abroad. He saw migration to Japan and securing employment with a port-entry visa as an opportunity to overcome structural barriers he faced in Bangladesh. Unlike popular assumptions about migrants being solely motivated by the availability of greater income opportunities (known as pull factors) or by structural factors (known as push factors, such as poverty), Jamal made a choice based on his assessment of the constraints (i.e., inability to find success in Bangladesh due to not studying enough) and opportunities (i.e., information about port-entry visas and employment in Japan) in his own migration. Moreover, his story identifies brokers and the financial capability of his family as necessary for migration to Japan. This complicates our understanding of human migration in terms of structural factors and individual motivations. Instead, migrants make decisions from within their structurally embedded positions characterized by limits, as well as based on the available resources to overcome them, thereby demonstrating both the role of the individual and their social position in shaping their actions.

In this chapter, I highlight the economic motivations as well as structural factors that shape Bangladeshi migration to Japan as a temporary journey. I outline the emergence and subsequent transformations of Bangladeshi migration to Japan in terms of the legal and sociocultural factors that offer Bangladeshis higher income opportunities but also deny them long-term stay and settlement by requiring them to repatriate. Thus, migrants can earn enough money to live a middle-class life but are unable to establish a home and raise a family in Japan. By sharing the stories of my interlocutors, I show how not being able to build a permanent home in Japan (and thus experiencing a lack of belonging) shaped migrant experiences of working, living, and socializing and had implications for their remittance behavior and other transnational activities.

History of Bangladeshi Migration to Japan

In the 1980s, Japan saw a strong economic boom with an acute labor shortage. In previous decades, required labor was drawn from rural areas, especially from the country's millions of repatriated former soldiers. However, the demand for labor increased as Japan's fertility rate declined below replacement level, its population aged, and its economy rapidly expanded.[2] Japanese employers, particularly small- and medium-sized entrepreneurs, were in such a dire situation that up to fifty companies went bankrupt every week because they could not fill orders for lack of workers on their factory floors.[3] The conservative bureaucracy in Japan, unwilling to allow a large number of migrant workers into the country, offered visa-on-arrival to people from Iran, Pakistan, and Bangladesh.[4] These people would immediately take employment in Japanese companies and frequently overstay their visas. Some enterprising individuals in Bangladesh found earning opportunities by migrating to Japan while others established businesses that arranged migration to the country for others. Since this migration, which began only in late-1980s, most Bangladeshi migrants in Japan seemed to know and often talked about migrating to Japan as a tourist and earning large sums of money in a short time by evading immigration authorities.

The visa-on-arrival policy for citizens of Bangladesh, Iran, and Pakistan was launched in 1987, which allowed them to legally stay in Japan for 15 to 30 days. However, an overwhelming majority of the tourists from Bangladesh would take employment and overstay their visas. Between 1987 and 1989, the number of Bangladeshis in Japan jumped from a few hundred to over 34,000.[5] This first wave of Bangladeshi migrants mostly included middle- and lower-middle-class men from a few villages in, for example, Munshiganj District, south of Dhaka. They were mostly young, some coming right after college graduation.[6] Two-thirds had been employed or self-employed before their migration and one-fifth were still students.[7] Since Japan did not allow unskilled or low-skilled foreign workers, Bangladeshis used informal networks of co-ethnics to help them enter Japan as visitors, tourists, students, etc.[8] My informants among the earlier batch of visa-overstayers mentioned two travel agencies that advertised income opportunities in Japan and arranged the migration of hundreds of aspirants for a fee. These agencies continued their "business" of sending Bangladeshi migrants to Japan through international airports in Tokyo and Osaka during the entire period of the visa waiver program between 1987 and 1990.

These early migrants to Japan worked in small- and medium-sized companies and farms that were entirely staffed by Bangladeshis,[9] about 70 percent of whom worked in manufacturing industries like metal processing, printing, publishing, and rubber companies. Fourteen percent worked in construction and 13 percent in the service sector. There was a pattern of transition among migrants from hard and tedious jobs in manufacturing to the service sector. For instance, someone beginning as a handyman might switch to the job of driving a supply vehicle, or a floor worker would move up to the position of line supervisor or a foreman. In addition, as undocumented migrants, they stayed close to their workplaces and lived among co-ethnics to avoid arrest and deportation. The Japanese immigration authority turned a blind eye to the widespread abuse of the visa-on-arrival facility and allowed companies to hire these visa-overstayers. Despite high official's statements (without statistical proof) about the lax enforcement of immigration laws against the visa-overstayers, several of my interlocutors among the early Bangladeshi migrants in Japan shared stories about how the police were not interested in arresting them. As Shafiq said,

> I came to Japan in 1989 and landed at Osaka airport with other Bangladeshis. We all had port-of-entry visas as tourists. Our *dalal* [middleman] took me to a construction site near Inuyama town. I saw the police everywhere at the airport, on the road and in the town. But they never stopped us and asked for papers. I think everyone knew that we were "illegal" migrants. One day, a few weeks after I arrived, I took a wrong bus and ended up at another end of the town. I was lost as I did not know Japanese. A Japanese policeman picked me up in his car and dropped me at our makeshift dormitory near the construction site. But this attitude quickly changed after increasing reports of crimes committed by foreigners.

The visa-on-arrival policy did not last long as there was massive anti-immigration backlash. Local and national media were replete with reports of Japanese citizens' agitation and protests over the presence of large numbers of foreigners.[10] Consequently, the government rescinded the policy in 1990. Bangladeshis in Japan would also adopt this xenophobic public discourse and explain their anti-immigration stance in terms of a rise in criminal activities, including drug use and other petty crimes due to the sudden influx of "illegal" Bangladeshi migrants in Japan. As one of my interlocutors, Amin, told me,

> A lot of Bangladeshis came without work visas and began to work in Japanese companies illegally. But there were a few unruly young men among them who began to get involved in antisocial activities. Some of them would get drunk at night and fight with their friends. The Japanese police would arrive at the scene and find nothing serious. But such incidents created a fear among the locals as well as the authorities about the growing number of antisocial occurrences, which could ruin Japan's reputation. So, the government passed a law banning "port visas" [the visa-on-arrival] for Bangladeshis. The government also declared that the illegal migrants would be allowed to leave Japan without any punishment if they voluntarily surrendered. Most such migrants returned home after this law was passed.

Amin was referring to the changes in immigration law in Japan in 1990 that ended the visa-on-arrival opportunity for Bangladeshis and was followed by a crackdown on undocumented migrants. While Amin and other Bangladeshi migrants with whom I spoke in Tokyo explained this in terms of some migrants' antisocial behavior, reflecting their uncritical adoption of media narratives in Japan, it in fact resulted from a combination of pushback from Japanese society against a rapidly growing foreign population, the unwillingness of the state bureaucracy to incorporate migrants, and the discovery of another source of cheap labor in Latin America.[11] Changes in Japanese immigration law and enforcement drastically curbed the number of Bangladeshi migrants in Japan. However, word of high earnings had already reached Bangladesh. This encouraged hundreds of aspirants to look for alternative ways to get into Japan and earn their fortune. Entering as a self-funded language student emerged as an effective alternative.

In 1984, the Japanese government inaugurated its policy of internationalizing higher education.[12] Except for a few dozen Bangladeshi students supported by the Japanese government's Monbusho scholarships, Bangladeshis hardly applied for student visas before 1990. The primary reasons for this lack of interest included the absence of knowledge about income opportunities in Japan and the availability of on-arrival visas. The early cohort of the migrants entering Japan with tourist visas spread the news about entry and work in their origin villages and helped many of their relatives and friends to follow them to Japan. Once the visa-on-arrival policy was rescinded in 1990, these migrants recognized an alternative route to entering Japan as self-funded students in Japanese language schools. They also recognized that international students were allowed to work legally up to twenty-eight hours a week, which might even be extended by various techniques. The expanding service sectors in big cities such as Tokyo and Osaka had high a demand for foreign workers. Thus, Bangladeshis realized that entering Japan with student visas was better than entering as tourists. Given the rising demand for migrating to Japan among aspirants in Bangladesh, applying for student visas quickly became the primary channel for Bangladeshis to migrate to Japan throughout the 1990s and 2000s.

Unlike the early migrants, who would simply buy plane tickets and enter Japan as tourists, those migrating as students needed to navigate a complex process involving their intended language school, the immigration authority in Japan, and the Japanese Embassy in Bangladesh. The Japanese Embassy required every student applicant to provide proof of admission to a language school, financial solvency, and a guarantor in Japan. Generally, Japanese language schools (*nihongo gakko*) posted information about admission, courses, fees, etc., in Japanese, and aspiring Bangladeshis needed to find someone to translate the information for them. After completing school admission, the aspirants would need to procure the certificate of eligibility issued by the immigration department in Tokyo and Osaka, which was required in their visa application as proof of their eligibility. In addition, these aspirants needed support to find accommodations and jobs once they arrived in Japan. To manage these requirements, aspirants sought assistance from intermediaries, including relatives and agents.[13]

The majority of my informants reportedly paid intermediaries, known as *dalals*, large sums of money ranging from a few thousand to around twelve thousand U.S. dollars. This might seem surprising since a few studies recognize that migrants often tap into migrant networks to access free information about opportunities abroad.[14] However, even those with access to migrant networks did not always find free information, as I observed in Japan. In fact, nearly all my informants paid handsome amounts of money to brokers. This contradicts the academic assumption about access to free information and resources for migrants and others belonging to certain migrant networks. The practice of searching for agents and referring aspirants to them was so well known among migrants that I found them sharing information about their agents without any hesitation.[15] This confirms the observation in other migration contexts that migrants actively seek out intermediaries to get access to network resources and often pay agents large sums of money.[16]

A small number of Bangladeshis enter Japan through a formal channel as students supported by the Japanese government's scholarship program. According to the Japanese Embassy in Bangladesh, a total of 3,991 Bangladeshi students studied in Japan with Japanese government scholarships between 1955 and 2018, of whom 3,753 (or 94 percent) pursued a master's or PhD.[17] These highly educated students aspiring to further higher education in Japanese universities contact potential mentors at Japanese universities. Once they find mentors, they obtain admission to Japanese universities or research institutes, which then recommend the students for the *Monbukagakusho* (popularly known as *Monbusho*) scholarship. The academic mentors and universities assist scholarship recipients with the required paperwork and help them find accommodation and get settled after arrival. A small number of these scholarship awardees are also selected directly through open examinations conducted by the Japanese Embassy in Bangladesh, which then arranges their paperwork, supplies air tickets, and holds an orientation session about travel and initial challenges in Japan. Once the students arrive in Tokyo, representatives of the Japan Student Services Organization (JASSO) receive them at the airport and escort them to their place of stay in Japan. JASSO representatives also provide an allowance for initial expenses and give students directions to nearby shopping centers and hospitals. Finally, they take them to the local administrative office to apply for residence cards and health cards. These Bangladeshis migrate to Japan through legal channels and get all the necessary support, from procuring their visas to managing travel and initial settlement in Japan, through various parties, including both the Japanese government and non-government bodies.

Earning money defines Bangladeshi migration to Japan. The opportunity to earn money by working in the booming manufacturing and construction sectors attracted the first wave of Bangladeshis to Japan to enter as tourists. Once the visa-on-arrival policy ended, aspirants from Bangladesh continued to migrate to Japan as self-funded students in language and vocational schools and work in service sector jobs. While they were students on paper, they would work in multiple part-time jobs that often exceed full-time hours. Bangladeshis entering Japan with scholarships for higher education are distinguishable from their compatriots in Japan in terms of their high level of education and the quality of their engagement with Japanese authorities and society. Perhaps they too are influenced by the "money motive" for migration to Japan. Some of the Monbusho scholarship awardees among my interviewees in Tokyo acknowledged their mixed motivation, involving both education and money. For instance, Babu (a twenty-four-year-old student who entered Japan five years ago as a Monbusho scholarship awardee) told me,

> Some guys in the educated class, they come to Japan with the aim of earning and sending large amounts of money home. When I won the Monbusho scholarship, I was already admitted to the Bangladesh University of Engineering and Technology (BUET), the best reputed educational institution in the country. So, my father did not want me to come to Japan. But my mother supported me. I am from a village [referring to his lower-middle-class background]. I heard that the scholarship would give me 135,000 yen each month, pay for my air ticket, and also give me 25,000 yen right after I landed in Japan. *Subarashi* [large amounts of] money! I was very excited. Education never entered my thoughts. To those who are very close to me, I still admit that I did not come for education, but for money.

I learned this from my own experience, too. After completing my education in Bangladesh, I was awarded a Fulbright scholarship from the United States Embassy and a Monbusho scholarship from the Japanese Embassy for higher education. In Bangladesh, the financial value of these scholarships varies significantly, with Monbusho paying much higher sums. When I declined the Fulbright scholarship and accepted the Monbusho scholarship, many friends and relatives assumed that I did this for financial reasons. People in Bangladesh simply had a misconception that nobody going to Japan for higher education was serious about their studies and were instead interested in the opportunity to earn higher income.

In fact, the Monbusho scholarship does not pay more than other scholarships for higher education in other countries. However, unlike many other developed countries, Japan allows students to take part-time work outside their university campuses in addition to receiving scholarship stipends. Moreover, the spouses of migrants can easily procure work permits, work full time, and maximize the family income. By contrast, foreign students in the United States are allowed to work only limited hours on their university campuses and their spouses are not allowed to work at all. In addition, Japan offers foreign students more benefits, including subsidized housing, health insurance, and public transport. So, foreign students in higher education can earn and save money while pursuing their degrees in Japan. Many use their savings to purchase apartments or invest in other income-generating sectors in Bangladesh. One startling example of this is the establishment of many medical and dental clinics (mostly named after Japanese places or popular objects) in Dhaka and other big cities in Bangladesh by people with PhD degrees from Japanese universities. Inadvertently, all this bolsters the idea that Bangladeshi migration to Japan—regardless of the migrants' class, occupation, or visa status—is mainly to earn money.

By now, it is apparent that opportunities to earn money primarily define Bangladeshi migration to Japan regardless of the migrants' mode of entry, age, education, and other demographic characteristics. This explains why Japan remains one of the top desired migration destinations among Bangladeshis. Despite the relatively small Bangladeshi migrant population in Japan, the total remittances originating from the country place it in the list of top remittance-sending countries for Bangladesh.[18] The salience of remittance from Japan is also seen in the establishment of housing estates named after Japan (such as Japan Garden), medical and dental clinics, businesses in Japanese used cars and electronics, and so forth. Almost all these are established by someone with migration experience in Japan or their families. Comparing the remittances sent from all other countries to Bangladesh, I observed that Bangladeshis in Japan sent the highest portion of their income in remittances.[19] This might allude to the presence of a strong and vibrant Bangladeshi expatriate community in Japan. But, in fact, Bangladeshis in Japan live an extremely marginal and temporary life. Despite higher income opportunities, the migrants encounter insurmountable legal, social, and cultural barriers that deny them settlement and make their return inevitable.

Understanding the Temporariness of Bangladeshi Migration to Japan

As I discuss in the previous section, Bangladeshi migration to Japan is largely understood as a solely economic enterprise whereby individuals migrate for a specific period to maximize economic gains and enhance material success, as we see in the opening vignette in this chapter.[20] This fits the neoclassical economics approach. Like Jamal in the opening story, most migrants I met in Tokyo explained their migration as a voluntary act based on personal choice. Similarly, they discussed their future return to Bangladesh as a given. They shared with me the timing of their return to Bangladesh, the reasons for returning home, and what they would do afterwards in a manner that sounded like their decision to leave Japan was voluntary. I found this particularly confounding as I saw how excited they were to be in Japan and earn substantial amounts of income. During my fieldwork in Tokyo, I noticed that these migrants would frequently compare their manifold income and access to the modern facilities in Japan with the experiences of their peers in professional careers back in Bangladesh. So, if these migrants were happy about being in Japan, why would they decide to leave the country on their own? However, as soon as I began to ask my informants about why they decided to return home, I understood that their decision was not a voluntary one, but was shaped by legal, social, and cultural factors in the context of reception.

All my informants in casual jobs reported to me that they knew about the extreme difficulties of trying to stay on in Japan and eventually returning to Bangladesh, which supported the assumption about temporary migrants making choices about going abroad for a short period and then returning home.[21] Implicit in this understanding is the ability (i.e., agency) of the migrants and their families to decide to go abroad and return home after a certain period. While my initial conversations with these migrants indicated that their decision to migrate to Japan and leave the country were made voluntarily, closer attention to their lived experience contradicted this assumption by identifying how various structural limits make their decision to leave Japan the only reasonable option.

Migration scholars have long recognized that destination states induce migrants to leave the country by deploying various legal instruments, and hence make their stay abroad a temporary phenomenon. For instance, sociologist Michael Burawoy[22] observed how the influx control and the pass law required migrant workers from Black territories in South Africa to return home to reservations if their employment contract ended and they did not have a subsequent contract, or if they became unemployed due to retirement, disability, or simply a scarcity of employment. He argued that the lack of those migrants' legal right to continuously reside at the destination compelled them to maintain contact with family in the places where they would eventually return. The family also needed the migrant's financial support to subsist because of hardships in the local economy. It is important to note here that the destination state's role in keeping the migrants from family unification and permanent settlement created a mutual dependency between the migrants and their families. Such state-induced family separation and the consequent interdependence of the migrants and their families was a key reason for the migrants to engage in cross-border interactions with their families in the origin community through remittance. One of the most explicit examples of such temporary migration was the so-called "guest-worker program," whereby destination states admitted individual foreign workers legally for a certain period and repatriated them afterwards.[23] Although guest-worker programs in the United States and Europe have ended, similar schemes currently regulate migrants in destination societies, for instance, the *kafala* system in Middle Eastern countries.[24] As both the guest-worker programs and the kafala system are criticized for violating labor and human rights,[25] Japan could not adopt such a strictly controlled labor migration policy. But it also could not have an open-border policy because of the risk of a strong ethno-nationalist backlash and the unwillingness of its bureaucracy.[26]

In this contemporary age of hyper-globalization,[27] one might assume that migrants can move freely across national borders[28] and that the nation-state has lost its ability to control migration.[29] This may be supported by the steadily increasing number of migrants worldwide, from a little over 1 percent of the world's population in 1960 to nearly 4 percent of the global population in

2020.[30] Despite greater freedom in border crossing, more expansive migration networks, and a more developed migration industry, however, destination countries are tightening, not loosening, their grip on immigration. In fact, many scholars maintain that the role of the nation-state in migration control and regulation is ever present and significant.[31] For instance, reception states use various measures to manage these temporary migrants and ensure their repatriation, which include immigration laws constraining migrants to certain labor market sectors by attaching them to a particular employer or job, housing them in designated housing, and restricting their labor market mobility. States also launch frequent raids and strict security checks to prevent people from overstaying their visas. Moreover, these destination states do not allow migrants, especially those in low-skilled and low-paid jobs, to bring family and settle permanently.[32] I find Japan to be one of these destination states that heavy-handedly regulate migration with the consequence of making the country unfavorable for permanent settlement.

Besides controlling entry and repatriation, destination states also use immigration and border control policies to classify foreigners into different categories with different rights: for example, "permanent residents," "temporary workers," "visitors/tourists," and "undocumented" foreigners who must evade the legal procedures upon entry.[33] These different legal statuses set limits on migrants' ability to exercise choice in maximizing income, which is what motivated their move abroad in the first place. For instance, studies show that migrants entering with proper legal status earn significantly more than undocumented migrants.[34] The transition from undocumented status to legal permanent residency[35] and citizenship[36] increases migrant earnings and illustrates how the legal instruments deployed by the state shape migrant experiences abroad.

So, it is expected that, as a country of reception, Japan can exercise profound influence over Bangladeshi migrants from their entry until they leave the country. However, we should not assume that the state has total control as migrants can navigate through the restrictive measures Japan puts in place to control them. The very fact that most of these migrants could enter Japan and stay despite the absence of any legal framework to import migrant workers to Japan demonstrates the migrants' capacity to sneak through the weak points in Japanese immigration control mechanisms. With the help of migration intermediaries (people who offer various kinds of support for the migrants at different stages of their journey abroad)[37] and networks of relatives and friends, these migrants sought out ways to enter Japan and found employers in the manufacturing and service sectors who needed foreign workers to sustain their businesses. The migrants would pay large amounts of money to the intermediaries for processing paperwork for visas, finding lodging and employment, and providing several other necessary services in Japan.[38] While common sense might suggest a conflicting relation between the state and migration intermediaries (since they help migrants evade immigration control), scholars recognize how the state—often unintentionally, but also intentionally—facilitates the emergence and development of the intermediaries' business of migration facilitation.[39] Moreover, migrants find support from various local groups (such as employers' associations and civil society organizations) and individuals in Japan. Yet, the state has the ability to set limits on the intermediaries' ability to facilitate migration by its sovereign authority over foreigners' admission, stay, and return.[40] Elsewhere, I discussed how Japan plays a critical role in shaping the contours of this migration by controlling the admission, length of stay, and repatriation of the migrants.[41]

Unlike the economic approach's assumption that economic migrants often voluntarily leave a country to return home , I discuss in the following section how my informants were caught up in structural features that forced them to leave Japan at certain points by making permanent settlement an unfavorable choice and finding a sense of belonging in Japan impossible.

Forever Foreign

I went to Funabashi station to meet Amin. I had first met him at the Bangladeshi curry festival at Ikebukuro West Park, when one of my acquaintances introduced me to him as a researcher. Learning about my research, he seemed interested, so I asked him for an interview. He said he would be available the following Saturday, but he would not come to Tokyo. So, we decided to meet in Amin's neighborhood in Funabashi, about a forty-minute train ride from the Tokyo station. On a Saturday morning, I took a Chiba-line train to Funabashi, where I saw Amin waiting for me at the station exit. We entered a nearby McDonald's, and he ordered coffee for both of us. After a few minutes of chitchat, Amin began to share his migration story:

> It was after the big flood in 1988. I was lazing at home, as the flood damaged our college to the point that it was shut down. One afternoon, my uncle visited us from Dhaka. He was sitting with my father on the veranda after lunch. My father called me and told me that I would go to Japan. My uncle smiled at me, giving assurance. I do not remember how I felt at that moment. My uncle said that he knew someone who had sent many Bangladeshis to Japan, and everybody was making "big" [unspecified but large amounts of] money. My father thought I would do better to go to Japan than to complete my college education in the local college. I was too young to have any say in the matter. But I believe my father did what he thought was best for me and the family. So I went to Dhaka with my uncle the next morning. He contacted a *dalal* [broker] who worked for Noor Ali. They completed my paperwork and got me a passport in four days. On day five—it was a Monday—I went to the airport in a group of nine people. I was very nervous, but I saw two other people in the group from my village, which gave me some comfort that I was not alone.

Amin's story captures the social and cultural factors involved in shaping the earliest flow of Bangladeshi migrants to Japan. Amin was the second son of his parents' eight children. His family lived in Munsiganj, one of the newly formed districts in Dhaka division about 60 kilometers outside Dhaka. Middle-class parents in Bangladesh assume responsibility for their children's futures and make the major decisions regarding their education and career. They also expect a financial contribution from their grown-up children, especially their sons. Customarily, daughters are married off and considered members of their husbands' families, which absolves them from obligations toward their parents, including financial support.[42] This, together with the state's restrictive policy against female migration,[43] explains why Bangladeshi families tend to send only males abroad. Bangladeshi migrants entering Japan as tourists and language students are almost all males; those who migrate to Japan with scholarships for higher studies (especially women) often do so with their spouses.

Like Bangladeshis in other destination countries, migrants in Tokyo organized various community events all year round, and generally, some of the early migrants who married Japanese wives assumed leadership roles. Amin, for example, held a leading position in the Japanese branch of the present ruling political party in Bangladesh. He was an organizer of the Bengali New Year celebration committee and a liaison between the Bangladesh Embassy in Tokyo and expatriates and was recognized by many at gatherings of the Bangladeshi community in Tokyo. Amin had been working in a Japanese electronics factory for about fourteen years and had acquired permanent Japanese residency through his wife. During the weekends, he would help his wife with household chores until lunch, and then he would go out to join his Bangladeshi friends and spend the rest of the day with them, usually returning home by the last train at night.

Visa overstayers always faced the fear of being arrested and deported by the Japanese immigration authority. One strategy adopted to become a legal resident and stay on in Japan was to marry a Japanese woman and acquire permanent residency. While it is often assumed that marriage and family lead a migrant to permanent settlement in the new country, these migrants continued to struggle settling down. All of my informants reportedly found life with their Japanese wives "too Japanese" to adjust. Isolated from their Japanese in-laws and the local community and ridiculed by their Bangladeshi friends, they planned to return home to Bangladesh as soon as they could—with or without their Japanese wives. Scholars studying other migrant groups in Japan observe similar patterns whereby their respondents shared their difficulties settling down in Japan.[44]

I noticed that almost all Bangladeshis with Japanese wives[45] followed a similar weekly schedule. Once, returning from a party, I met four Bangladeshi men on the train heading to Ikebukuro station. It was already 10:30 P.M., and they were planning to go to a café for *adda*,[46] the most common leisure activity among Bangladeshi males. They invited me to join them and, noticing my hesitation, one of them asked if I had a Bangladeshi wife at home. When I replied that

I did, he promptly suggested that I should return home. With a smile, one of them commented that their Japanese wives would not mind them returning late at night, but a Bangladeshi wife would certainly get upset. Despite their fluency in Japanese and familiarity with social and cultural aspects of daily life in Japan, these migrants generally lived a marginal social life and had limited interaction with their wives, in-laws, and Japanese relatives and friends. If they were not occupied with their children or doing household chores, they would generally "hang out" with other Bangladeshi men during their leisure hours on weekends and holidays. For instance, during my fieldwork I met about a dozen Bangladeshis in a coffee shop at Ikebukuro station almost every Saturday evening.

Bangladeshi migrants were more involved with their relatives in Bangladesh than their in-laws and friends in Japan. For instance, Wajed (a salesman in his mid-forties working in a Japanese store, and a permanent resident with a Japanese wife) reported that one of his sisters called him every weekend. In addition, he talked to people in Bangladesh almost every other day. He recounted attending a Christmas party at the house of his parents-in-law, where he did not like the food and could not participate in elaborate and intricate cultural interactions with Japanese guests. He felt totally out of place. Since then, he avoided such gatherings with his wife's relatives, and his wife did not insist he join her. However, I observed that some migrants with Japanese wives and children had a greater involvement in Japanese society. For instance, Islam (a travel agent in his mid-forties working for a renowned Japanese travel agency and a permanent resident of Japan) lived with his Japanese wife and two children near his parents-in-law. He would spend one day on the weekend with his wife and children at a park in the neighborhood and eat out with them. He would spend the other day with his Bangladeshi friends. Mehdi (a professional migrant in his mid-thirties, who entered Japan as a Monbusho scholar and worked for a Japanese bank) seemed to have the most engaged relationship with his Japanese wife and her family, relatives, and Japanese colleagues. He would spend most of his weekends with them. I noticed an important difference between Islam and Mehdi and the early visa-overstaying migrants. Whereas the early migrants married Japanese women out of necessity to regularize their legal status in Japan, both Islam and Mehdi acquired their permanent residency through their professional employment before their marriages, which they presented as involving true love. However, Islam and Mehdi were exceptions, as most migrants in professional careers returned to Bangladesh to marry a Bangladeshi woman.

In Japan, marriages between citizens and migrants from a relatively poorer Asian country generally involve Japanese men and foreign women.[47] Scholars have recognized the considerable utility for both spouses in such unions: Japanese men looked for foreign brides for lack of marriageable Japanese women, while female migrants needed legal and economic sponsorship from Japanese men.[48] However, the gender composition was reversed in the case of Bangladeshis, particularly among those who entered as tourists and overstayed their visas. These migrants realized that their best option to stay on in Japan legally was to find Japanese wives. So, they actively sought friendships with Japanese women and at a certain stage would propose marriage. As most Bangladeshis in Japan considered such pragmatism deplorable due to its connection with gaining legality and permanent residence, someone married to a Japanese wife would always say that he had fallen in love and gotten married. However, informal conversations occasionally revealed the truth.

At a dinner party, I was in an *adda* with Emran (a supply store worker and a permanent resident in his late forties) and five other men, including one of Emran's longtime friends. The intimacy between the two was obvious in the way they teased each other. At one point, Emran's friend jokingly commented that Emran had tricked his Japanese wife into marrying him by showing fake love. Emran immediately protested, giving a detailed narrative of how his love had begun and grown. He said that as an illegal (i.e., visa-overstaying) migrant, he had lived near the factory where he worked on the outskirts of Osaka. He was all alone without any other Bangladeshis working in his factory. To avoid police arrest and deportation, he stayed within the factory premises and his nearby residence, going out only to buy groceries at the neighborhood store, where he met his wife, who was a salesclerk. He said that he immediately fell in love with her and began to speak to her whenever he visited the store. Over time, their relationship developed, and they began to date for a few months at his apartment (this was, in fact, unlikely, as visa-overstayers usually lived in shared rooms with other single male migrants). Emran said that the following spring she went to her parents in her village and asked for their permission to marry him. Since her parents disapproved, she came back and asked Emran to leave Osaka for Tokyo with her. So, they relocated to Tokyo. Emran took her to the mosque near Shinjuku (known as the Tokyo Jama Mosque, which was established and run by the Turkish government) where she converted to Islam and they registered their marriage.

However, this exciting and rosy tale did not take much time to fall apart. The focus of the adda, characteristically conversations on random subjects, continued to move back and forth between life in Japan and Bangladesh, personal to family and community issues, and business to politics. At one point, all the men began talking about what they would do in the future. They all were Japanese permanent residents and had Bangladeshi wives and children in Japan, except Emran, who was married to a Japanese woman. All except Emran said that they would return to Bangladesh once their children grew up and moved out as independent adults. Emran said that he would not wait that long; instead, he would return to Bangladesh in a few years, when his two-year-old son would be able to stay with him without his mother. We all turned to him in shock. I asked him why he wanted to do this. He replied, "I do not like this life. I cannot go to movies with my wife. I do not enjoy the TV at home. My wife does not cook the food I like, but only Japanese food. You know how tasteless their food is, right? I do not have any relatives in Japan. So, why should I stay?"

He looked at us, perhaps for our support that what he was saying was right. I asked him, "Then why don't you plan to take your wife with you?" Emran replied, "She will not go to Bangladesh. So, I'll take my son with me and go back home forever." While he did not say it, Emran implied that he would divorce his wife. Interestingly, I often heard Bangladeshi migrants predicting that a Japanese wife would eventually divorce her Bangladeshi husband. This notion was more prevalent among those who had overstayed their visas and then regularized their undocumented status by marrying Japanese women. There were no statistics available on divorce among Bangladeshi–Japanese couples or on who took the decision to file for divorce. So, it was difficult to know why these men would blame their Japanese wives for the divorce. One possible reason for this, I think, was to avoid the negative sociocultural repercussions of divorce. In Bangladeshi culture divorce is severely stigmatized.[49] While it is the women who endure most of the negative repercussions of divorce, divorced men are also seen as incompetent and unreliable. And since Bangladeshis are already suspect for marrying Japanese women to stay on in Japan, a divorce makes them subject to more ridicule for not being able to stay in Japan even after going to this length. This would show these men's weakness as it was believed they still could not manage to find a successful life.

However, marriage between a Bangladeshi man and a Japanese woman was not always a pragmatically calculated decision, as some of my respondents shared with me. I found some bi-national couples in Tokyo who reportedly had fallen in love and gotten married and were living happily in Japan. In such marriages, the men were generally Bangladeshis who had come to Japan as recipients of the Japanese government's scholarships and had found professional employment, as in the case of Mehdi, who had come to Japan at age nineteen. He completed an undergraduate degree from Tokyo Agricultural University and a master's from the University of Tokyo and entered a professional career in banking. He learned the language and culture and was able to make friends among the Japanese at his universities and workplaces. Somewhat unusually for a Bangladeshi migrant with a Monbusho scholarship, he dated and eventually married a Japanese girl. In 2013, when Japan introduced new immigration laws allowing naturalization for highly educated and skilled migrants, Mehdi immediately applied for and obtained his citizenship. Many others like him, who entered Japan for higher studies, told me how comfortable they were in Japan compared with Bangladesh or the other countries in which they had traveled. They rarely complained about their lives in Japan or about Japanese society. As Mehdi told me, "I have no complaint about living in Japan. My employment is very good. I know the Japanese language and culture. I have a Japanese wife and several Japanese friends. I have Japanese educational degrees. So I feel safe and comfortable in this country.

I am very much happy personally. In fact, who does not like being treated as a guest?"

As scholars document, migrants tend to look for better opportunities for themselves and their families and may settle permanently in their destination countries if they find such opportunities.[50] In addition to legal options to settle in these countries, migrants need to find a comfortable and decent means of earning a living and an accommodating community where they can establish their families. Mehdi appeared to have met all these socioeconomic and legal conditions. Moreover, he was fluent in Japanese and well-connected with the Japanese community through his wife, in-laws, and extensive networks of Japanese friends and colleagues. So, I was surprised to hear that he planned to move out of Japan. He told me that he had applied for immigration to Australia and Canada and been granted permanent residence status in both countries. When I interviewed him again in May 2014, he was making plans to travel to these countries so he could explore his future in them. But another surprise was awaiting me as Mehdi said that being treated as a guest was one of the reasons why he wanted to leave Japan with his wife. He explained this by using a Bengali metaphor, *ghar-jamai*, to describe his position in the country:

> Japan treats foreigners as guests. Everyone admires the Japanese people for their hospitality. In Bangladesh, we treat guests with special attention, as we know that they will leave soon. But you know, I have been living in Japan for about two decades. I have a Japanese passport. Yet, if I tell anyone that my country is Japan, he or she will think I am joking. In America, for example, a Chinese can claim to be an American, but that is not possible in Japan. Here, one must look Japanese. I always feel I'm a *ghar-jamai* here: respected, well-treated, but not as one of them. That's why I have acquired permanent residency in both Australia and Canada.

In Bangladesh, as in other South Asian countries, the patrilocal family is the norm; a woman moves out of her family home to join her husband's family. In the absence of a son, some wealthy families may ask a son-in-law to move in with them after marriage. These sons-in-law are called *ghar-jamai*, which literally means a son-in-law living with his parents-in-law. According to the social custom of treating the son-in-law as a special guest, a *ghar-jamai* is treated specially. However, he has no voice in decision-making in the family, which is customarily regarded as a man's role. Isolated from important decision-making and other responsibilities in the family, he always remains an outsider and eventually becomes an object of ridicule. Therefore, none wants to be a *ghar-jamai*, and those in such a position always seek to establish their own families, independent of their in-laws' influence.[51] Mehdi's plan to move out of Japan resonated with his use of this Bengali term. It indicated how marginalized Mehdi felt in Japan and how frustrated he was at not being able to become incorporated into Japanese society because of his different physical appearance. In fact, all my interviewees in professional careers shared similar perspectives about social marginalization, and most told me about plans to leave Japan. Four of my interviewees among the scholarship recipients, who had already been granted Japanese citizenship, left Japan for higher studies in the USA after my fieldwork, and subsequently found jobs and permanently settled there. On several occasions I interviewed one of the leaders of the Bangladeshi migrant community who was married to a Japanese professional and had raised their two children in Tokyo. After marriage, both children moved out of the parental home. This man told me about business plans in Bangladesh. I recently learned that he had established a business in medical tourism in Bangladesh and was staying most of the time there, while his wife lived in their family home in Tokyo.

Currently, most Bangladeshi migrants enter Japan with student visas to attend language and vocational schools. A close look at such migrants demonstrates how Japan's immigration policy and the migrants' social class in Bangladesh together make their migration temporary and return to Bangladesh inevitable.[52] Of all Bangladeshi migrants in Japan, the language students live the most marginal life with hardly any social bonding with Japanese society. Through working in the service sector, most often in Japanese restaurants with Japanese co-workers and serving Japanese clients, they quickly acquire fluency in colloquial Japanese and a basic knowledge of Japanese society and culture. However, their life in Japan is almost entirely devoted to working in multiple part-time jobs and commuting between these jobs, as well as attending school to maintain the legality of their stay in the country. The centrality of their work shapes their unvarying daily routine. Jakir, who was twenty-six years old and unmarried, came to Japan as a language student four years ago. He described his normal day. He woke up between 6 and 7 A.M., washed, and rushed to his first job. After working for five to six hours, he went to school, where he stayed for the next three to four hours, resting and going through the course material. After class, he went to his next job for another five to six hours. He then returned home, usually on the last train, took a shower, and prepared dinner. After dinner, he called home for several minutes to an hour, and stayed up until 2:00 or 3:00 A.M. Probably looking at the expression of disbelief on my face, Jakir smiled and asked me to compare his routine with those of others like him. Before I could speak, one of his roommates began telling me about his own schedule. He had morning classes. After school, he went to work at two jobs back-to-back, and also finished late at night. During the weekends, both worked extra hours because they had no classes. Most such migrants said they organized their daily schedule around work throughout their entire four-to six-year stay in Japan. Most migrants I approached agreed to be interviewed but often could not find the time. So I accompanied them on the train to or from school or work and had multiple shorter interviews with them.

From the beginning, those entering Japan with language student visas focused totally on earning as much money as possible, working in part-time jobs rather than studying. Most of them began as dishwashers (*araimono*) in restaurant kitchens. At the start, it was a great culture shock, as menial jobs in restaurants are seen as dirty and low-class in Bangladesh. But there were several reasons why they had to take any kind of job and begin earning. They were under tremendous pressure to send money to their families, who needed to repay the loans they had taken to finance their sons' migration to Japan. These migrants also had to take care of their living costs and tuition fees as well as send remittances for their families' monthly expenses and health problems, the education of their siblings, social and religious occasions, etc. Furthermore, both the origin and destination communities of the migrants emphasized the importance of earning money— the more one earned and sent home, the higher one's status. As Ashoka (a twenty-seven-year-old who had come to Japan as a language student five years ago) said, "We come to Japan for success, which is measured solely in terms of money, nothing else. I must send a lot of money to my family. No one will ask about what I do in Japan as long as I send money. If I cannot send money, everyone will start saying that I have failed."

While in Bangladesh work in menial jobs was not considered a way to achieve success, Bangladeshis at home did not see this link between restaurant jobs in Japan and migrants' social status. Still, migrants doing such work did not tell the truth about their jobs in Japan. My interviewees said that they often created stories of working in semiprofessional jobs, as hotel managers and cashiers, to tell their families and friends in Bangladesh. However, in Japan their status-related concerns about working menial jobs were so inconsequential that I even found many fully funded Bangladeshi students in PhD programs doing part-time jobs at restaurants to increase their income. In fact, on several occasions, my interviewees offered me part-time jobs to earn more money in addition to the stipend I received as a Monbusho student.

The motivation to work menial jobs, especially for those entering Japan as language students, was further bolstered by the way migrants came to see their school attendance. They found learning Japanese *kanji* (Chinese) characters a daunting task. Since most students in their classes were Chinese proficient in kanji, Bangladeshi students could not keep up and quickly fell behind. They also heard from senior Bangladeshi students that the schools did not recognize special efforts made in studies and every student received the same certificate, which simply indicated substantial progress in learning the Japanese language. So, they concluded that studying was useless[53] and that it made more sense to work hard in part-time jobs and earn as much as possible. However, they still had to attend classes regularly to maintain their student visas. Their school attendance turned into a mere excuse to maintain their legal residence in Japan, while they were almost entirely engaged in earning money at part-time jobs. This was why, as several of my interviewees told me, they were called *uso gakusei* (fake students) by the Japanese police and some unsympathetic local employers.

In some ways, migrants entering as language students mimicked the lives of the early migrants who overstayed their visas. While the visa-overstayers had to live outside the cities and Japanese residential areas to avoid detection and deportation, language students could live in cities with their residence or alien cards. Moreover, they learned Japanese almost like natives and learned basic social and cultural information. Yet, they had to deal with the issue of maintaining their legality as students by concealing a portion of their work hours, which exceeded the legally permitted twenty-eight hours per week. So, they would send their savings home immediately to avoid getting caught. Extended work hours and the fear of getting caught violating the law for working over the permitted amount discouraged them from interacting with other Bangladeshis or Japanese outside of their workplaces, which severely limited their feeling of belonging to Japan. While they would occasionally meet other co-ethnics in their homes and at ethnic stores, they were almost never able to develop friendships with Japanese people and eventually came to believe that the Japanese could not be their true friends. As Rahman (the owner of a struggling Indo-curry restaurant in his early thirties, who had entered Japan as a language student eleven years ago) explained,

> I never feel at home in Japan. I know that life here is far better and more comfortable than that in Bangladesh. Yet I do not like the "mentality" of people here. To tell you simply, there is no interaction. For example, I am having coffee with you now. This opportunity rarely comes with Japanese people. Friendship with them is only possible when you meet someone, have coffee and talk a little. After that you board the train and your friendship ends there. This is true in nine out of ten cases. You again meet after five or six months and behave like friends. Then, you part again. This is normal for them, but I cannot take it.

Although Rahman complained about the "mentality" of Japanese people, it was in fact structural barriers that kept him isolated and denied him the feeling of home. His only social interactions beyond work and language school were a few minutes spent with co-ethnics while shopping at ethnic stores and international phone calls to his immediate family, relatives, and friends in Bangladesh. Almost all my language student interviewees reported that they found it difficult to make friends with Japanese people, and therefore felt socially unwelcome in Japan. This structurally induced isolation of migrants in casual jobs was common among foreign nationals in Japan. For instance, Parreñas[54] observes that Filipino women working as entertainers in Tokyo bars start thinking about their departure almost as soon as they arrive because they have hardly any integration into Japanese society. Consequently, they organize their daily schedule around their work and virtual socializing with their families and friends back in the

Philippines. Similarly, Bangladeshi student migrants spent their days working multiple part-time jobs, attending school, and calling their parents, relatives, and friends in Bangladesh rather than seeking regular social life in Japan. Thus, these migrants' stay in Japan becomes solely for the purpose of earning money and developing any attachment to Japan is meaningless, as this will not lead to experiencing social belonging.

Compared with the student migrants, highly educated migrants in professional careers who were married to Bangladeshi women were less ambivalent about their position in Japan. These migrants were more likely to settle permanently in Japan because of their higher education, professional career, citizenship, and long-term residence in the country. They maintained very close ties with other Bangladeshi families in Tokyo, frequently socialized among themselves, and took the lead in celebrating ethnic and national cultural events—preparing participants (including child performers), helping organize events, and hosting delegates from Bangladesh. They appeared to have found their place within their ethnic/national community, as I noticed at several community events during my fieldwork in Tokyo. They also felt a sense of accomplishment at being able to migrate to Japan with their families and satisfaction about their living experience in the country. Nevertheless, social marginalization and consequently the pressure to move out of Japan would grow because of their concerns about raising children, as Leemon (a professional in his early forties, living in Tokyo with his wife and a daughter) explained. After graduation, Leemon had joined an IT company in Tokyo and had gone back to Bangladesh to get married. He was granted a Japanese passport through his employer's sponsorship, which allowed him greater flexibility in his job and made him eligible to buy an apartment in the country. Yet he was reluctant to do this:

> The problem now is that I must make a choice for my daughter. Either we settle here permanently, return to Bangladesh, or go to Australia. My daughter is growing up fast. She is now three-and-a-half years old. If she enters a Japanese school, we will not be able to return to Bangladesh before she completes the twelfth grade as her education will not be transferable to Bangladesh due to [the] incompatibility of Japanese education there. So, her education in Japan will be totally useless and she will fail to enter and catch up with her university education and professional career in Bangladesh. She will also find it extremely difficult to find friends due to her lack of social and cultural knowledge appropriate to Bangladesh. That's why I am looking for a job in an English-speaking country where the education system is compatible with that in Bangladesh. Moreover, I have seen that any Bengali child who goes to a Japanese school will never go back to Bangladesh. This happens in 99.99 percent of such cases. Children attending Japanese schools learn independence and live separately from their parents after graduating and entering adulthood with their own earnings. They become closer to their

friends and colleagues than their parents. So, my daughter will also go away from us eventually. Moreover, Japanese law does not allow parents to impose their decisions on the children, which means I will not be able to take my daughter to Bangladesh against her will in future. So, staying longer in Japan for me will mean losing my daughter, which I do not want. That's why I am planning to leave Japan before my daughter begins to go to school.

Leemon's narration explains how the most likely Bangladeshi migrants to permanently settle in Japan, professionals with legal permanent residency or citizenship, were actually less interested in settling permanently. While those in casual jobs (i.e., the early visa-overstayers and the student migrants) faced both legal and sociocultural barriers, the professional migrants faced only sociocultural challenges in permanently settling in Japan. Legal provision to bring their wives and children with them to Japan would create an opportunity for these migrants to establish their home and find belonging in Japan. However, the sociocultural barriers—as Leemon's concern about raising his daughter in Japan demonstrates—would prevent them from experiencing a sense of belonging, leading to their moving out of Japan. The case of Khan (a computer engineer in his mid-thirties) is even more revealing in this regard. He came to Japan in his late teens on a Monbusho scholarship for undergraduate studies. After completing his bachelor's degree in computer engineering, he began his career as a professional engineer at a major IT corporation. He went to Bangladesh to marry a Bangladeshi woman, returned with her to Japan, acquired Japanese citizenship, and bought a modern apartment in an expensive neighborhood in Tokyo. When I interviewed him in 2014, he had already applied to MBA programs in some high-ranking universities in the United States. Two years later, I learned that he had been admitted to an MBA program at a prestigious business school in Boston and received funding from a Japanese scholarship. In my most recent communication with him, he told me that he had joined an American corporation in Denver, bought a house in a gated community, and sent his five-year-old daughter to an expensive private school. He also mentioned that he had applied for a green card through his employer, and he and his family would renounce their Japanese citizenship once they became U.S. citizens.

In sum, the early Bangladeshi migrants came to Japan as tourists and took jobs, overstaying their visas despite their awareness that they could be arrested and deported back to Bangladesh. Those who entered Japan as self-funded language students also knew about Japan's strict enforcement of immigration law and would planned to return to Bangladesh as soon as their student visas expired. The Japanese immigration regime and sociocultural barriers pushed them to the margins of society. They had extremely busy daily schedules, working in multiple jobs and socializing minimally with the Japanese. Even marriages to Japanese women and legal permanent residency or citizenship could do little to help them overcome barriers to integration into Japanese society. Those in higher education and professional employment living with family also experienced marginalization and isolation. All my interviewees, regardless of their legal status, education, occupation, or length of stay in Japan, reportedly experienced an acute lack of belonging and consequently thought of their stay in the country as temporary.

Bangladeshis' experience of feeling marginalized and excluded in Japan is not unique. It is an outcome of government policy and Japanese society's attitude toward migrants in general. As Shipper[55] observes, Japan created a racial hierarchy in the labor market for foreigners in which *Nikkeijin* (descendants of former Japanese immigrants to South America) and *Zainichi* (Koreans stranded in Japan during World War II) occupy higher positions with better pay and other benefits than South Asians, who are often at the bottom of the ladder, with casual jobs, poor pay, and dangerous working environments. The Nikkeijin were well received by the government because of their Japanese ancestry and were therefore more likely to settle in the country permanently. When the Japanese government revised the Immigration Control and Refugee Recognition Act in 1990 to offer them long-term visas, several hundred thousand people of Japanese-origin from Latin America "reentered" the country. The Nikkeijin were mainly attracted by the opportunity for higher earnings; indeed, they gave themselves Japanese names, *dekasegi*, which literally means "go out and earn money." Most came from Brazil, followed by those from Peru, Argentina, and other Latin American countries characterized by limited income opportunities. Within two decades after 1990, the number of Nikkeijin in Japan mushroomed, from fewer than 5,000 in the mid-1980s to more than 300,000 in 2005.[56]

Initially, the Nikkeijin held on to their belief that they had returned to their ethnic homeland. But it did not take them long to feel marginalized as foreigners in Japan.[57] Their interactions with Japanese society, which were frequently marked by tension and disappointment on both sides, disproved the Japanese government's assumption that common descent would facilitate not only harmony but integration. Tsuda[58] describes how this ethnic rejection led the Brazilian Nikkeijin to withdraw to their own ethnic communities, increasing their social isolation and alienation from Japanese society through self-segregation. When the Japanese economy entered a recession in 2008, a number of these migrants lost their jobs, and in 2009–2010, a government program offered cash payments of nearly $4,000 to defray travel expenses on condition that the recipients leave Japan permanently (a proviso that was subsequently amended to three years). Approximately 20,000 South American nationals took advantage of the offer.[59] By 2011, the population of Japanese Brazilians in Japan had fallen by about a third, and more Brazilians were leaving Japan than arriving.[60] If even migrants with recognized ancestral ties to Japan experienced marginalization and went home, total strangers like Bangladeshi migrants would surely always see Japan as a foreign country.

Conclusion

Several aspects stand out about Bangladeshi migration in Japan: Bangladeshis migrate to Japan for higher income opportunities and their stay in Japan tends to be temporary. And even if they live in Japan for decades, sociocultural barriers make it difficult for them to settle permanently and find belonging.

As one of the most densely populated countries in the developing world, Bangladesh has been a major source of international migration. People in Bangladesh look for income opportunities abroad due to lack of employment opportunities and limited room for upward socioeconomic mobility. Some enterprising Bangladeshis saw Japan's visa-on-arrival policy as opening Japan's otherwise closed border to foreign workers and they were part of the first flow of labor migrants to Japan. The preference for migrant workers among Japanese employers offered them employment while the lax immigration law enforcement allowed them to stay in Japan without legal papers for a few years. However, Japan closed its border in about three years due to increasing anti-immigrant opinion and began to strictly enforce immigration laws by arresting undocumented migrant workers, including Bangladeshis. A small number of migrants were able to acquire legal residency by marrying Japanese women, but they lived a marginal social life and remained excluded from mainstream Japanese society. They maintained close connections with their families and relatives in Bangladesh, which further spread the idea of higher income opportunities in Japan among Bangladeshis and encouraged aspiring individuals and families to enter Japan by other available means. It was this perception of Japan as the destination with the highest income-earning opportunities among Bangladeshis that would draw subsequent migrants to Japan. The belief that they could earn more in relatively shorter period in Japan was so strong that individuals already admitted to universities in Bangladesh often would leave their studies to seek admission in Japanese language schools, which would not give them a credential useful for finding professional jobs. Moreover, those entering Japan for higher education with Japanese government scholarships, as well as their spouses, would frequently take paid employment. Hence, the generalized perception among Bangladeshis is that migration to Japan is a financially motivated act.

The ability to enter Japan and find income-earning opportunities, however, would be accompanied by legal exclusion and social and cultural marginalization. The visa-overstayers were outright illegal migrants and would have to live in constant fear of being arrested and deported to Bangladesh. Those entering as self-funded language students would also have to navigate between legality (as students) and illegality (for breaking the law on work limits). Those staying longer as legal residents through marriage or professional employment would experience social and cultural marginalization due to the sociocultural barriers that prevented them from entering the mainstream of Japanese society. As a result, all Bangladeshis in Japan—regardless of their employment, education, occupation, and marital status—find it difficult to settle permanently and raise a family. They all come to the realization that Japan cannot be their final destination. So, they must plan to move out of Japan to Bangladesh or some other country where they can establish their home and find belonging.

Getting education and finding a career is followed by beginning a family and building home to raise the family. Migration to Japan offers Bangladeshis the chance to earn higher amounts of money—which often surpasses income in professional jobs in Bangladesh by a huge margin—and allows them and their families to live a middle-class life. However, unlike other migration destination countries that allow migrants to settle permanently and raise a family, Japan does not offer opportunities to stay permanently. Consequently, Bangladeshis in Japan turn to Bangladesh and other traditional immigrant countries to settle. As the following chapter shows, these migrants send remittances to their original home, Bangladesh.

2

Narratives of Remittance
from Japan

•••••••••••••••••••••

Bangladeshi migration to Japan is characterized by the expectation of earning large sums of money, with young, educated, male individuals and their middle- and upper-middle class families viewing it as a status-enhancing opportunity. Thus, it is an aspirational journey, as the goal of migrating to Japan is to achieve a better future than is possible in Bangladesh. Migrants decision to migrate to Japan includes migrants' immediate families and relatives, demonstrating the social embeddedness of this aspirational migration, in contrast to migration as a matter of individual choice or one that is socially forced upon them. Migration scholars have explored the role of the belief that leaving would be better than staying in various origin communities.[1] These studies show that an individual's interest in migration exists within a particular social context and is only possible in that social formation.[2] In the previous chapter, I showed how Bangladeshi migrants' decision to leave Japan involves their realization of the impossibility of establishing a home and finding belonging in Japan, which makes them look beyond Japan for other migration opportunities or return to their home. In this chapter, I discuss these migrants' perceptions about their home, including their immediate families, relatives, and the locations where they establish their homes to raise families. In particular, I focus on narrative constructions of home through their remittance. Thus, I share stories of remittance among Bangladeshi migrants in Japan, spanning nearly thirty years since the Japanese bubble economy—a period over which several economic recessions gradually reduced their numbers.

I begin by introducing three men who represent three broad categories of Bangladeshis in Japan in terms of their legal status and socioeconomic standing and without mention of their original social background in Bangladesh. Amin (a pseudonym), a permanent resident, entered Japan under the visa-waiver program for Bangladeshis during 1987–1989 and prolonged his stay by first becoming undocumented and later acquiring Japanese legal permanent residence by marrying a Japanese woman. Amin represents the oldest cohort of Bangladeshi migrants in Japan. Rahman entered Japan as a self-funded student in a Japanese language school (*nihon gakko*); he later transferred to two vocational schools (*senmo -gakko*) and finally to a four-year undergraduate program in a private university. He represents the most recent and the largest segment of Bangladeshi migrants in the country. Rafi is a Bangladeshi with a Japanese passport who came to Japan as a student on a *Monbusho* scholarship from the Japanese government in 2001. After graduating from university, he was employed in a multinational corporation in Tokyo and was later naturalized. He represents the small number of educated middle-class Bangladeshi expatriates in Japan. While the first two groups typically work in the secondary labor market,[3] this last group occupies a relatively higher position in Japan's formal labor market. Certainly, not all Bangladeshi migrants precisely fit these categories. So, I intersperse the narratives of these three migrants with stories from others to construct coherent narratives[4] about their homemaking through remittance. The ways these migrants explain their remittance help us to understand the development of their perceptions of self, home, and belonging.

Amin is a forty-six-year-old Bangladeshi migrant who lives in Tokyo. He came to Japan in 1988 after completing high school (the twelfth grade) at age twenty-one. He is the third child and second son of his parents. His elder brother knew a broker who helped Amin migrate to Japan as a tourist and find a job in a Japanese construction company. Amin overstayed his visa and turned "illegal." He worked in his first job without any problem, until 1990, when his employer asked him to leave because immigration law enforcement was tightening. Amin found another job in an electronics manufacturing company outside Tokyo to avoid police detection. However, he felt insecure every day because of increasingly stringent immigration law enforcement. As a result, he began to look for a Japanese woman willing to marry him so that he could get legal papers to stay in Japan. With the help of some friends in the Bangladeshi migrant community, Amin met a Japanese woman who was seven years older than him. After spending a couple of days with her, Amin married her in 1994 and acquired legal permanent residency. Since then, Amin and his wife have been living in an apartment in Saitama Prefecture.

Like other migrants of Amin's generation, he migrated to Japan to earn money. He eventually married a Japanese woman and started a family in Japan. Yet, the social and cultural barriers were so great that he was unable to feel at home in

Japan. The relational distance between him and his wife and in-laws in Japan coincided with his continuous attachment to his origin family in Bangladesh, which shaped his financial decisions, including remittance. Amin explained, "I migrated to Japan as a bachelor. I left my parents and siblings, my family, in Bangladesh. I thought that whatever happened to me in Japan, I would honor my responsibility to my family. So, I sent them money without thinking whether I needed to send it. Besides, I thought I would return home someday. So, I purchased land in Bangladesh and developed an apartment building on it. All this I did by sending home money from Japan." Here, Amin talked about his sense of responsibility to his family in Bangladesh as one reason he faithfully sent remittances. It is a social norm in Bangladesh for working sons to provide for their parents financially, and I have not come across any Bangladeshi migrant who disregards this norm.[5] Amin explicitly mentioned the parents and siblings he left behind in Bangladesh, which he referred to as "home," a place where he anticipated returning one day. Amin told me that his wife had never interfered with his money management. She did not even ask how much Amin earned or how much he spent in Japan or in Bangladesh. She has a job in a Japanese daycare center. Instead of asking for Amin's money, she even helped him to construct an apartment building in Bangladesh with her savings. While it was difficult to confirm the reliability of Amin's story about his wife's support of his plans to return to Bangladesh, Amin's own perception of lacking home in Japan and his aspiration of having one in Bangladesh, where he left his family, is clear from his narration.

So, despite his being the second son, Amin assumed the role of breadwinner for his family in Bangladesh after his migration to Japan. His elder brother was helping his father with the family business and his two younger brothers were in school. Therefore, Amin sent all his income to his father in Bangladesh—about $2,200 per month. His father would spend the money on the family's maintenance and also on the education of his younger brothers. The excess amount would be deposited in his father's bank account in Bangladesh. Amin explained that he could never think of separating his personal assets from those of his father and he could not conduct banking until he became Japanese permanent resident through marriage.[6] When his father died, he was still undocumented in Japan and was not able to open a bank account. So Amin used his mother's bank account to save his money in Bangladesh. By the time his mother passed away, he had already acquired legal papers, visited Bangladesh, and opened his own account where he put his savings. Amin and his wife had no children and did not expect to have any because of his wife's age and other physical problems. But he had property in Bangladesh, including an apartment building and significant savings. With a job and a wife in Japan, and no urgent reason for going to Bangladesh, Amin was reluctant to give serious thought to his savings and future in Japan. He was certain that he would return to Bangladesh someday, though he did not know when.

Rahman, age thirty-four, migrated to Japan as a self-funded language student in 2005 after completing a bachelor's degree in English literature at a university in Bangladesh. He was the eldest son of his parents and had a brother and three sisters. With the help of his cousin in Japan, Rahman contacted a broker to help him get a student visa. He paid the broker $1,000 to obtain his admission to a Japanese language school and complete other formalities for a student visa. Once he was issued the visa, he paid the remaining amount (about $11,000), which included his tuition for the first year at the language school. After arriving in Japan, Rahman stayed with his cousin, who helped him with the initial paper-work at the ward (local administrative) office and opening an account with Japan Post. He also helped Rahman find his first part-time job at a Japanese restaurant. Rahman worked four days in the restaurant while attending the language school as a full-time student. Soon he started another part-time job at another Japanese restaurant. With two jobs, he worked over sixty-five hours every week and attended school. Although the length of Rahman's work hours may seem astonishingly long for any student, this was common for self-funded Bangladeshi students in Japanese language and vocational schools. A student visa often func-tioned as pretext for migrants to maintain legal status while they worked as much as full-time workers or even longer.[7] Sociologist Gracia Liu-Farrer[8] has observed the same practice of acquiring visas and maintaining student status at language schools as a way for Chinese migrant workers to enter and stay in Japan.

Like Amin, Rahman also sent remittances to Bangladesh as soon as he began to earn money. Getting married to a Bangladeshi woman and starting a family in Japan for these young, single, male Bangladeshis was out of question due to both a legal restriction on bringing a spouse and living an extremely marginal life between school and multiple part-time jobs. So, their sense of belonging to their origin (i.e., parental) family in Bangladesh remained unaffected after they migrated to Japan and left behind their family members (e.g., their parents and unmarried siblings). As the norm suggests, Rahman assumed the role of the pri-mary breadwinner for his family. He told me:

> I send money to my parents because the whole family is now dependent on me. My father had a business, which he sold to pay my broker, and rented out the store. So, I regularly send money for my family's maintenance. Moreover, I send extra money on special occasions. I believe it is my responsibility to spend money on my parents' needs. I saw my father do the same for my grandparents and his siblings (as much as he could). I suppose I have inherited this mentality from my father. I believe that if you do for your parents, your children will do the same for you.

Rahman's explanation of his remittance uses common economic conceptions of repayment, as his father had to sell his business to finance Rahman's migration. But Rahman also recognized that regularly sending remittances for family maintenance and other occasions was a normal practice socialized in the family. Thus, he sent money to Bangladesh every month, initially to his father's bank account. After the family's needs were met, the remainder of the money accumulated in his father's account. He was able to pay for the marriages of his three sisters and his younger brother's education. Like many other Bangladeshi migrants, he bought two plots of land in Dhaka and an apartment in his hometown, and deposited the rest in a savings account in a bank in Bangladesh. Finally, he managed to bring his brother to Japan as a self-funded student like himself. How Rahman used his remittance points to Bangladesh as his perception of home, where his parents and siblings reside.

Unlike Amin, who acquired permanent residency by marrying a Japanese woman and living with her in an apartment in Japan, Rahman was completely excluded from Japanese society. Moreover, he—and migrants like him with student visas—did not see acquiring permanent residency as a viable choice. Yet, Rahman extended his stay in Japan and maximized his earning potential as much as he could by seeking admission into different schools. Thus, he had spent the longest possible time in Japan on a student visa—two years in the language school, four years in two vocational schools, and another four years in a private university. So, he suspected that his forthcoming visa renewal application would be denied. Moreover, he had gotten married during his previous visit to Bangladesh a year ago, which showed that Rahman's home was in Bangladesh where his most intimate relatives—parents, siblings, and wife—were living. When I met him for the last time in February 2014, he mainly spoke about his plan to return to Bangladesh in the next few weeks.

Rafi, age thirty-one, migrated to Japan in 2001 to study on a Monbusho scholarship. He was the eldest child in his family, with a younger brother and a younger sister. His father had passed away when he was in the eleventh grade. After he graduated from high school, Rafi was admitted to the Bangladesh University of Engineering and Technology (BUET), the best university in the country. He was also selected for the Monbusho undergraduate scholarship through an extremely competitive screening process. Many BUET students would not have considered entering Japanese universities for undergraduate studies, because many BUET graduates had opportunities to go to the United States and other Western countries for higher studies. However, Rafi accepted the scholarship, anticipating that it would enable him to immediately contribute financially to his family. He told me:

> My education was all that my parents and I looked up to. You know, this is how middle-class families in Bangladesh think. With my parents' support and encouragement, I did really good in my classes and eventually got admitted into BUET. But my father's untimely death left me no option but to come to Japan with [a] Monbusho scholarship and financially [support] my mother while also continuing my higher education. My father did not have much

savings and his business took a downturn in his absence. So, I had to step in to take some of the family responsibility as the eldest son.

At nineteen years old (in 2001), Rafi left home to study in Japan. He became the primary breadwinner for his mother and two younger siblings and sent money every month to support them. His mother also received a small return from what was left of his father's business, which was barely enough, and his younger brother and sister were growing up and advancing in school, which substantially increased their educational expenses. Rafi took a part-time job to earn extra money in addition to his stipend to be able to keep up with the growing financial needs of his family. Gradually, he became the main financial contributor to his family in Bangladesh. In addition to sending money to maintain the family, he sent some money to one of his cousins, who was "more than a brother" to him, every month, which took care of about one-third of his cousin's monthly family budget. Rafi also invested $15,000 in a joint business with this cousin. Occasionally, he also sent money to other relatives for various purposes, including the educational expenses of one of his cousin's children, the marriage ceremony of another cousin, a one-time allowance to the manager of his father's business, and a donation to the local religious school.

After graduating with a bachelor's degree in electrical engineering from a top Japanese university, Rafi took employment in a U.S.-based multinational networking company in Tokyo in 2008. As his income increased in his highly paid job, he increased his allowance to his mother. In 2011, he married a Bangladeshi woman, also an engineer, who was working in Canada. They were first introduced to one another by a common friend, who also mediated between the two families in discussing the marriage. Rafi reported that he did not save anything for himself and sent all his money to his family in Bangladesh. Moreover, he incurred a huge debt for his wedding expenses, which he had to pay back with savings from his income. This debt burden substantially limited his ability to send as much money to his immediate family and relatives in Bangladesh as he had done before his marriage. Fortunately for Rafi and his family, his younger brother had graduated with an engineering degree from a university in Bangladesh and found a fairly well-paid job. So, his brother began to share family expenses and reduced Rafi's financial burden.

While he shared with Amin and Rahman a perception of home in Bangladesh consisting of parents and siblings, Rafi had a different understanding of his future home in Canada, where he planned to move and settle permanently. He told me that he was trying to find a vacancy in his company in Canada. The last time I met with Rafi, he told me that he had been transferred to the Canadian branch of his company.

As I describe above, Amin, Rahman, and Rafi all migrated to Japan in their early twenties, primarily to earn money. While the early visa-overstayers and the self-funded students in language schools have clear financial motive, other students sponsored by Japanese government scholarships are also financially motivated. As unmarried sons, they identify with their parental families and share their financial responsibility by regularly sending money home. Amin, Rahman, and Rafi considered their stay in Japan temporary and planned to move out of the country someday. However, there were also crucial differences among them. Amin married a Japanese woman to regularize his stay in Japan by acquiring permanent residency, Rahman married a co-ethnic woman in Bangladesh, and Rafi married a Bangladeshi woman living in Canada. All three worked in casual and part-time jobs in Japanese factories and restaurants. However, both Amin and Rahman continued to work in their casual and part-time jobs, while Rafi ascended to a professional career in a multinational organization. Moreover, they demonstrated varying patterns of remittance despite assuming the role of main financial provider for their families in Bangladesh. In addition to providing their families with financial necessities, Amin and Rahman invested large amounts of money in income-generating activities, buying land, developing apartments, and saving in bank accounts, while Rafi neither invested nor saved anything in Bangladesh. The differences in their motivations to send remittances are likely linked to their future plans—Amin and Rahman planned to return to Bangladesh and thus wanted to establish income sources for themselves in the country. But Rafi did not need any income in Bangladesh, as he planned to migrate to Canada and settle there permanently.

Despite coming from the same origin country and leaving for the same reason (to earn money), Bangladeshi migrants in Japan exhibit varying patterns of remittance that correspond to 1) their inability to settle permanently in Japan and raise a family, 2) their access—or lack thereof—to upward social mobility in Japan or another destination country, and 3) their experience of feeling "at home" by establishing a home and finding belonging with intimate relatives beyond Japan in Bangladesh or a third country.

Motivations to Send Remittance

All Bangladeshi migrants in Japan sent remittances to their home in Bangladesh. As young single males, they left behind their families, including parents, dependent siblings, and other relatives. With increased incomes, they took responsibility over the family budget, purchasing family property, education, healthcare, marriages, and parents' pilgrimages, as well as helping with job searches and committing money to charity and joint investments. In addition, they sent money to other relatives, friends, and occasionally neighbors. I found widely varying degrees of involvement, from remittance being completely voluntary (i.e., sending remittances without being asked by the remittance recipients) to almost absolutely nonvoluntary (i.e., sending remittances under unavoidable pressures), and the migrants also had various levels of understanding of social-cultural factors and of rational calculation in regard to remittance.[9]

Sending remittances to the family was one of the most common acts of transnationalism for Bangladeshis in Japan. Contrary to academic assumptions about rationally calculating economic interests or sacrificing self-interest for loved ones, migrants explained their remittance as a "normal" act, which they did without much prodding. For instance, Rashed (a twenty-seven-year-old professional engineer, who entered Japan years ago in 2006 as a Monbusho scholarship awardee) sent money to his mother every month for regular family expenses. He was the oldest son in his family, with another brother and a sister. Rashed's father had passed away before he migrated to Japan and his mother remained a widow and a housewife, so the family was totally dependent on him as the only income earner. Jaman (a twenty-nine-year-old married IT professional, who also had entered Japan as a self-funded student eight years ago) also sent money to his family regularly, although his father was alive and was the head of the household. Besides sending money for ordinary family expenses, Jaman also sent money for special occasions, such as the marriages of his two sisters, and to finance the migrations of a brother-in-law and a younger brother to Japan. Instead of seeing the recipients of their remittance as separate entities than themselves, or as people at arms-length in economic transactions, both Rashed and Jaman described their remittance to family members as part of their role of family breadwinner according to the prevailing norms in Bangladesh. Jaman explained that "Sending money to the parents is my responsibility. It is our family tradition. I saw my father spending for my grandparents, uncles, and aunts. And I believe my children will do the same if they see me following the tradition. This is natural and I believe it is transmitted to younger generations not by reading books, but by family practices." This statement suggests that Jaman did not feel compelled or coerced, but sent money as a member of his family, which socialized him to accept providing for them as "normal."

However, norms cannot not always ensure complete compliance, which, at times and for some people, must be elicited through the concept of obligation. For instance, Kabir (a thirty-one-year-old banker who had entered Japan twelve years ago as a Monbusho scholarship awardee) sent large amounts of money to his family to renovate their home and purchase land in Dhaka and to fund his parents' pilgrimage to Mecca and the marriages of his brother and sister. He also sent a regular amount to his mother for the family's monthly expenses. Despite being the youngest member of his family, he felt this obligation because he believed that his father had spent more on his education than he could afford, which had depleted his family's resources and deprived his siblings of the same opportunities. This realization grew as he looked at his achievements in an elite school in Bangladesh vis-à-vis those of his elder brother and sister, who had attended the local school. In addition, as a practicing Muslim, he attributed all his success to the blessings of God, which his parents earned for him through their daily prayers. Indeed, Kabir's father had performed a special prayer for him during the Hajj pilgrimage at Mecca. So, Kabir tried to please his parents in the belief that his good fortune would be with him as long as he had their blessings. Kabir told me that he often reassured his mother, "Never worry about money. As long as I eat, I will also feed you."

Additionally, many of my informants talked about a sense of reciprocity in sending remittances to their families in Bangladesh. They recognized that their families had "invested" a great deal of money, time, and effort in raising them: sending them to the best schools, taking care of their health, and so forth. Therefore, even if their parents did not need money or ask for it, they felt obliged to pay them back. This was particularly true of those working in professional jobs. As Mamun (in his late thirties, the owner of a halal shop who had entered Japan as a language student sixteen years ago) said, "I send money to my parents because I cannot help them physically. As a son, it is my duty to take care of them. They have brought me into this world and they took the best care of me. My debt to them is inestimable. No amount of money can compensate them. Still, I try as much as possible to repay them."

Mamun's conception of reciprocity is different from how we understand the term in a market situation. In a market, one exchanges something with another interested party with the expectation of reciprocity in an equal or agreed-upon return in cash or kind, which is a legal obligation. Neither Mamun nor his parents thought of Mamun's remittance as obligatory. In fact, he told me that his mother would always ask him if his income was sufficient for him to live comfortably in Tokyo, which she knew was the most expensive city in the world. Thus, while Mamun's explanation alludes to reciprocity, this was not legally binding and no legal action would be taken if he did not send remittances to his mother. Yet he strongly felt that he should send remittances, which came from his feeling of indebtedness to his parents for taking care of him. His sense of gratitude perhaps grew even stronger due to his affection for his mother, so much so that he knew that no amount of money would be sufficient to pay back the favor he received from her. Thus, despite his implicit knowledge about an absence of legal obligations, Mamun sent remittances, which made his mother and younger brother happy. This reveals Mamun's deeper feelings for his family, who remain the relational core of his perception of home.

While migrants' stories about their remittance almost always included their immediate family, some also sent remittances to help people outside their immediate family, which indicates an expanded sense of home. For instance, Rafi (introduced at the beginning of this chapter) gave a detailed account of such remittance:

> One of my cousins is struggling financially, as she is the only income-earner and her husband is unemployed. While her teaching job provides enough for their monthly expenses, it is difficult for her to arrange the large sums of money required at the beginning of her son's school year. So, I help her. I have also set up a joint fund with my other cousins for another cousin who is a

widow with two children. I asked all my cousins to contribute to the fund as much as they could to pay for the educational expenses of her children. I also send money occasionally to my father's ex-manager, who lives next to our house. We feel a strong emotional bond with him, as he has been very close to us since our childhood. However, there is a practical interest in helping him as well, since his family takes care of my mother and sister, and I depend on them for the latter's security.

Rafi's remittance to his father's ex-manager involved a kind of reciprocity; in contrast, those to his cousins involved no expectation of return. Whereas Rafi felt close to the former through years of familial closeness, the latter are connected to him by blood. This shows that individuals who are not blood related may become part of the family through long-term services to the family, but those related by blood are members without offering services to claim some kind of reciprocity. As Rafi explained, blood relatives are automatically entitled to support from migrant relatives. These remittances indicate the presence of what Gouldner[10] called benevolence, and demonstrate Rafi's sense of obligation and reciprocity to people he perceives as members of his family and who belong to his "home."

In addition to the immediate family and closely related individuals, Bangladeshis sometimes send remittances to distant relatives and unrelated neighbors. One informant, Shams (thirty-two years old; he entered Japan as a student with funding from an nongovernmental organization [NGO] and became a sales executive) told me that he sent small amounts of money to a neighborhood boy he had known for a long time. He called the boy *parar sele* (nonkin, literally "a son of the neighborhood"). Another informant, Saleem (forty-six years old; he entered Japan as a tourist and later regularized his legal status by marrying a Japanese woman) said he sent money to his mother to feed around thirty poor neighbors every Wednesday so that they would pray for his deceased father, a common religious practice among Muslims in Bangladesh. Moreover, he often sent money to his mother to simply donate to her needy neighbors. While this may be seen as a way of supporting his mother to maintain higher status among neighbors by offering financial assistance, Saleem mentioned that he occasionally sent money against his mother's wishes (such as by donating to the neighborhood boy's football club). These remittances show his extended conception of obligations to people in his community of origin beyond the immediate family.

It is clear from the examples above that Bangladeshi migrants send remittances to their immediate families, relatives, and neighbors out of their social-cultural obligation to family, reciprocating family investment in their upbringing, including migration and the benevolence of kin and nonkin. Migration scholars have already recognized these motivations behind migrant remittance; those adopting sociocultural approaches highlight social and cultural factors and those adopting the NELM approach recognize rationality in the determination of remittance. What is common to both approaches the assumption that migrants' membership in the family and origin community (in the sociocultural approach), or rationality (in the NELM approach) is a given. While surveys and structured interviews with migrants might confirm both the sociocultural and economic understanding of remittance, a closer look into their stories about their life experiences in Japan reveals more. Their stories show us how they make decisions about remittance. They have their own agency that is based on their perception of common belonging to the family (and by extension to kin and the neighborhood). One key element common in all these stories is the geographical separation between the migrants and the family to which they reportedly belong and their perception that they maintain their membership by sending remittances. While the opportunities to earn more money in a shorter amount of time in Japan draws these migrants abroad and they leave behind their families in Bangladesh, they encounter insurmountable barriers to bringing their families with them to Japan, which necessitates sending remittances. Socialization into the culture of sharing family expenses, a deep feelings of gratitude and affection for the family, and a sense of obligation to the origin community all make it necessary for the migrants to send remittances. Thus, while migrant remittance is financial, it demonstrates their continued sense of membership in a family, from which they derive their sense of self and find belonging.

Home Beyond Japan

It is common practice for individuals to grow up, earn a living, and establish a home to raise a family. This is especially true in contexts characterized by a culture of migration, as sociologist Syed Ali identifies among Indian Muslim communities.[11] I concur with several other scholars in observing that migration is a way for young males from middle-class families in rural Bangladesh to maintain their family's livelihood.[12] Thus, I expected a significant number of Bangladeshi migrants to settle in Japan by building a home to raise their families there. The popular narratives depicting migration to Japan as a matter of individual and family decision also allude to the likelihood of these migrants settling in Japan. However, as I discussed earlier, migrants' ability to enter and stay in Japan, as well as their eventual return to Bangladesh or elsewhere, is decisively shaped by the institutional context in Japan. As I observed, migrants' entry and stay in the destination country and eventual return to the home country is strictly conditioned by the destination state's policy of denying the migrants permanent settlement and the right to establish a home.[13]

The nearly insurmountable barriers to establishing a home in Japan were well known among the migrants I encountered. Most interviewees among the early visa-overstaying migrants knew how easy it was to enter Japan with tourist visas, and some had very amicable encounters with police, especially before the cancellation of port-of-entry visas in 1990. However, they also faced numerous structural barriers. For instance, they were unable to open bank accounts and pay rent on their own as they were visa-overstayers and hence undocumented migrants. They were paid in cash, which they immediately sent to their families in Bangladesh using an informal money transfer system known as *hundi*.[14] As undocumented migrants, they avoided visiting Bangladesh because of they feared being fined and jailed and would not be able to ever re-enter Japan and resume their lucrative jobs. After 1990, their mobility within Japan also became severely limited. Employers were legally responsible for employing undocumented migrants, and police raided construction sites and residences to arrest and deport these undocumented migrants. Except for the few who marry Japanese women, their entire stay in Japan is marred by the fear of arrest and deportation, which results in them sending all their income to their families in Bangladesh as remittance. Their social isolation and lack of opportunities to establish home in Japan causes them to turn to their families and origin community for social membership and belonging, which they maintain through remittance.

Without the opportunity to enter as tourists and overstaying their visas, most Bangladeshi migrants entered Japan as language students after 1990. Like their predecessors who came to Japan as tourists, these migrants knew about the difficulties of trying to stay on in Japan and accepted their inevitable repatriation as a given. Common sense suggests that as "students" they would experience much better conditions in Japan than the visa-overstayers. However, I found this group equally vulnerable to institutional surveillance and restrictions. They were required to renew their student visas after two years, with supporting papers from their schools showing their regular attendance and bank statements showing that they had enough money. However, while they could get satisfactory progress reports from their schools as long as they paid tuition, they needed to conceal their additional income from work beyond the legally permitted limit. So, they would get direct deposits from one of their employers that would remain within the 28 hour a week limit; for the remaining work they would receive payment in cash and immediately send the money to Bangladesh through informal channels to avoid detection.

The self-funded student migrants learned from earlier Bangladeshi migrants that visa-overstaying was risky and uncertain and not worth trying. The undocumented migrants had to move out of Tokyo, cut all ties with their friends, and live in isolation in remote workplaces to avoid capture. So, the self-funded student migrants did not overstay their visas—unlike their Chinese counterparts, the majority of whom would become undocumented and accessed the extensive Chinese co-ethnic networks.[15] These Bangladeshis rejected the idea of obtaining permanent residency by marrying Japanese women because of family pressure to marry Bangladeshi women[16] and their own perceptions of the difficulties of raising a family in Japan. Moreover, the migrants' extremely tight work and school schedules severely reduced their opportunities to meet local women and form friendships. Consequently, they rarely dated Japanese or other foreign women. Likewise, there was no possibility for them to stay on in Japan legally through professional jobs that provided work visas, as some of the Monbusho students did. Plus, most did not study seriously, and professional jobs demanded long working hours while offering low net savings compared to what they could save by working in part-time jobs. Additionally, finding professional jobs involved paying exorbitant fees to job brokers without the certainty of being able to change their student visas to work visas. Realizing that having a professional career and establishing a home in Japan was out of reach, these migrants sent all their savings to Bangladesh for family support and income generation for their futures in Bangladesh, where they would return to form their own families. They should have been able to do so with the large sums of money they earned in Japan; however, their middle- and upper-middle-class family background demanded they find careers upon their return to Bangladesh that would generate both income and social status.

Shakil, a thirty-one-year-old who entered Japan in 2005 as a language student, lamented, "I had earned a BA degree before coming to Japan. Now, my classmates have already advanced in their career as bureaucrats, professionals, and businessmen. What will I do with my Japanese diploma? I cannot even tell them what I studied or what I worked at in Japan. I have just wasted my life." Although my interviewees always emphasized their identity within their parental families, Shakil's statement revealed that, in addition to their family backgrounds, migrants' future careers determined their sense of self and their respective positions in society. His peers in Bangladesh finished university education and entered professional careers in respectable jobs or in businesses that provided both financial income and social status. While Shakil earned significantly large sums of money in Japan compared to his peers in Bangladesh, the diploma earned in a Japanese school would not help him get a professional job in Japan or Bangladesh. Nor would his work experience in Japanese restaurants offer him any career path in Bangladesh due to the low social status of restaurant work in Bangladesh. Thus, Shakil and other migrants like him would invest a certain portion of their remittance in projects that produced enough income for them to afford a lifestyle comparable to that of their peers with a career, income, and status in Bangladesh. I argue elsewhere[17] that this rational (i.e., individualistic, or selfish) perception of remittance emanated from a combination of the migrants' realization of their institutionally circumscribed position in Japan through their lived experiences of marginalization and their aspiration to establish a home and find belonging in Bangladesh.

Monbusho students who migrated to Japan had a different experience (and often different aspirations) than previous migrants from Bangladesh. Every year, over two hundred Bangladeshis entered Japan with Monbusho scholarships for higher education. Unlike the other migrants, they received a number of institutional supports from the very beginning and were preselected by Japanese universities and the Ministry of Education and supported by the Japanese Embassy in Bangladesh and the Japan Student Services Organization (JASSO). Within a few days of their arrival, they received residence and health insurance cards and were able to open bank accounts. Some months later, those who were married would be allowed to bring their spouses (and children, if any) to join them in Japan. Moreover, both the migrants and their spouses were legally permitted to earn money in Japan in addition to their scholarship stipends. But except for the tiny proportion of scholarship awardees who entered undergraduate programs and learned Japanese thoroughly, most needed to transfer their visas to one of the professional categories but failed to find professional jobs due primarily to their lack of Japanese language and cultural proficiency. While a few could extend their stay for a couple of years as postdoctoral researchers, most knew that leaving Japan was imminent and unavoidable. For career development, a higher standard of living, and a better future for their children, the majority would look for migration opportunities in developed countries such as Australia, the United States, the United Kingdom, and Canada, as Rafi did.[18] Most would qualify to become permanent residents through the merit-based immigration systems in these countries, and some would find professional jobs that allowed them to relocate there with their families. Researchers observe similar "twice migration" among Bangladeshis in Italy,[19] who respond to marginalization there by further migrating to the United Kingdom. This pattern of migration is also common among other Asian migrant groups such as Indians,[20] Filipinos, and Indonesians.[21] These highly educated professionals could earn and save their incomes in Japan legally, unlike their compatriots in low-skilled jobs. They kept most of their income with them in Japan while sending a small portion in remittance to maintain their connections with family and their origin community in Bangladesh to retain membership and belonging. This confirms researchers' observation that migration to Japan is often not the final step for any foreigner, but rather an interim step during which further options can be explored.[22]

Those migrants who remained in Japan as permanent residents and citizens with Japanese wives were the most likely to achieve integration and find belonging. Nevertheless, they maintained close connections with their relatives in Bangladesh because of their socially isolated and marginalized life in Japan. Perhaps this was why nearly all expressed their intention of spending their old age among relatives in Bangladesh. Even the scholarship awardees in professional careers in Japan reportedly experienced social marginalization and lack of belonging, which encouraged them to leave Japan and either remigrate to another country or return to Bangladesh.

Earning Money, Making Home

Simply put, Bangladeshi migrants in Japan earn money for their families, both the one they were born to and the one they aspire to begin. Thus, sending money to the family in Bangladesh is one of the most common practices of Bangladeshi migrants in Japan. To understand common reasons for the migrants to send remittances home, I collected 200 copies of money transaction forms for Bangladesh in the month of July 2014 from a money transferring agency (MTA) in Tokyo by promising to remove the personal information of the senders. The vast majority of the migrants (184 out of 200, or 92 percent) reported "family maintenance" as the reason for their remittance. My interviews and fieldwork also identified the family as the main recipient of migrant remittance. The stories in this chapter show how migrants responded to a social norm in Bangladesh that stipulates that the eldest son take over responsibility for the family once he grows up and begins to earn, because sons have full rights of inheritance and so remain family members all their lives. However, while Bangladeshi society places the greatest burden of family responsibility on the eldest son, migration modifies this to make the migrant son most responsible, regardless of birth order. For instance, Nayeem, a forty-six-year-old professional in hotel management, who was married to a Japanese woman and had a child with her, said:

> I'm the second son in our family. My elder brother is a doctor and brigadier general in the Bangladesh Army. As an honest officer, he faces difficulty in maintaining his own family with his limited income. Thus, he cannot give money to my parents and younger siblings regularly. He told me, "You are working abroad, that's why I see hope." I understand his difficult situation. So I do not accuse him of not sharing family responsibility, and I provide for the family as much as possible. In fact, the financial burden of the family ultimately comes upon those who live abroad. And no one refuses to take this responsibility unless he is an animal.

The influence of migration in transforming traditional social roles has been recognized in other contexts as well. For instance, Thai[23] observes that migration makes married daughters in Vietnam responsible for providing financial support to their aging parents. My interviewees shared a strong sense of identification with their parental families in Bangladesh, in some cases even after getting married and forming their own nuclear families. As Jamil, a businessman in his mid-forties who had lived in Japan for nearly two decades and had a Japanese wife and two children, said,

> You see I have a good earning. I am wearing branded clothes. I am living in a safe country. I am doing well. I think my father, mother, and siblings should also have such a comfortable life. You see the feeling—I send them money because I have this feeling for them. People can only raise the question about sending money if they do not have this feeling. Sending remittances is a way of expressing love for the family. Except [for] one or two people I have known, all Bangladeshis have this feeling, I think.

Jamil's sense of belonging to the parental family was further enhanced by physical distance:

> I am now living abroad. I have left my parents and all my relatives behind in
> Bangladesh. I feel I am living like an orphan here. If I were in Bangladesh, I
> would see them on weekends or other vacations. But I cannot do that now.
> This distance increases my love for them. I miss them every moment. But I
> want them to feel that I'm with them. So I send money. I cut off many luxuries,
> and even some necessary spending, to save and send them money. This
> remittance is actually a bridge between them and me.

As an explanation for why they feel such obligation to provide financial assistance, Jamil and other Bangladeshis in Japan repeatedly said that they were members of their parental families in Bangladesh and they derived a sense of belonging from them. But they also talked at length about remittance as an expression of love.

Membership in the family and origin community would sometimes put these migrants under pressure to send remittance. Moral attributes (such as "good/ bad" son, successful, caring, reliable and so forth) used to assess individual behavior and compliance with existing norms and values in Bangladesh exerted considerable influence on migrants, leading to remittance. As Ashfaq, a twenty-eight-year-old who had come to Japan as a language student five years previously and worked part-time, said,

> There is family pressure for sending money, especially in my village. You know,
> lots of people from my area came to Japan. They all sent large amounts of
> money with which their families made their fortune. Therefore, the families do
> not only ask for money, but also want to see you successful. To them, success
> means having lots of money, houses and apartments in Bangladesh.
> If you do not send money, the family, relatives, and neighbors all say, "People
> made so much money, what did you do after living in Japan?" It is hard to
> ignore such pressure. For some, their parents would make repeated phone calls
> to ask for money and put emotional pressure on their sons if they did not send
> them money.

Ashfaq is talking about two informal social mechanisms that elicit migrant compliance with norms—public shaming and exploitation of the emotional bond within the family, particularly with the mother and father. Shaming by the community is particularly effective in areas with a culture of migration.[24] Migration scholars have recognized how societies with a migration culture make migrants send remittances by linking this with their status in the society. As long as the migrants derive their identity from their origin communities, this obliges them to send remittances. Both the feeling of love for the family and the submission to social pressures to conform to existing norms and values about financially providing for family can shape migrants' actions, since the migrants identify with their family left behind in Bangladesh. Thus, I argue that migrants' connection to the family is necessary for remitting to occur. However, it is not sufficient. For instance, migrants would not need to send remittances to the family if they were able to bring them to Japan and permanently settle there. That is, if the migrants were able to establish their home in Japan with a dependable job and immediate family members, they would not need to send remittances. Thus, separation of the migrants from their families—and by extension, relatives and the origin community—to which they maintain belonging—leads migrants to send remittances.

Regardless of their families' needs and demands for money, my informants sent remittances because they saw their migration as temporary (due to a lack of integration and belonging) and moving out of Japan inevitable—to Bangladesh or, for a tiny few, to a third country. Besides supporting their parental families, they were also concerned about establishing their own families in Bangladesh. As Amin explained,

> After spending for essentials, we sent all our income to Bangladesh. This was because we knew we would ultimately return there. None of us thought we would settle here permanently. So we focused on earning as much as possible and sending all our savings home. We never thought of saving money here. This was because we knew that we could not stay here for a long time. We must return to our origin. We would need an income there, an address [meaning own house] in Bangladesh. So we must purchase assets there. Therefore, we would send remittances home.

Amin was compelled to make this choice because of his inability to establish his family in Japan as a foreigner. In fact, he and his fellow migrants had a strongly positive attitude toward Japan and had experiential knowledge that life was far better in Japan than in Bangladesh. Had they been free to choose, they would have settled in Japan with their families permanently and established their homes there. Studies among Bangladeshis in other destination countries confirm this assumption by recognizing large portions of Bangladeshis settling abroad permanently and raising families. In fact, migrants' temporary stay and inability to settle permanently has been found to strongly correlate with their remittance to home in the origin country.[25]

In addition, of course, my interviewees realized that separating from their parental families and forming their own families was inevitable. As they grew up, their siblings would have their own families. And their own family membership and belonging would eventually give way to their own separate nuclear families. This would reduce the need to financially support their families through remittance, which was reflected in Amin's narrative. As Amin told me, his brothers and sisters in Bangladesh got married and had separate families of their own. So he did not send money to them regularly like before, but only on special occasions such as the annual Eid festivals. Moreover, as his brothers and sister had their own careers and families, he sent money to his nephews and nieces as gifts. He told me,

> I do not give money to my brothers and sisters anymore. All but one of my brothers is younger than me. So I do not have any responsibility for elder siblings. But I know they will be happy if I give money to their children. So I send money to all my nephews and nieces during both Eid festivals. I send my money to one of my sisters and tell her how much to give to whom. I have set a standard amount for each of my nephews and nieces based on their grades in school.

Here, we see how the parental family eventually disintegrates into separate families of grown-up siblings leading to transformation in their family membership and corresponding changes in family responsibilities. Once grown-up family members establish their own nuclear families, they cannot expect to share financial burdens with their siblings. While they still maintain their membership in the extended family through gift exchange and other social interactions, they do not share the core family responsibilities with their siblings. Upon separation, each of the newly established nuclear families inherit a small portion of the parental family wealth, which often is not enough for them to sustain middle-class status. Thus, they must find a career of their own with enough income to maintain their original middle-class status. However, most Bangladeshis in Japan did not study enough and worked in menial jobs; they could not find a respected career and earn a decent living in Bangladesh. Thus, they had to use money they earned in Japan as the primary capital with which they would build their future family in Bangladesh. While my interviewees did not deny their financial obligation to their parental families, they admitted that they were actively engaged in making investments toward their personal income and that this often led to disputes and conflicts within their families (elaborated on in chapter 5). Most interviewees among the language students (29 out of 35) said they heavily invested in their own sources of income separate from the parental family. The majority (22) planned to establish their own businesses in Dhaka, 6 wanted to set up and run agro-based businesses in their villages, and the remaining 7 wanted to join and expand their family businesses. Their preferred businesses included importing Japanese used cars, electronics, medical equipment, etc., and exporting garments and agricultural products from Bangladesh.

As I explain above, among all Bangladeshis in Japan, students with scholarship support were the least constrained in material and social ways. Moreover, they could typically find jobs that made them eligible for long-term professional visas and citizenship in Japan or other developed countries. That is, they were able to foresee settling permanently with their family and establishing home in Japan or another country. Therefore, they did not see returning as inevitable and felt no need to invest in Bangladesh. Except for those in medical and dental schools, who wanted to go back to Bangladesh and establish their own clinics, none of these migrants reported sending remittances for business purposes, though many did purchase houses and apartments, primarily because they wanted a place to call home in Dhaka. They did not worry about having their own income sources in Bangladesh like other migrants. Instead, they bought houses and apartments in Japan, prepared for their next migration by visiting their targeted countries, explored the process of being granted permanent residence in these countries, and networked with friends and co-ethnics there.

Conclusion

Although migration to Japan is characterized by high income and Bangladeshis—particularly young, educated, male individuals and their middle- and upper-middle-class families—talked about their financial gains, they accomplished much more than mere financial outcomes: these migrants sought to maintain their membership and belonging to the family and their original middle-class social status through remittance. Thus, an apparent economic migration to Japan becomes more than an economic endeavor; for them, it is an opportunity to maintain family membership and enhance their middle-class status. This idea about migration to Japan is shared by both the aspirants and their families and origin community, thereby demonstrating the social embeddedness of this aspirational migration.

Bangladeshis of all social backgrounds in Japan perceive themselves as members of their origin family and maintain this belonging to their families and communities in Bangladesh through remittance. While the generalized understanding is that sending remittance is a "normal" act, many also explain their remittance in terms of their family responsibility, reciprocating their parents' contribution to their upbringing and migration, social obligation, and benevolence. What is especially worth noting is how they come to perceive their migration to Japan as an opportunity to earn large sums of money but also recognize how it limits their option to settle abroad and makes return to Bangladesh inevitable (except for the small number of highly educated professionals who further migrate to a Western country).

Japan is a land of opportunity for these migrants in terms of higher income opportunities and an updated lifestyle with modern amenities. Yet, their entry and stay in Japan is severely restricted by the Japanese immigration regime. These migrants can enter Japan through strategic loopholes condoned by the state, including visas-on-arrival and lax enforcement of immigration laws in certain periods, but there are also periods of stricter enforcement when it is deemed politically necessary. And despite the successive changes in Japan's immigration regime to allow and dissuade foreign workers from entering and staying, the state has always put forth measures to deny foreigners permanent settlement in Japan. Japan draws Bangladeshis to disproportionately highly paying jobs compared to available income opportunities in Bangladesh. These migrants also reportedly live well in Japan with modern facilities. Many of them tried to stay longer in Japan and settle permanently there. Yet, the state set up numerous barriers to prevent migrants from permanently settling, which, together with the local society's unwillingness to accept foreigners, resulted in a generalized perception of the migrants that Japan is not a country to settle in. As a consequence, my informants unanimously defined their stay in Japan as temporary and their moving out of Japan as unavoidable.

Despite higher income opportunities and access to a developed lifestyle, all my informants talked at length about their inability to see Japan as their future home to raise a family in. Those in so-called blue-collar and semi-professional jobs entered Japan through "backdoors" and "side doors" in the Japanese immigration regime[26] and remained in the liminal space between legality and illegality. This shows the ability of the destination state to effectively regulate migration and exercise overwhelming control over who enters and stays and who must leave the country. Those few migrants entering Japan for higher education with government funding were better off as they received the Japanese government's patronage and a range of supports (e.g., financial stipends, administrative support, subsidized housing, and healthcare) throughout their stay. However, they were equally marginalized by the native Japanese society, which encouraged them to migrate to another country in the West with a multicultural society. This contradicts the assumption about legality of entry and stay as sufficient for migrants to permanently settle in any destination country by identifying the important role of the native population in migrants' integration.

Having denied legal provisions for permanent settlement and lacking sociocultural backing from both the state and co-ethnic communities in Japan, Bangladeshis must look beyond Japan to build their home and raise families. While they all earned enough money to establish a home and raise their family abroad, many lacked sufficient legal, social, and cultural resources to achieve such a goal. Except for a tiny few who are able to move out of Japan and into traditional immigrant countries to settle permanently (e.g., Australia, New Zealand, Canada, and the United States), most viewed their return to Bangladesh as inevitable.

In sum, Bangladeshis migrated to Japan to earn a good living and have better lives than they had at home in Bangladesh. Apart from those with scholarship support, migration was primarily a family affair, with families arranging for the migration of their sons or other relatives in anticipation of receiving remittances. Early visa-overstayers and those migrating as self-funded language students were all single males between twenty and thirty years old. The majority of scholarship awardees were also single males, with only a few married males and females. Regardless of their legal status and socioeconomic standing in Japan, these migrants all sent remittances to Bangladesh. As they explained, they belonged to and identified with their parental families and considered it natural to assume the role of breadwinner after their migration. Over time, all the migrants would separate from their parental families and form their own nuclear families. The highly educated and professional migrants differed from their counterparts in low-skilled and part-time jobs as they could settle in Japan or other developed countries, while the others would have to return to Bangladesh to establish families. That is, the lack of an opportunity to establish a home and raise a family in Japan would lead Bangladeshi migrants to look to make their own home in Bangladesh (or abroad for a few), which they realized by sending remittances.

3

The American Dream

•••••••••••••••••••••••

Hakim, a single male who migrated to the United States after winning the diversity visa (DV-1) lottery in 2007, recounted the process of obtaining his visa:

> I had been applying to the U.S. Diversity Visa Program [DV lottery] each year since 1999 but never won, and so in 2006 [I] didn't plan on applying. Meanwhile, I took a job in a small factory and moved out of my family home to Dhaka after graduating with a diploma in mechanical engineering. One day in 2006, a thief broke into my room and stole everything. Thoroughly frustrated with my life, I went for a walk and noticed people sending their DV lottery forms. One of my neighbors insisted that I complete and send one, too, which I did so reluctantly. About five months later, my younger brother called me from home and told me that I had won the DV lottery, and the first letter had arrived. I became extremely happy, but also cautious, and asked my brother to keep the news secret so that I would not be embarrassed if I failed to get the visa at the end. I went home by a four-hour bus trip the next morning. I consulted with my father and brother and found an experienced *dalal* [colloquial Bengali word for "broker"] to fill in the first form. After another four months, I received the second letter, with the visa interview date to be held in about two weeks in Dhaka. The broker helped me prepare all the necessary paperwork. I was very nervous about the interview and its outcome. Three weeks after the interview, I received a call from the U.S. embassy asking me to collect my visa. When I came out of the embassy with my visa, it felt like I was flying in the sky!

Hakim was cheerfully describing how his dream of migrating to the United States came to fruition. Typical of most children of middle-class families in Bangladesh, Hakim wanted to become an engineer and have a decent life. He had also developed a strong preference for living in a Western country, preferably the United States, through watching Hollywood movies and TV serials and hearing stories from one of his neighbors who migrated to New York a few years before. He saw an opportunity in the Diversity Visa Program (popularly known as the green card lottery) to realize his dream. Because he did not have sufficient educational credentials, language competency, work experience, or family members residing in the United States that might qualify him for other available visas, the DV-1 lottery was the only way for Hakim, and other aspirants like him, to migrate to the United States. So, Hakim began to take part in the DV-1 lottery program as soon as he became eligible after he graduated from high school and turning eighteen. He continued to send DV-1 lottery forms for six years without luck. So, he gave up on this plan thinking that luck was not on his side. The seventh time he participated in the DV-1 lottery, he won. In his conversation, Hakim particularly emphasized his extremely low mood due to a theft from his room and loss of all his possessions. He noted his reluctance to fill out the lottery form to highlight that he won the DV-1 lottery not by his own trying. While he had been participating in the lottery for years with plans about how to manage the subsequent stages in his migration processing as well as to settle in the United States, he was unsuccessful. The success came when he gave up!

I came across similar stories among Bangladeshi immigrants in Los Angeles who had entered the United States as legal permanent residents (i.e., as green card holders) by winning the DV-1 lottery. Common in all these stories is the idea that the immigrants were able to come to the United States through nothing but their luck. This defies the assumption about migration as a planned undertaking based on rational calculation by migrants and their families. For most of these DV-1 immigrants, moving to the United States would have been impossible without this lottery program. They reportedly knew about a few Bangladeshis migrating to the United States through higher education or family connections. Once they were picked in the lottery, they would invest all their resources in completing the visa process with utmost sincerity and dedication so they could finally get move to the United States[1] and become U.S. citizens. Since the United States allows citizens to sponsor immigration of their immediate family members, including parents and siblings and their respective families, the entire family of a DV-1 lottery winner would come to see this as an opportunity to migrate to the United States and be part of the American Dream.

From the perspective of Bangladeshi immigrants in the United States, migrating to the country truly is a dream. Although many of my informants shared details about how much they loved the idea of migrating to the United States, almost all, including those migrating through the DV-1 lottery program, higher education, or family unification policy, talked about their own migration as something they did not plan; it just happened to them. In this chapter, I present a historical overview of Bangladeshi migration to the United States, with particular focus on the incipient Bangladeshi immigrant community in Los Angeles. Then, I offer a brief scholarly review of immigrants' permanent settlement and incorporation into the United States, followed by Bangladeshi immigrant accounts of settling down in Southern California. Finally, I draw attention to their efforts to establish a home and find belonging to show how various structural factors shape their settlement and integration into the United States, with important implications for understanding their perception of home and strategies of finding belonging.

Ticket to Hollywood: Bangladeshi Immigration to Los Angeles

The United States of America is at the top of preferred migration destinations among Bangladeshis. Regardless of their education, occupation, and social status, almost all Bangladeshis look forward to opportunities to migrate to the United States, an interest driven by U.S. television,[2] the Internet,[3] and Hollywood, in addition to stories about affluence and comfort communicated by those Bangladeshis already residing in the United States. More crucially, in the mid-1990s the U.S. government began to actively encourage Bangladeshi immigration through the DV Program. By 2011, the year before Bangladesh was eliminated from the list of eligible countries, Bangladeshi applicants to this program outnumbered those from any other country. In colloquial Bengali, what people say about America translates as "the country where dollars fly in the air." Ordinary Bangladeshis believe that anyone who goes to America can achieve economic success, whereas Bangladesh has widespread poverty, rampant corruption, and various structural barriers to upward mobility for most people.

The desire to migrate to the United States grew so strong that many Bangladeshis invested significant amounts of time, effort, and money in search of opportunities. As Hakim recounted,

> The whole process of winning the DV lottery to collecting the visa took about eleven months. I could not sleep a single night properly due to worries about how I would be able to do everything correctly so that I would not miss getting the U.S. visa. I did not have any savings, but still I agreed to pay the broker $8,000, as my father suggested that I should not miss this "once in a lifetime" opportunity. My parents and an uncle arranged for all the money I needed to pay the broker and pay for my trip to Los Angeles. When I first stepped out of the airport, I took a deep breath and felt like I had entered another world full of hope and prosperity. It felt like my dream had come true. I still remember those moments.

Knowing about family sponsored immigration to the United States, Bangladeshis regarded one family member winning the DV-1 lottery as the whole family winning the opportunity of migrating to the United States. One of my informants told me that his youngest brother changed his undergraduate major from political science to English language and literature, anticipating that it would be more useful for him once his immigrant brother sponsored his migration to the United States. Thus, everybody in the family would invest as much as possible in procuring the visa and sending the DV-1 lottery winner to the United States. Once in the United States, the individual would immediately find jobs and begin to send money to the family, reinforcing their belief that the United States is a land of opportunity and prosperity.

The desire among Bangladeshis to migrate to the United States goes back more than a century: as Bald[4] recounts, one of the three earliest South Asian immigrant groups at the turn of the twentieth century originated from Bangladesh (then known as the Bengal province of British India and then after the British left as East Pakistan). Well into the 1960s, migrants arrived on U.S. shores as sailors in British ships. They came primarily from rural farming households in what are now the Bangladeshi districts of Sylhet, Noakhali, and Chittagong. The exorbitant tax imposed by the British colonial state and the risk of losing lands to moneylenders forced these middle-class families to send their young sons to work on British ships as *lascars*, or lower-class workers. But the extreme working conditions and paltry wages would encourage many seamen to jump ship in U.S. ports. They ended up working in growing industries in the northern and midwestern United States, where they experienced racism and formed extensive networks of ex-seamen in cities including New York, Detroit, and Baltimore. They found allies primarily among African Americans and Latin American immigrants. Focusing on Bengali Harlem, Bald describes how these ex-seamen married into Puerto Rican and other working-class communities of color, established their homes and organized their social lives. Creating their own community by setting up restaurants and boarding houses, organizing regular religious celebrations, and socializing with other Bengali families, they developed a multiracial community of "true companionate relationships"[5] characterized by equal rights for wives and acceptance of their religions and culture. The Immigration Reform Act of 1965 led to increasing numbers of professional migrants from Bengal, who congregated in different neighborhoods while preserving a distinct national identity as Bangladeshis. At the same time, many seafarers retired and returned to Bangladesh. Thus, Bengalis gradually dissipated into other ethnic groups and finally disappeared from the history of South Asians in the United States.

Contemporary Bangladeshi immigration to the United States began a few years after Bangladesh's war for independence in 1971. A few Bangladeshis entered the United States as students and political asylum-seekers, but their numbers remained small until the introduction of the DV Program in 1994, when

Bangladeshis began to enter the United States in thousands. From 5,800 Bangladeshis in the 1980 census, the number of Bangladeshi immigrants climbed to 57,412 in 2000 and 147,300 in 2010. Economic hardship and failed dreams of an emergent middle class in Bangladesh, which led to the war of independence,[6] were the main motivations for those migrating to the United States for higher education and better professional careers. As Tauhid (an IT company manager in his late fifties who lived in Los Angeles with his wife and two daughters) recounted,

> I wanted to study medical science and become a doctor. But everything changed after the independence war in 1971—a huge social disaster, which I could not adapt to. My father was an honest government officer and never did anything wrong. After completing my university degree, I took a government job. But I was not happy, as I saw others around me quickly becoming rich by "doing this and that" [a reference to corruption], you know. I had only one determination—to get established through education. So, I came to the U.S. in 1981 at the age of thirty. I lived in a shared apartment with much younger Bangladeshis, who came here immediately after high school graduation. I heard only negative things from them, such as no job, no income, no prospect for permanent settlement, and so forth. This made me very sad and disheartened. They would ask me, "Brother, why did you leave your job in Bangladesh and come here for nothing? I would never do this like you." They would discourage me from taking casual jobs in fast food restaurants and gas stations, telling me that those jobs were unsuitable for me. Thus, instead of supporting me to survive, they made me very depressed. But I was extremely determined. I came to the U.S. spending so much money and leaving my secure job in Bangladesh. I could not simply give up and return home. I told myself, "I have to survive in this country. If I have to go back, it will be my dead body. I cannot fail [at] my own dream, my family's dream to become successful." So, I stayed on and began to work in part-time jobs besides my master's degree program at California State University.

Most of the early Bangladeshi students who came to the United States for higher education in the 1980s shared such stories of determination and persistence. The aspiring middle class in Bangladesh found their aspirations for better living unrealized, owing mainly to the government mismanagement and a lack of necessary resources after Bangladesh's independence in 1971. Some young male students from these families, frustrated at seeing some of their peers quickly getting rich while they struggled to find decent employment and a "respectable" lifestyle, applied for admission into higher education programs abroad. And once they were admitted, the whole family would pull the necessary money from their small savings and borrow from relatives to arrange the students' travel abroad. Students would exert themselves in the foreign universities and in part-time jobs in the secondary labor market to earn their living. Their backbreaking struggle would generally end happily with their graduation and landing a professional job. They would gradually settle permanently by acquiring citizenship and bringing their families to join them in the United States.

While Bangladesh has made significant economic and social progress over the last five decades,[7] the frustration of the middle class continued to grow and the number of young individuals willing to migrate abroad increased substantially. The statistical yearbooks of the U.S. Immigration and Naturalization Service documented only 154 Bangladeshi immigrants in 1973 and 787 in 1983. The introduction of the OP-1 visa lottery (the predecessor of the DV-1 visa lottery) in 1990 resulted in the admission of 10,676 immigrants from Bangladesh,[8] and thereafter, immigrants entering through this visa lottery system outnumbered those entering the United States by any other means. Each year several thousand Bangladeshis entered the United States through the DV-1 lottery, until they reached the numerical threshold that excluded Bangladesh from the program in 2012.

However, Bangladeshi's attraction to the United States did not subside with exclusion from the DV-1 Program. Those with family members and close relatives who are U.S. citizens continued to enter the United States as immigrants in significant numbers. According to U.S. Department of State statistics, 14,946 Bangladeshis entered the United States with immigration visas in 2018. Almost all of them (14,818, or 99 percent) obtained visas through sponsorship by immediate family or close relatives. The State Department statistics show that from 2012 to 2018, the total number of immigrants from Bangladesh remained more than 12,000 per year. Vaughan and Huennekens[9] observe that for the period 2000–2016 the Bangladesh chain migration multiplier was 4.44, much higher than the most recent worldwide average chain migration multiplier of 3.45.

The number of students going to the United States for higher education has also grown substantially in recent years, particularly young men from Bangladeshi cities. According to the United Nations Educational, Scientific and Cultural Organization (UNESCO), the number of Bangladeshi students going abroad increased by more than 100 percent between 2006 and 2016.[10] UNESCO reported that every day 90 students left Bangladesh to study abroad, and most of them would remain abroad for a better life. As Bal[11] observes, economic growth, rapid urbanization, and increasing investment in education infected emerging urban middle-class youth with new desires for a "modern" lifestyle that could not be fulfilled in their home country and generated a sense of disengagement from Bangladesh. The destination countries of international students, such as Australia, Canada, Malaysia, the United Kingdom, and the United States, have taken measures to encourage their migration, thus contributing to the trend. The U.S. ambassador reported that there were 7,143 Bangladeshi graduate students in the United States in 2018, making Bangladesh ninth among the top 25 student-sending countries.[12] The flow of Bangladeshi students to the

United States grew significantly as the U.S. Embassy in Bangladesh eased student visa processing. Between 2012 and 2017, the number of Bangladeshi students in the United States increased by 53.5 percent, with a 9.7 percent increase in 2017 compared to the previous year, while the international average increased by only 3.4 percent, according to a 2017 report by the Institute of International Education (IIE).[13]

While Bangladeshis are recognized as one of the biggest groups of "illegal" migrants who enter Europe by navigating the Mediterranean Sea,[14] they are almost unheard of among undocumented/illegal migrants in the United States. Perhaps this is due to the vast geographical distance between the two countries and the absence of transnational underground networks like those serving other well-known migrant groups. Nonetheless, a small but significant number of undocumented Bangladeshi migrants in the United States enter as tourists and visitors and then overstay their visas. Most manage to legalize their stay through marriage, while a few remain undocumented.

Settler Migration: Understanding Migrants' Permanent Settlement in the United States

All Bangladeshi immigrants I met in Los Angeles told me that from the very beginning of their journey, they intended to settle permanently in the United States. Their settlement plan not only included themselves and their immediate families but also the families of their siblings and in-laws. Most of their relatives back in Bangladesh had a strong desire to migrate to the United States with the sponsorship of their U.S.-citizen relatives. This desire to settle permanently was motivated, as my informants reported, by their knowledge of the United States as a country of immigrants that actively encourages people from all over the world to come and settle. This is entirely different than the experience of Bangladeshi migrants in Japan who perceived their migration as temporary.

Etymologically, the word "settle" means "to seat" or "to come to rest" in Old English. Scholars of U.S. migration use the term "settler" to refer to European colonists who migrated to the so-called New World in the mid-seventeenth century. Sociologists looking at the U.S. context use the term "settlement" to understand the accumulation of experiences, patterns of residence, and probability of homeownership for immigrants in the host society.[15] For instance, well-known migration scholar Douglas Massey[16] used the term settlement to refer to immigrants' living periods or integration processes in the host society. In his study of Mexican immigrants in the United States, Massey defined settlers as immigrants who lived in the United States for three continuous years and differentiated settlers from seasonal migrants, who only worked and lived for several months in the United States. In Massey's view, the probability of settlement is based on an immigrant's accumulation of experiences in the host society. In other words, settlement is likely to take place when immigrants develop interpersonal, institutional, and economic links with the host society. Thus, settlement is both quantitative (duration of stay) and qualitative (nature of experience). Migration scholars also use the term settlement to explore the location of residences[17] and homeownership[18] in the host society and find homeownership to be a strong indicator of permanent settlement.[19]

Unlike the early European settlers who established the foundations of North American society, Bangladeshi immigrants find themselves in an already developed Euro-American society upon arrival in the United States. Thus, the issue for them is whether or not to blend in with the existing society by embracing its culture—a process referred to as assimilation.[20] A widely accepted definition of assimilation, the "decline of an ethnic distinction and its corollary cultural and social differences,"[21] assesses whether migrants and people in the host society become more similar over time in terms of, for example, their inclusion in the labor market. Scholars have questioned the process of assimilation as a linear progression toward a specific goal with the implicit expectation being one of conformity to Anglo-Saxon norms. Such a teleology, heading inexorably toward a stable and identifiable endpoint, hinges on the belief that a single mainstream culture constitutes American society.[22] Thus, segmented assimilation theory recognizes how migrants assimilate into different cultures rather than a single "melting pot."[23] Additionally, migrants do not simply shed their original culture and identity and adopt a new identity by embracing the culture of their destination country.[24]

Compared to classical accounts of assimilation theory, neo-assimilation theory emphasizes that the focus of assimilation is "on the process, not on some final state and [that] assimilation is a matter of degree. Assimilation designates a direction of change, not a particular degree of similarity."[25] However, even a dynamic definition of assimilation may not appropriately describe migrants' sociocultural adaptation over time. Therefore, scholars began to use the term "migrant integration" instead of assimilation to examine migrants' experience after they permanently settle in the United States.

The term integration is used to understand migrants' participation in the receiving society, often stimulated by special policies and in public debate. This term clarifies many confusions associated with the term assimilation (i.e., absorption into the dominant society). As recent studies show, migrants do not necessarily "melt into" a presumed mainstream in the destination country; rather, they establish a relationship with the receiving society while at the same time maintaining their ethnic identity.[26] This framework applies quite well to Bangladeshi immigrants in the United States, an overwhelming majority of whom entered the United States to settle permanently thanks to favorable policies such as the DV Program, family unification policies, and numerous services that assist new arrivals to get started in their life in the United States. Once they enter the United States, they immediately find a place to stay and a job to earn a living. While they primarily depend on co-ethnic networks at the initial stage, they also eke out basic supports from various public and non-profit organizations (detailed in the following section). Migration scholars[27] observe four domains of integration: 1) *Structural integration* refers to rights and status within the core institutions of the receiving society; 2) *cultural integration* refers to learning the norms and language of the receiving society; 3) *social integration* refers to the establishment of social contacts in the destination country; and 4) *psychological integration* relates to an emotional bond with and a feeling of inclusion in the destination country. A growing body of literature focuses on the structural[28] and cultural[29] aspects of integration. Migrants' economic status and language proficiency are considered objective indicators of their degree of integration, which can help determine the likelihood of migrants staying or returning to their origin country. The establishment of social bonds between migrants and the native/local population through social integration is understood to increase the benefits of settlement in the destination country through building stable location-specific social capital. By looking at various dimensions of integration of Bangladeshis in the United States, I observed how my informants faired in terms of integration into the country upon their permanent settlement.

Entering the American Dream

The U.S. immigration policy of family unification and the social encouragement of the origin community in Bangladesh usually result in migration of the entire family. As a consequence, Bangladeshi immigrant neighborhoods have sprung up in most big U.S. cities, such as New York, Los Angeles, Detroit, Atlanta, Dallas, Houston, Boston, Indianapolis, Chicago, Phoenix, and so forth. By contrast, there is no visible Bangladeshi ethnic neighborhood in Japan due to the lack of opportunities for family unification and permanent settlement.

Recently, the Bangladeshi neighborhood in Los Angeles (LA) has been officially named "Little Bangladesh." It is a four-block stretch on 3rd Street between Alexandria and New Hampshire Avenues, two miles west of Downtown LA. On any given day, women in brightly colored traditional dresses can be seen walking along the tree-lined residential streets, often pushing strollers with babies or accompanied by small children. On the weekends, they are joined by men. Among the many Latino and Korean residents and businesses in the area, Bangladeshis have registered their presence by six restaurants and ethnic stores, two video stores, two liquor stores, a secondhand store, two 99-cent stores, a mosque, and a community center hosting two afterschool prep centers. Although Bangladeshi immigrants began to arrive in this area in the early 1980s, they formed a visibly distinct ethnic neighborhood only after the introduction of the DV Program in the early 1990s. The first ethnic store and restaurant was established in 1993, followed by two more in 1995. In addition to selling groceries and other necessary ethnic goods, these stores serve as places to socialize for many Bangladeshi immigrants in Southern California, who often frequent the stores before going to work and return after finishing their shift. They come to watch Bangla news on the big flat-screen TVs hanging on the walls and read Bangla newspapers available for free. Especially for single immigrants, these stores facilitate interactions they used to have in extended families and friendship circles in Bangladesh. Those settled with their families in the valley areas far away from the neighborhood visit these stores on weekends.

I met Ahmed in one of these stores one evening in the summer of 2012, four years after he landed in Los Angeles through the DV-1 lottery. After living in his cousin's house for two days, Ahmed saw a rental vacancy notice posted on the wall of a desi restaurant and moved to an apartment with three other Bangladeshi immigrants who worked at liquor stores and gas stations. As with other single immigrants, Ahmed's life in Los Angeles revolved around his apartment, his workplace, and ethnic restaurants. On any given day, Ahmed would get up early in the morning and take a one-hour bus ride to South Central LA, where he opened his cousin's liquor store at 8:00 A.M. Finishing at 4:00 P.M. when the other employee checked in, he would take another bus to return to Deshi.[30] There he would have light snacks and tea while watching Bangla TV or reading Bangla newspapers. Meanwhile, some of his friends would appear, as they did almost every day. Ahmed would spend a few hours with them until dinner at around 9:00 P.M. in the restaurant and then retreat to his apartment. This schedule changed slightly on the two days Ahmed attended an ESL class at Los Angeles Community College. On Saturday, his day off, he would spend more time in Deshi with his friends, in addition to cleaning and other household chores and relaxation time. Thus, Deshi (and other ethnic restaurants in the neighborhood) occupied a central place in the lives of Ahmed and other Bangladeshi immigrants like him in Los Angeles.

The restaurants symbolize the ease with which Bangladeshis permanently settle in the United States and create their own social spaces. The glass storefront of this restaurant is decorated with a hand-painted picture of a landscape in Bangladesh: a sailing boat, a green rice field, and a few cattle grazing on the bank of a river. The signboard on the front door is written in bold Bangla letters followed by smaller English letters. A strong, spicy smell of cooked food blows out of the open door to pique the appetite of passersby for authentic Bangladeshi cuisine. When somebody enters the door, a smiling salesperson greets him or her in Bangla (also known as Bengali). Together with the ethnic goods on display, the constant presence of a few Bangladeshi customers inside and the ongoing Bangla programs on the TV transform the restaurant into a unique and exquisite Bangladeshi social space. It is so ethnic that Bangladeshis feel at home in this place, whereas a non-Bangladeshi immediately feels out of place. For instance, one non-Bangladeshi commented on the Yelp about one of these restaurants: "As soon as I walked in, I swear I was in Bangladesh, lol. There's raw meat, flies, and Bangladeshi people. . . . The food was pretty good. I had the curry goat. I can definitely assure it tastes very ethnic."[31] The ambience in these ethnic stores and restaurants is so homelike that they attract all kinds of Bangladeshi immigrants. For instance, Mukul and his family lived a few blocks away from one of these businesses on 3rd Street and he would often walk to the restaurant with his wife and two daughters to taste ethnic snacks and sweets that his wife did not prepare at home. He would also bring his wife to the stores so she could purchase spices and other ethnic goods, which she accused Mukul of not recognizing. Besides, they often met friends from faraway suburbs, who would visit these restaurants and stores for ethnic groceries on weekends.

Ahmed, Mukul, and others like them accommodated to life in the United States thanks to U.S. immigration policies that encourage legal permanent residency and family unification and the ethnic community that helps reproduce a lifestyle akin to what they were used to in Bangladesh. While their legal status made them eligible to work and their co-ethnic networks helped them get started with casual jobs shortly after arrival, their credentials did not help them find jobs commensurate with their education. I interviewed more than two dozen immigrants with university degrees working in casual jobs in LA. Rashid (forty-seven, a medical school graduate who migrated as a DV-1 lottery winner in 2009 with his wife and two children) shared his experience as follows:

> After graduation from Dhaka Dental College, I joined a private medical college as a faculty member and set up my own dental clinic in Dhaka. But I had to make a tough choice between staying in Bangladesh and moving to the U.S. when my wife won the DV lottery in 2008. She had her two cousins already living in the U.S. They talked about a number of supports for immigrants from the U.S. government, including subsidized healthcare, housing, education, job training, and so forth. With their encouragement and at my wife's insistence, we decided to move on. I came to LA because I had a senior friend from my dental college who settled in LA a long time ago and established his own dental clinic. My friend helped me to find a one-bedroom apartment on West 4th Street. He also gave me information and necessary preparatory books for the license examination to become a registered dentist in the U.S. In a month, however, I realized that I would not be able to pass the examination. Besides, the money I brought with me was clearly falling short to support my family beyond a few months more. So I had to take a job in a gas station to earn money and support my family. I worked there for more than two years. In the meantime, I completed a four-month course in phlebotomy from UCLA extension and joined a hospital lab [the name has been omitted to conceal the interviewee's identity] as a phlebotomist. Besides, I found a two-bedroom apartment in government-subsidized housing near the USC [University of Southern California] campus and moved there.

Like a few other immigrants I interviewed, Rashid left an upper-middle-class life of honor and affluence in Bangladesh for an uncertain life in the United States, characterized by downward mobility, because he was convinced that his children would have better opportunities in there. I interviewed a few former mid-level bureaucrats and corporate professionals who migrated to the United States through either the DV lottery or family sponsorship and took jobs of much lower status than they had in Bangladesh, confirming the observation that first-generation immigrants often experience downward occupational mobility in their destination country.[32] However, my interviewees were generally satisfied with a number of other aspects of their life in the United States. For instance, Rashid was very disappointed about leaving his career as a dentist in Bangladesh to end up working as a phlebotomist in LA. However, he was happy about finding a much safer and more comfortable life in America than in Bangladesh, with fresh and healthy food, a crime-free neighborhood, free English-language schooling for his children (English-language schools in Dhaka are prohibitively expensive), free healthcare for the family, and other support from the U.S. government. Contrary to general media perceptions about high crime and increasing gun violence situation, nearly all of my interviewees appreciated American law and order, finding everything under systemic control by the federal and state governments as well as the local administration. It was obvious that they compared their experience in the United States with their experience in Bangladesh. They also shared their feeling of gratitude toward the U.S. government for supports in education, health, housing, and so forth, and accepted the regulations as necessary to enjoy the quality of life they lacked in Bangladesh because, as they would argue, the government could not perform either supportive or regulatory roles there.

These immigrants, however, were not appreciative of the United States at the beginning and were surprised and often frustrated to find their ideas about America wrong. The glittering image of the USA they had developed from American TV shows and Hollywood movies, and the ease of life they had heard about from their friends and relatives in the country, contrasted sharply with what they found for themselves upon arrival. The LAX airport with its ongoing construction work, the highly congested traffic on the way out of the airport to downtown, the age and shabbiness of apartments in the neighborhood—all would come as a surprise. As Rashid told me,

> We came to America in July 2010. It was a very hot and humid day and I felt like we were still in Dhaka. I was not impressed by the dirty surroundings at the arrival area of [the] Los Angeles airport. Our taxi waited for almost thirty minutes to pass through the traffic until we entered the freeway. The afternoon traffic on the freeway also reminded me of the super-slow and congested transportation in Dhaka. But what made me most frustrated was the apartment we rented. My friend had told me that he arranged a good apartment for us in the neighborhood. After visiting some neighbors' apartments later, I realized that ours was better. But when we stepped into it for the first time, I compared it with my apartment in Dhaka and got very upset.

Coming from a middle- and upper-middle class backgrounds in Bangladesh with unrealistically high expectations of life in the United States, these immigrants were disappointed at the kind of life they entered upon arrival in America. The working-class neighborhood and casual jobs were far below their expectations and qualifications. The sub-standard housing and crowded, poor community spaces (e.g., neighborhood parks, grocery shops, and footpaths) would compound the hardships in their daily lives and lead to growing disappointment.

Despite recognizing racism against immigrants in the United States—mainly Muslim immigrants—in both academic[33] and public discourses,[34] my informants hardly talked about experiences of racial encounters. Their lack of attention to racial encounters was perhaps due to their initial busyness settling in the United States and their initial struggles to find necessary resources, including housing, income, and supportive social networks. They would turn to their relatives, friends, and acquaintances for information about affordable housing and immediately available income opportunities, which eventually would direct them to the emergent ethnic neighborhood known as Little Bangladesh. They found material and social support from their co-ethnics, so much so that most of them saw the ethnic neighborhood as a place to begin and seek relief from the difficulties of their new life in the United States. However, this did not mean they overlooked anti-immigrant racism, Islamophobia, and occasional experiences of xenophobia. They often chose not to pay attention to it. For instance, I was entering the Southern California Islamic Center (the largest mosque near Little Bangladesh) with a group of Bangladeshis to have breakfast during Ramadan in 2013. A group of white men in a truck shouted at us: "Go back, terrorists!" We all looked at them momentarily and entered the mosque without commenting. Later that evening, Mustak—a community leader—explained that such incidents were not worth noticing due to "the bigger concerns," including earning a livelihood and raising children, which echoed Rashid's narrative. Kamal, who graduated from a university in Bangladesh and worked as a front desk clerk in a motel in Downtown LA, reported derogatory comments and sideways glances directed at him in his workplace. While understanding these incidents as racial profiling, he explained that these incidents were associated with his low working position. He expected that he would be able to avoid these experiences by moving into a more professional job with greater social status. Mustak's perspective alludes to a generalized reluctance to discuss towards racism and Islamophobia among Bangladeshi immigrants, who understood being racially profiled as a natural outcome of being settlers in a new country and were optimistic about overcoming it with their gradual settlement and upward social mobility.

Almost all immigrants from middle- and upper-middle-class backgrounds in Bangladesh experienced downward mobility in the United States, especially those who migrated with the DV-1 visa or through family sponsorship. Like Rashid, they could not immediately find professional jobs despite having university degrees from Bangladesh. They could afford to rent only cheaper apartments in working-class neighborhoods like Little Bangladesh. With time, they began to recognize the positive aspects of their migration. They made new friends among co-ethnics and others who offered them useful information about jobs, schools, groceries, leisure activities, and so forth. They began to socialize with co-ethnics on weekends and on special occasions, and to enjoy their uninterrupted electricity and running water at home, fresh fruits and vegetables uncontaminated by harmful preservatives and pesticides, cheap and timely public transportation, and above all, absence of bribery/corruption, as well as a lack of government regulation in professional and daily life.

Single migrants reportedly had an easier time at the beginning than those coming with family. One reason, Ahmed explained, was that the single immigrant did not have to worry about other family members while struggling to settle into their new life in LA:

> I was doing well in Dhaka. But I knew that my life would change forever once I migrated to America. So I did not care about the low quality of my apartment or my job in the liquor store. My earnings were still higher than in Dhaka. I missed spending time with my university friends and relatives. I did not mind living in my shared apartment, as everyone like me did it to save money. Having no family, relatives, or close friends in fact helped me save both money and time that I used for productive purposes. You see, I was able to take English language courses at LACC, another course on stock market investment, and also the tax preparation training course with H&R Block. When I am able to establish my own consulting business besides investing in the U.S. stock market, I will earn more income and status. I'll also be able to bring my siblings to America, which I would not be able to do from Bangladesh. Therefore, I always feel very lucky that I won the DV lottery and came to America.

Like Ahmed, other single migrants were better able to cope with the difficulties and challenges of their early days in LA, as they had more flexibility in finding suitable housing and jobs and had higher savings. They were also able to accommodate themselves to the hardships in their new lives by exclusively focusing on earning and saving money for their families and relatives. This, perhaps, was why the single immigrants I talked to reported more positive impressions of their life in LA than those migrating with family. They would not have to worry about helping a wife and children settle in.

Unlike Japan, which deploys several direct and indirect measures to discourage migration and permanent settlement by foreigners, the U.S. government offers various kinds of support for immigrants to settle in the United States permanently. For instance, most of my informants reportedly attended ESL (English as a second language) courses for multiple years at Los Angeles Community College (LACC) and other publicly funded institutions. The government-paid stipend for low-income immigrants and their families enrolled in ESL courses were strong incentives for them to persevere in language classes. The resulting improvement in their English helped many of them to find semiprofessional jobs with better pay and employee benefits. For instance, like most migrants, Ahmed arrived in LA with very limited English. By attending ESL courses for three years, he improved his English substantially and was able to take the advanced courses he mentioned. Compared to single immigrants, those with family received greater government support in the form of subsidized housing for low-income families; tax benefits; free medical treatment for the wife, children, and infants; and financial support for the education of their children. Moreover, a few families received food stamps during extreme economic crises due to the household head's unemployment or critical health problems. Thus, my informants shared a strongly positive impression of the U.S. government and often compared it with the dismal government support in Bangladesh.

The ethnic community also plays a vital role in helping Bangladeshi immigrants get settled in LA. Most migrants found their residences and jobs through networks of relatives, friends, and acquaintances. For instance, Ahmed depended on his cousin to find his apartment and job, and Mukul had a neighbor in LA from his village in Bangladesh. During my fieldwork, I met several dozen new immigrants at the ethnic stores and restaurants looking for information about jobs and cheaper housing. I also saw advertisements for vacant apartments—both for families and individuals—and jobs written in Bangla and posted on the walls in front of the restaurants and the Bangali mosque. The role of the ethnic community was further enhanced after the official inauguration of the neighborhood as Little Bangladesh. Many new immigrants and students now come directly to this neighborhood after arriving at LAX International Airport. One community leader claimed that he had helped over 200 new students from Bangladesh find transportation and information about other Bangladeshi residents near their universities in Central California in the summer of 2013. One of the neighborhood council members claimed that the council had helped over 250 Bangladesh immigrant families find government-subsidized affordable housing, which substantially reduced their expenses on rent.

In addition, there are over twenty-five community organizations that bridge the gap between these immigrants and mainstream America. Because of their limited English proficiency and marginal presence in the job market, Bangladeshi immigrants often remained stuck in their co-ethnic community. Those with higher education and contacts with the mainstream (i.e., the professional and middle class, including both white and non-white Americans) stepped forward as leaders in various community organizations. For instance, Sharif had been the president of a Bangladeshi cultural organization in the San Fernando Valley and had organized a Bangladeshi stall in the annual multicultural festival in Pasadena for six years. The owner of one of the LA restaurants was a prominent community leader who mobilized Bangladeshi immigrants in support of the incumbent mayor in the 2013 mayoral election. This resulted in the mayor's first visit to the neighborhood and recruitment of some Bangladeshis to his staff. Close contact with the mayor also inspired Bangladeshis politically. As a result, two Bangladeshis were elected to the neighborhood council in 2014, and four in 2015. A few also successfully ran for the governing bodies of neighborhood schools, and one was elected chair of a school governing board in 2017. However, their political aspirations took a massive blow in 2018 when Bangladeshis campaigned to expand the area officially recognized as Little Bangladesh into a much bigger area cutting through Koreatown. The proposal lost by an overwhelming margin of 97 percent, severely reducing the political ambitions of Bangladeshis and generating fear of retaliation by Korean owners of apartments and stores. Besides showing competition between Koreans and the Bangladeshis, this episode also exposed growing rivalries among the leaders of the Bangladeshi community that lowered Bangladeshi turnout in the referendum.

Except for this failed initiative, Bangladeshis in LA have had positive intercommunity relations with Koreans and other immigrants from Latin American countries in the neighborhood. A dentist and prominent leader of a Bangladeshi hometown association often invited Korean and Latin American community leaders to Bangladeshi programs. An information booth of the South Asian Network (SAN), the largest NGO among immigrants from South Asia in California, was a common feature at all community events, offering information and consultation on legal matters to everyone, including non-Bangladeshi immigrants. Thus, the community organizations facilitated not only a smooth beginning, but also interethnic interactions by connecting the ethnic community to the mainstream, with the possibility of helping some migrants obtain upward mobility.

Although the highly educated and professional immigrants were less dependent on the ethnic community for residences or jobs, they found community support necessary for their children's upbringing. Like many other Asian communities in the United States,[35] the Bangladeshi ethnic community played an important role in shaping the life of the second generation. Regardless of their own social position in the United States, immigrant parents placed extreme emphasis on the education of their children. Afterschool programs and home teaching among Bangladeshi families offered additional preparation for children so that they might succeed in school and enter competitive universities. Parents I spoke with at social gatherings emphasized the importance of education by linking their children's educational success to their achievement of the American Dream. Perhaps this was why Sharif showed me two letters of admission for his niece from the medical schools at New York University and UCLA when I interviewed him. I also heard immigrant parents proudly talking about their children's admission to Ivy League schools or graduations from the prestigious University of California system. While most first-generation Bangladeshi immigrants struggled in their jobs and failed to get formal education in the United States, they would try every possible way to send their children to good universities. For instance, Mukul—a salesclerk at a gas station—sent his elder daughter to the University of California, Berkeley and his younger daughter to the University of Southern California. Their concern for education and the upward mobility of their children encouraged them to keep working hard and cope with unpleasant experiences, including occasional racial profiling. They would often compare their challenging lives and marginal sociocultural experiences to their lives in Bangladesh.

In sum, Bangladeshi immigrants experienced both economic and social integration to a certain extent after migrating to the United States, which allowed them to establish homes and enter sustainable lives. Moreover, they found opportunities for upward mobility—though limited—not only for themselves, but for the next generation, opportunities that they had not found accessible in Bangladesh. Collectively, they established their own ethnic neighborhood, which provided them with homelike public spaces. Despite their limited ability to connect to mainstream (i.e., white American) culture, these immigrants were not left out, as their community acted as a bridge between them and other Americans. While low-paid jobs enabled the first generation to survive, their emphasis on higher education for their children and available supports from the U.S. government and the ethnic community facilitated quick improvement in social status for many in the second generation, substantiated by numerous instances of highly educated Bangladeshi youth coming out of working-class families. As a consequence, these immigrants were able to integrate into the United States by establishing a permanent home and seeking social belonging. Getting settled in this new home went smoothly enough that even an undocumented immigrant could see a future in the United States. This also encouraged immigrants to sponsor their parents, spouses, and siblings: all my respondents among the low-income families and most among the professional immigrants applied for the immigration of their parents and siblings as soon as they got U.S. passports. Establishing their new home and finding social belonging in the United States followed by bringing their family members shaped almost all aspects of their lives after migration, including their remittance.

Home Away from Home

Unlike economic migrants, who go abroad for a short period to earn money and return home (like the Bangladeshi migrants in Japan and the Middle East), those who migrated to the United States would settle permanently, bring their families, and raise children. This would allow them to stay focused on their life in the United States instead of looking back to their homeland. Choudhury (a man in his seventies who migrated in the early 1980s and an owner of a restaurant in Little Bangladesh) told me:

> After independence, some of the young sons of middle- and lower-middle-class families in Dhaka began to migrate to the U.S., mainly as students. They considered America as a gateway out of Bangladesh. For example, I studied general history at Dhaka University [the flagship university in Bangladesh]. I asked myself: What would I do with my bachelor's degree other than working in a museum or entering the bureaucracy? I did not see my future in those jobs. Neither did I think of pursuing higher education further. I came to America and wanted to earn some education so that I could get a decent job and settle here. There were few among us who did not take education seriously at all. We were satisfied with earning money in whatever jobs or business we found as long as we could stay here.

Here, Choudhury is talking about the early wave of Bangladeshi migrants to the United States from urban, middle-class families. Their disenchantment with their prospects in Bangladesh and perceived opportunities to earn money and stay permanently in the United States shaped their motivation to settle there. My interviewees among the early Bangladeshi immigrants to the United States who came for higher education talked about this motivation, which was further emphasized by their naturalization through the Immigration Reform and Control Act (IRCA) of 1986. This act was practically an amnesty offered to seasonal, agricultural, and undocumented immigrants. During the application and interview, candidates were required to swear they had not committed any crime; that they had entered the country before January 1, 1982 and stayed on; and that they possessed at least minimal knowledge of U.S. history and government and the English language. Tauhid (introduced earlier) described his experience of being naturalized as follows:

> I came to the U.S. as a student in a master's degree program at Cal State LA (California State University, Los Angeles) in 1981. After graduation in 1984, I joined a private company located in Burbank. So, I rented a one-bedroom apartment near my office and brought my wife from Bangladesh. My employer told me that we would need to wait a couple of years for the company to apply for our green card. It would also involve money that I thought was too much for my income at that time. But President Reagan signed a law in 1986 that was a blessing for us. I purchased a fake employment contract paper certifying that I had worked in an agricultural firm in the Central Valley for eleven months. I paid $580 for the certificate. I also claimed undocumented status on my application. I had not committed any crime. I could also speak good English. This was the biggest event in our life! We were extremely lucky. Both my wife and I received our interview letters,

interview dates, and times together. There was no uncertainty. We received our green cards in about six months after the interview, whereas I saw many applicants waiting for a year, five years, seven years, or even never getting the green card. I was so fortunate! That was what helped us most in becoming how you see us now.

Here we see Tauhid's strong determination in pursuing his dream of permanently settling in the United States. Finding his education and professional job inadequate for acquiring U.S. citizenship, Tauhid took advantage of the IRCA amnesty and procured U.S. citizenship for his wife and himself. Generally, transferring from a professional visa to permanent residency through an employer's sponsorship involves navigating complicated legal procedures for years, which slows incorporation and upward mobility.[36] As Tauhid's experience shows, the IRCA allowed many foreigners to successfully acquire legal permanent residence by bypassing the complicated and slow process of transferring their visa status. This was, perhaps, why many of the early Bangladeshi migrants to California took advantage of the 1986 act.

While interviewing Tauhid in his four-bedroom house in a newly developed suburb in the San Fernando Valley, I looked around the living room. It was decorated with a stylish sofa and chairs, traditional showpieces from Bangladesh and elsewhere his family had traveled, as well as contemporary paintings. Noticing that I was looking at the paintings, Tauhid told me that his elder daughter was interested in painting and had collected all of them. When she moved out to live with her husband in Miami after getting married, Tauhid and his wife wanted to keep the paintings with them. His wife gave us coffee and snacks using expensive cups presented on an ornately decorated tray. The overall décor of the house was indicative of their relative affluence and upper-middle-class social standing. However, Tauhid was candid in reminding me that the beginning of his new life in the United States was modest:

Don't get me wrong, but I was struggling in early days like all other Bangladeshis here. I had to work in part-time jobs besides my studies. To be frank, I took a temporary job in the Central Valley area one summer, although not in an agricultural firm [he smiled, alluding to his fake certificate of employment]. I lived in a shared apartment and cooked at home to save as much as possible. Sometimes I even had to borrow money from my elder sister, who was very rich in Bangladesh. My only concern was to survive and settle here anyhow. Gradually, I got better-paying jobs and promotions in my career. Our daughters were born. So we purchased this house on loan and moved here. After I became a U.S. citizen and got my passport, I applied for my brothers and sisters. My two brothers and three out of five sisters migrated to the U.S. with their families and successfully settled here. Neither we nor anyone in our village in Bangladesh thought that we could come to America. But Allah made us successful!

For the early migrants, who often entered the United States as students, success was measured in terms of their ability to find a professional job after graduation and settle permanently with their family and close relatives in the United States. After naturalization, immigrants would bring their spouses from Bangladesh; those who migrated as bachelors would be called on by their families in Bangladesh to marry a bride through their family's arrangement. Gradually, as their income rose and their children entered school, they would move out of their initial modest residences to "better" neighborhoods. In the meantime, they would get their citizenship and immediately apply for the immigration of their parents and siblings.

The beginning for recent immigrants entering through the DV-1 lottery and family sponsorship is far more difficult than those coming earlier for higher education like Tauhid. These immigrants' strongest motivation for persevering in low-paying, temporary, and precarious jobs was the chance to settle permanently and acquire citizenship in the United States. In fact, the aspiration for de jure citizenship[37] motivated even highly educated and skilled migrants to take on casual jobs. In an interview, a paralegal practitioner working among Bangladeshis in LA told me that his Bangladeshi clients applied for the immigration of their parents and siblings immediately after naturalization. This was confirmed by my informants, none of whom delayed applying for the immigration of their spouses, parents, or siblings. I helped Moinul (who entered the United States by winning the DV-1 lottery in 2008 and naturalized in 2014) fill out his application form for citizenship. I also helped him with the application forms for the immigration of his three brothers the day after he received his naturalization certificate, while he was still waiting for his U.S. passport. Ataur (a former schoolteacher in Bangladesh, who entered the United States with a DV-1 visa in 2011 and is now a cashier in a gas station, told me,

> My work is very painful. I have to stand behind the cash counter for the whole period of eight to ten hours each day for six days a week. This causes severe pain in my back and legs. But I cannot leave the job, because I need money to send home for my family. Therefore, I take pain medicine so that I can endure the pain. It is just for a few years until my family joins me here [he smiled, indicating optimism]. I'm working here because I will be able to bring my parents and younger brothers to the U.S. This is an unimaginable success for a schoolteacher like me.

Unlike migrants in Japan, who would evaluate success in terms of the amounts of money they earned, Ataur and other immigrants like him measured their success in terms of access to U.S. citizenship for themselves and their immediate family members. Given the relatively large family size in Bangladesh (5.7 children on average), each immigrant would eventually sponsor the migration of more than a dozen others, including the sponsor's spouse, children, parents, and siblings. Sharif (fifty-four years old at the time of our interview, married with two children, migrated in late-1970s) told me that he had sponsored the immigration of both his parents and four brothers with their families, totaling 23 individuals:

> I'm the Columbus of my family. I came to the U.S. without any knowledge of what my life would be, except my strong belief in achieving the American Dream. I sacrificed my relatively easy middle-class life in Bangladesh and worked hard in America so that I could settle here. Eventually, I also brought my parents and brothers and they have been doing well. It was like discovering a new homeland for my family.

Like Sharif, other immigrants also considered their ability to sponsor their family's immigration as a significant part of their perception of success in America. A number of my informants who entered the United States before 1995 had already sponsored the immigration of as many as twenty or more of their immediate family members and respective families. As I noted earlier, the U.S. government statistics report that 99 percent of Bangladeshis naturalized in 2017 had gotten their immigration visas through family sponsorship. The near universality of the practice was indicative of a deep craving for the company of loved ones as well as a duty toward the family, who would complete these immigrants' efforts to settle in the United States and experience the ease of feeling at home.

Conclusion

Based on my fieldwork and conversations with Bangladeshi immigrants in Los Angeles, I found two main characteristics of this migration: First, Bangladeshis have strong desire to live the "American Dream" by migrating to the United States, and second, they tend to settle permanently in the country and sponsor their immediate relatives. Bangladesh has a long history of both emigration and immigration. Currently, it is recognized as a major source country of international migration. While Bangladeshis move to most countries in the world, the United States is a special place for them among all migration destinations. Unlike migration to the Middle East and East- and South-East Asian countries that are relatively close and less expensive to travel to, migration from Bangladesh to the United States is challenging due to the long distance, expensive and time-consuming travel, and stringent documentary screening by U.S. authorities. Yet, the influence of Hollywood, other cultural industries, and word-of-mouth from Bangladeshis already in the United States indicated a much better future there, with affluence, comfort, and prestige. The desire to live in the United States has grown so strong that most Bangladeshis would leave everything behind to move to the United States and settle permanently with family. It was in this context that the Diversity Visa Program launched by the U.S. government in mid-1990s emerged as a blessing. Shortly, Bangladeshis outnumbered most other countries in terms of the yearly number of migrants entering the United States through the DV-1 lottery. People from all over Bangladesh would participate in the lottery program with the hope of winning an immigration visa and eventually migrating to the United States. While Bangladesh was dropped from the DV-1 lottery program due to surpassing the threshold[38] in 2012, the nearly universal practice among Bangladeshis to sponsor the immigration of family members resulted in a steady influx of new immigrants, and Bangladeshis came to be recognized as the fastest-growing immigrant group in the United States. New ethnic neighborhoods began to appear in most major cities around the country, including New York, Detroit, Los Angeles, Atlanta, Houston, and Dallas.

Migration is seen as a matter of the individual and their families motivated by economic consideration. While my research confirms this idea, Bangladeshi immigrants I interviewed reported much more than economic considerations for migrating to the United States. For them, to entering and settling in the United States was a matter of accessing better economic opportunities, but also social and cultural security, and the comfort and prestige associated with being an American. Thus, many immigrants left professional careers and income in Bangladesh to migrate to the United States through the DV-1 lottery or family sponsorship. For instance, several Bangladeshi medical doctors and professional scientists with PhDs migrated to the United States knowing that they would have to work in semiprofessional or casual jobs. Their apparently irrational decision in economic terms only makes sense when we consider their decision as collective one that will bring opportunity to the entire family. Thus, the first immigrant in a family usually goes through a lot of personal sacrifice; however, most are able to eke out a leaving and provide opportunities for upward mobility for the second generation, thereby fueling their American Dream of achieving success in the United States.

The overall perception of these immigrants about the U.S. government is overwhelmingly positive. Despite their initial loss of career and status, these immigrants worked hard and were able to establish their home and bring immediate relatives to the United States, thereby creating an entire extended family and eventually a community. Perhaps this is why their first impressions of their new lives are generally positive. Ironically, they also experience a dissatisfaction due to their lack of belonging due to sociocultural barriers toward upward mobility and the family disintegration. The supports these immigrants received from the government and nongovernmental organizations were hardly enough to leave a comfortable life and access upward social mobility as well as experience a comfortable retirement in addition to supporting children and grandchildren like their parents had done in Bangladesh. Hence, these immigrants, who were at all socioeconomic levels in the United States, eventually turn to their origin community in Bangladesh and send remittance—a theme I discuss in the following chapter.

4

Narratives of Remittance
from the United States

• •

As detailed in the previous chapter, Bangladeshi migration to the United States is characterized by the expectation of naturalization and family unification. Therefore, this migration is seen by Bangladeshis as de facto family migration and permanent settlement in the United States. Since this migration involves attempts to build a new life in one of the most prosperous countries in the world, it is an aspirational journey for both the individuals and their immediate relatives. So, the entire family engages by mobilizing family resources and connections to facilitate the migration of the first family member, who is expected to sponsor further immigration of the rest of the family. Migration scholars observe that in origin communities characterized by a culture of migration, success is measured in the amount of money remitted home.[1] This is not necessarily the case for Bangladeshi migration to the United States because migrants a) plan to bring their families to the country and b) do not plan to return to Bangladesh. Therefore, their standard for evaluating success is their ability to settle permanently and sponsor the immigration of the remaining family in Bangladesh.

In the previous chapter, I showed how Bangladeshi immigrants found their residences and jobs in the United States with support from the U.S. government, non-profit organizations, and their co-ethnic community, which together made it relatively easy for these immigrants to establish home and seek belonging in the United States. In this chapter, I discuss their experiences settling down with their families and relatives and raising children. Particularly, I focus on immigrant narratives about their remittance to demonstrate how varying degrees of integration into the United States correspond to differences in remittance. I share stories of remittance among Bangladeshi migrants in Los Angeles (LA), spanning nearly twenty-five years since the beginning of the DV Program in mid-1990s.

I begin this chapter by introducing four immigrants who represent four broad categories of Bangladeshis in the United States. Two entered the United States by winning the DV-1 lottery and naturalized as U.S. citizens—one migrated as a single man and the other with his wife and children. Both worked in casual jobs as salesclerks to support their families. I call the single man "Ahmed" and the married one "Mukul" throughout this chapter. They represent the newest and largest wave of Bangladeshi immigrants in the United States. The third entered the United States as a student at a university in California in the late 1970s. After graduating with a business degree, he worked for a bank until he established his own financing company. I call him "Sharif." Unlike the immigrants coming through the DV-1 lottery, who were mostly from modest rural backgrounds, Sharif came from an upper-middle-class urban background in Bangladesh. He represents the oldest and most successful wave of Bangladeshis to the United States. The fourth person, "Hasib," is an undocumented Bangladeshi immigrant who entered the United States by walking across the U.S.–Mexico border with the help of a transnational network of migration intermediaries. He represents the few undocumented Bangladeshi immigrants in LA. Like the immigrants coming with DV visas, Hasib came from a modest rural background in Bangladesh and worked in casual jobs in LA. However, his position in the labor market was significantly weaker because of his lack of legal status. Hasib is also distinct from the three others for his previous migration experience to the Middle East. Again, I present the narratives of these four immigrants as ideal types in the Weberian sense,[2] and since not all Bangladeshi immigrants precisely fit these categories, I intersperse these four narratives with stories from others to fill in gaps.

The following immigrant narratives give us a sense of how their remittance behavior reflects their sense of self and their social belonging in the United States. In addition to recognizing the structural opportunities and constraints of attaining social integration and belonging in the new destination, the narratives recognize an unsatiated urge for belonging that encourages the migrants to look back to their origin in Bangladesh through transnational engagements, including remittance.

Ahmed

Ahmed, aged forty-three, migrated to the United States in 2007 by winning the DV Program. He is the second son in his family; his elder brother lives in the Middle East and three sisters live with their husbands and children in Bangladesh. Before migration, he managed a dental clinic in Dhaka, which was the family's major source of income. Being a business studies graduate, he knew about investing in the stock market and played the Dhaka stock market to earn extra income.

As a legal permanent resident of the United States, Ahmed was eligible to work immediately after his arrival. He took a sales job in a liquor store in South LA owned by one of his cousins, who had migrated three decades earlier. Working about seventy hours a week, Ahmed earned approximately $2,500 a month. He lived in a one-bedroom apartment with three other single Bangladeshi immigrants, sharing expenses for rent, food, and utilities totaling $340 per month. His mobile phone bills and a few other miscellaneous expenses added up to $150. Thus, he had about $2,000 per month to save and send to his family in Bangladesh. Ahmed explained:

> My family [parents and a widowed sister with two children] depends on my income. So, I send them money every month. My father has been severely ill and on bed rest. I need to send a large amount for his treatment. After I came to America, I brought my widowed sister to our house to look after my parents. She also helps in managing our dental clinic. I send money for my nephews' education in an English-medium school. My brother sends money from Saudi [the Kingdom of Saudi Arabia], too; but that is small and irregular. So basically, it is my responsibility to maintain our family now. In addition, I am doing stock market business in Bangladesh, as the return is very high. I've already invested about $20,000 there and will invest more. We have a three-story house in Dhaka, so I do not intend to buy apartments or housing plots like many others. Instead, I invest money in the stock market, which I can easily bring to America whenever I want to. I will build my career in America. So why should I invest in Bangladesh?

Ahmed's narrative follows a typical scenario in which the immigrant son assumes the role of main breadwinner for the parental family. This is especially true if the son is unmarried. He provides for the family budget, medical care, education, and other necessary expenses. What is worth noting in this narrative is Ahmed's awareness that he would settle in the United States permanently and did not envision a return to Bangladesh. This was also apparent in his plan to move from working as a liquor store clerk to a semiprofessional or business career. He completed a tax preparer's course with H&R Block and earned a license from the IRS to begin working as a tax preparer. He also enrolled in an online course on the stock market in the United States and hoped to invest in the U.S. stock market immediately after his marriage, which was scheduled for winter 2013. Then, he would establish a consulting firm jointly with his wife, offering tax preparation services and brokering in insurance, travel tickets, and real estate.

Ahmed arrived in the United States with a dream of making America his permanent home, and his future plans centered on his life in the country. Yet he continued to send substantial amounts of money every month to support his family in Bangladesh, including his widowed sister and her two children. He told me his plans for them:

> I will get my passport in March [2014]. Then I will apply for all of my three sisters' immigration. I could bring my parents immediately after getting my passport. But they are too old—my father already has lost his ability to walk. My mother's health also will not allow long-distance air travel. I wish I could live with them [he sighs]! In this situation, I must keep sending them money so that they enjoy a better life in Bangladesh. I will do so as long as they are alive.

Ahmed's elder brother was a practicing dental surgeon in Saudi Arabia and was not interested in migrating to the United States at the risk of ending his career due to the extreme difficulty of acquiring a dental license. So, he would return to Bangladesh, live in the parental house, and take over the family owned dental clinic. Ahmed's sisters' families would happily migrate to the United States, as they were not leaving much behind in Bangladesh. So, once Ahmed's parents passed away, he would have no responsibility to send money to Bangladesh.

Mukul

Mukul, aged forty-four, had come to the United States with his wife and two daughters in 1998 by winning the DV-1 lottery. He is the eldest son in his family and has two brothers and four sisters. Before migrating to America, Mukul was a teacher in a local college (equivalent to an American high school). He lived with his wife, aged parents, and the youngest brother in his origin village just outside of Rajshahi city. The rest of his siblings were married and lived with their separate families. Besides teaching, Mukul looked after the family's farmlands and a pond with fisheries.

Mukul came to LA because he knew a family from his village who had migrated a few years earlier. When he left Bangladesh for the United States, he brought only about $4,000 with him, so he needed to earn immediately to support his family. Like most new immigrants from Bangladesh, he found a job with the help of another Bangladeshi immigrant (at a gas station). He worked about sixty hours a week and earned around $2,200 a month, just enough for his family to get by. He rented a one-bedroom apartment in Little Bangladesh for $850 per month. He spent about $300 on groceries, $100 on utilities, $200 on his car, and $250 on miscellaneous items. Thus, he had only a few hundred dollars at the end of the month to send to Bangladesh. He reported:

> It was my responsibility to send money for my parents as I was the eldest child. Just as I took care of them in Bangladesh, I continued to do so after coming to America. In fact, the demand for money increased after my migration, as

people thought that I was earning "big" money here. However, I also have a family to take care of in America. You see, it is not easy to maintain a family here. You cannot live cheaply like those without a family. So I could not send large amounts to Bangladesh. Yet I would send $100 every month for my parents. This was more than enough for them, you know, because they lived in our own house and had earnings from agriculture. So I would not worry much about them. Besides, I sent about $400 for my younger brother at the beginning of the year for his educational expenses at a college in Rajshahi [the nearby city]. Other than this, I did not have anyone to regularly send money to. In addition, I sent money to my parents on special occasions like Eids [Muslim religious festivals] or a relative's marriage, etc.

As legal permanent residents, both single immigrants and those with family are eligible to work in the United States. They find employment in certain low-wage jobs relatively easily with the help of co-ethnic networks.[3] While their work and earnings are similar, the lower living costs of single immigrants allow them to save more than half their monthly income, whereas those with family have only a small amount left at the end of the month.

Despite Mukul's limited saving capacity, he did not forget his parents and dependent sibling, whom he continued to regard as his own family. To be able to support them financially, he sacrificed luxuries and occasional expenses like eating out, going to movies, and so forth. One source of extra funds for Mukul was tax refunds. At the beginning of every year Mukul would receive all the money deducted from his paychecks, because his annual earnings were below the poverty line. Mukul and his wife would plan to spend this amount on new clothes, furniture, household utensils, etc., for their family in LA and on gifts and charity for relatives in Bangladesh. Additionally, both Mukul and his wife went to language classes at the local community college, which paid them a stipend sum to supplement their meager family income.

Four years after Mukul's migration, his father passed away in Bangladesh and his younger brother graduated from college [equivalent to a U.S. high school] and took a job. Mukul brought his mother to live with his family in LA. One of his daughters entered the University of California and supported herself through part-time jobs and the stipend she received from the government. His wife also took a part-time job at a nearby grocery store, while Mukul continued to work at the gas station. As his family income grew and financial responsibilities declined both in Bangladesh and in the United States, Mukul could now save a few hundred dollars each month. So, he started sending installments to purchase an apartment in Dhaka. He also bought a mango orchard in his village. He explained:

Saving money in America brings nothing. You know, the banks give you almost no interest on savings. Moreover, it would require big sums of money that I cannot save to buy a house here. So I bought an apartment in Dhaka with a down payment of $12,000 and monthly installments of $450 to be paid over ten years. Recently, I bought a mango orchard in my village at about $8,500. Both are valuable assets. I get a large income from the mango orchard every year. My apartment in Dhaka is already worth over $200,000 now and will continue to grow in value. My wife and I are planning to purchase another apartment in Dhaka.

After the dissolution of his parental family in Bangladesh, Mukul's remittance was driven not by his responsibility to the parental family, but by an economic calculation of how to maximize his income. Mukul planned to return to Bangladesh with his wife in their old age. By that time, both his daughters would finish their educations, find jobs, get married, and form their own families in the United States. He concluded that his wife and he would live in their apartment in one of the posh areas in Dhaka with the income from another rental apartment, their landed properties in Bangladesh, and their U.S. Social Security benefits.

Sharif

Sharif, aged fifty-four, is the third son in his family. He came to the United States as a student in 1978 immediately after graduating from high school. His upper-middle-class family was financially capable of sending him to LA for a university education, but the money they sent him every third month was not enough, so he had to earn extra money by doing part-time work:

It was an extremely tough life. I lived with six other Bangladeshi students in a two-bedroom apartment. We cooked together, as we could not eat American food. Cooking together was also cheaper and would allow us to live on a limited budget. To supplement the money we received from our parents, we would often work in part-time jobs. I even worked on painting a building wall [emphasizing that this was unimaginable for a Bangladeshi of his social background]! Most often we would work at a gas station owned by an Iranian Jew living next to our apartment. However, my focus was only on graduating as quickly as possible so that I might find an employment. After earning my bachelor's degree in management, and then an MBA, I began my career as a professional banker. I sent a $50 bill from my first paycheck to my mother in Bangladesh. That was the first time I sent money home. My parents never depended on my financial support. Moreover, my eldest brother was already an engineer working in the Middle East, who would send enough money to my parents. Still, I would send a few hundred dollars to my mother from my paycheck every other month until I visited Bangladesh for the first time after eight years. My parents arranged my marriage. I was surprised to find that my mother spent all the money I had sent her over years on purchasing gold jewelry for my wife!

Sharif's narrative represents the initial struggles of the early Bangladeshi immigrants in the United States. In the late 1970s, higher education was the only way for Bangladeshis to enter the country, and it was limited to a few financially solvent families. Moreover, educational facilities were mostly concentrated in the capital city, Dhaka. The expenses involved in applying to a U.S. university and the bank balance necessary for the visa application further restricted this opportunity to those from upper-class and upper-middle-class families in Dhaka. Because Sharif's family in Bangladesh had their own money, he never felt the need to send them remittances.

After joining Sharif in LA, his wife began to work part-time in a fast-food restaurant. Sharif took a new job in a corporate bank. By the time Sharif and his wife became U.S. citizens, their income was high enough to allow them to buy a house in a newly developing area in the San Fernando Valley. In a few years, Sharif left his job and started his own financing business with three employees. His wife left her job to look after their daughter and son. In the meantime, one of his brothers migrated to LA under Sharif's sponsorship, and his only sister migrated to New York with her own family. Despite Sharif's insistence, his parents refused to leave Bangladesh. They lived in their original house in Dhaka with several relatives. Sharif and his siblings visited their parents in Bangladesh every year until they died.

Sharif would send about $6,000 every year to Bangladesh as *Jakat* [the obligatory charity for rich Muslims]. Other than this, he did not send money to purchase land or save in bank accounts. He inherited a twelve-unit apartment building in a suburb near Dhaka, which generated considerable income for him. Sharif invested all his money in his business in LA, which grew to a total of twelve employees. He purchased two more houses in LA and rented them out. He sent his son to an expensive MBA program at a private university. His daughter graduated from the University of California, found employment, and married an IT engineer in Silicon Valley. Having both children well established in the United States, Sharif began to think about retiring:

God has given me everything. I have a good business. I own my house. My children are already in professional jobs. What else can I ask for? Now, it's time to retire. I think I will go back to Bangladesh. I feel that I still belong to where I was born—Bangladesh. I'm not alone in thinking like this, you know. I have friends from my elementary schools living in the U.S., the U.K., Canada, and Malaysia. They also talked about going back home after their retirement. So we opened a Facebook group among our childhood friends both in Bangladesh and abroad. Some of those in Bangladesh are very rich and powerful people. We have purchased a beautiful piece of land near the

Sundarban [the biggest mangrove forest in the world, in Southern Bangladesh, a UNESCO World Heritage Site] to develop retirement houses for each of us. One of our friends is a prominent real estate developer in Bangladesh, who oversees the whole project.

To develop this retirement home, Sharif sent substantial amounts of money until the project was completed. He also sent both religious and nonreligious charity to Bangladesh every year.

Hasib

Hasib, aged thirty-eight, is the fourth child in his family and has three brothers and two sisters in Bangladesh. He was married, but he came to the United States alone in 2008, leaving both his wife and a son in Bangladesh. Unlike the three men introduced above, Hasib entered the United States as one of the few undocumented Bangladeshi immigrants. Before coming to the United States, he spent four years as a migrant worker in Dubai. He began to plan his move to the United States once his brother-in-law won the DV-1 lottery and migrated to LA. With his help, Hasib contacted a broker who guided him to LA through several Latin American countries, a journey that cost him about $26,000 in cash and about five months of travel. His brother-in-law arranged his accommodation in an apartment with three other single Bangladeshi immigrants. He also helped Hasib find a job at a 7-Eleven store, where Hasib worked until 2012, when the employer asked all employees to provide valid Social Security numbers. Having no legal papers, Hasib had to leave the job and find another job at a gas station.

From the very beginning, Hasib felt tremendous pressure to send money to Bangladesh, primarily because he had spent all the savings he earned in Dubai, leased out a portion of his parents' agricultural land, and borrowed from a money-lender to arrange his migration to the United States. Although he worked seven days a week, his shifts were short and his pay was less than minimum wage. Thus, he worked 48 hours a week and earned about $1,400 a month. By sending home at least $1,000 every month, he was able to pay off the loans and take back the land by the end of his second year in LA. After that, Hasib sent money to his own savings account and purchased assets in addition to supporting his family. He concluded:

I'm far better off here in the U.S. than I was in Dubai. Now I earn three times as much as I earned in Dubai and can send more money. After spending on rent and other necessities, I have more than $1,000 to send home. With this money, I support my family in Bangladesh, including my parents, wife, and son. Besides, I have purchased one acre of agricultural land in our village and a store in the nearby town. Now, I'm sending installments [to buy] an apartment in Dhaka. I do not keep any savings with me here, but immediately send them to Bangladesh.

Unlike other Bangladeshi immigrants, Hasib sent all his savings to Bangladesh, perhaps because, as an undocumented immigrant, he could not open a bank account in the United States. Although there were very few stories about police arrest and deportation among Bangladeshi immigrants, Hasib talked about his persistent fear of apprehension. But this could not stop him from dreaming of settling permanently in the United States:

> My brother-in-law has applied for immigration of all his siblings including my wife. So, six years from now [practically, this could take a little longer given the time his brother-in-law applied], my wife will get a U.S. green card and come here. Then I will get legal papers through her as her spouse. I think I will be able to stay here until she comes, because the U.S. is not like Dubai. Anyone can stay here."

Despite his unfavorable work schedule and low pay, as well as his fear of being arrested and deported, Hasib was satisfied with his position in the United States because his income was higher than it had been Dubai and his long-term prospects were better.

Regardless of their social position in both the United States and Bangladesh, all four of these immigrants pursue a dream of making the United States their permanent home (at least before retirement). But their social position in the United States, determined primarily by the selectivity of U.S. immigration policy, plays a central role in shaping both their life courses and their remittance. Bangladeshis entering the United States through the DV Program, like Ahmed and Mukul, see their migration as a lucky chance to enter the land of the American Dream despite their modest social background in Bangladesh. They begin their life in America at the bottom of the labor market. Taking financial responsibility for their families, parents, and siblings in Bangladesh, these immigrants regularly send money home. Some move from casual work to semiprofessional jobs by acquiring necessary education credentials and find a comfortable and respectable life in the United States. However, the majority fail to acquire any useful credentials in the country and continue to toil in precarious jobs in the secondary labor market.[4] They send remittances from their small savings to buy properties and invest in other income-generating assets in Bangladesh and thereby realize economic success. Those who migrate as students come from higher social classes in Bangladesh and enter the primary labor market by finding professional careers after their university graduation. As in the case of Sharif, their families in Bangladesh do not depend on their money and they more easily establish themselves economically in the United States. Yet, they do send money to Bangladesh for religious purposes and often share a desire to retire to Bangladesh. Finally, the undocumented immigrants occupy the most marginal position in the United States. Like the unskilled workers among Bangladeshi legal immigrants, they work in the secondary labor market, but unlike them they can neither save nor invest in the United States. They send all their income to Bangladesh, where their remittance is spent on family support and on income-generating assets.

The most striking observed pattern of among all these immigrants is permanent settlement, which means all of them bring their immediate families and relatives to live permanently in the United States. Yet, there are important variations in their remittance. A closer examination of the relationships between immigrants and the recipients of their remittance reveals qualitative differences reflecting their diverse levels of integration and social belonging to the United States and Bangladesh.

Motivations to Send Remittances

The United States is one of the top source countries of remittance to Bangladesh. According to Bangladesh Bank data,[5] the United States has been the third-largest sources country of remittance to Bangladesh, after the Kingdom of Saudi Arabia and the United Arab Emirates, since 2017. I have shown elsewhere that Bangladeshi immigrants in the United States send considerably higher amounts of their income in remittances than Bangladeshi migrants in other destination countries.[6] A closer look, however, reveals that some immigrants, like Sharif, do not send remittances at all and others send only a small portion of their income, unlike their counterparts in Japan.

My first-wave informants repeatedly emphasized their struggles while studying and then navigating through the process of naturalization. They did not talk much about difficulties finding professional jobs and managing daily life, perhaps because their employment in formal sectors offered a clear path forward through regular promotion and because it was their wives who had to "manage daily life" in the United States. In both respects their experience contrasted with more recent immigrants entering the United States through the DV Program. Choudhury comments about the later migrants,

> During the OP-1 and DV-1 programs, anybody in Bangladesh could migrate to the US [this is not correct; the DV-1 application required high school graduation, a selective mechanism in a country where fewer than 30 percent complete high school]. These people came with the plan to earn and send money to Bangladesh, to purchase whatever they found on sale in their villages that they were not able to purchase before—land, house, business, cattle, [and] what not. They would take jobs in gas stations, 7-Eleven stores, liquor stores, and so forth. They saw migration to America as an opportunity to earn money and to achieve whatever dreams they [could not] realize in Bangladesh.

While professional Bangladeshis saw their migration to the United States as an avenue to higher income and upward socioeconomic mobility, immigrants who won the DV-1 lottery and were from relatively lower-class backgrounds would find earning and living in the United States quite challenging. Most came from modest social backgrounds, and their families invested large sums of money to arrange for their migration to the United States. Officially, the DV-1 lottery process cost about $1,000, including an application fee to the U.S. Immigration Department and a visa processing fee at the U.S. Embassy in Dhaka. However, I found that these immigrants had spent from $2,000 to $30,000 (with a median of $11,000) managing the visa process alone.[7] In most cases, their families and relatives lent money to the migrants. Many also borrowed from loan sharks at high interest rates and faced the urgent need to repay loans and replenish the family funds.

As Mahbub (a single immigrant in his early thirties who entered the United States after winning the DV-1 lottery in 2009) told me,

> Those who come to America are mostly from financially needy families in Bangladesh. No one coming out of a BMW car purchases a lottery ticket, you know. He who cannot afford to buy a car buys a lottery ticket. Similarly, rich people in Bangladesh do not send in DV lottery forms. Those who need money are the ones who send in DV lottery forms. Once they arrive here, they send remittance to fulfill their responsibility to the family.

Almost all my interviewees among the DV-1 lottery winners reported that they regularly sent remittances to their families in Bangladesh from the very beginning, like Ahmed, Mukul, and Hasib in the opening vignettes. The owner of a money-transfer agency in Little Bangladesh also confirmed that most immigrants, especially those with limited education and low incomes, regularly sent money to support their families in Bangladesh. To back up his claim, the owner showed me about forty remittance-sending forms filled out in one day by migrants and pointed out that most selected "family support" as their reason for sending money. In addition to loan repayment and replenishing family assets, this support can be explained in terms of the origin culture in Bangladesh, where sons are expected to share in the responsibility for their family once they grow up and begin to earn.[8]

The need for immigrants to send money to their families in Bangladesh tends to subside within a couple of years after their arrival. This is because they are able to repay loans and replenish family assets in a few years. Moreover, their naturalization after five years as permanent residents allows them to bring their immediate family to the United States. They also apply for the immigration of their siblings, who grow up and form their own separate nuclear families in Bangladesh while waiting to migrate to the United States. Thus, the initial pressure to earn in whatever jobs they can fades away. But as they have not earned any U.S. education credential that would allow them to enter higher-paying jobs, they continue to depend on the co-ethnic networks that initially helped them find casual jobs and apartments. Thus, these immigrants end up in similar jobs and neighborhoods to those they began with. Therefore, while it is possible for immigrants to enter the United States and establish a home through permanent settlement and family unification, upward social mobility remains unavailable for most of them, confirming research on segmented assimilation, or the process of immigrants integrating into different segments of U.S. society.[9]

As the days went by in their new home in the United States, my DV-1 lottery informants came to rely on government support. While it is likely they will work hard to earn more, sometimes these immigrants try to keep their benefits by maintaining their low-income status. For instance, they might understate their income on their tax returns to continue living in subsidized apartments, get stipends for attending ESL courses, and use other facilities. They realize they have settled in a marginal life with casual jobs at the bottom of the local labor market, which results in low incomes, little savings, and zero social prestige, as Mukul notes in the opening vignette. However, they recognize that their small savings are enough to invest in assets in Bangladesh that will bring them both income and prestige (for instance, as owners of homes and apartments). My informants reported a range of investment initiatives, including purchasing land and apartments, depositing in savings accounts, investing in the stock market, lending at high interest, and so forth. The most common investment project was purchasing residential land and apartments in Dhaka, followed by purchasing agricultural land in the village and depositing savings in a bank account in Bangladesh. The primary motivation for purchasing land or saving in a Bangladeshi bank was economic—my interviewees could not afford real estate in LA, but they could spend small amounts in monthly installments to buy land and apartments in Bangladesh. Moreover, the price of real estate was increasing very quickly in Bangladesh, almost doubling in five to eight years. Again, interest on bank savings in America was nearly zero, whereas banks in Bangladesh would pay more than 10 percent interest.

The amounts required to make investments in Bangladesh were small compared to income and savings in the United States. For instance, a typical monthly installment on an average-sized apartment in Dhaka would range from $300 to $500 U.S. dollars, according to the marketing executive of a renowned real estate company I met at a housing fair that took place at a Bangladesh Day celebration. The financial return was also relatively small. Once the apartment was handed over to the owner after several years of payments, the owner would rent it out at a monthly rate of about $200 to $250. However, the social gain from the newly acquired property was much higher. Despite living in poverty-stricken neighborhoods in LA and working nonprofessional jobs, the immigrants now could feel accomplished among their co-ethnics as homeowners in Dhaka. Most of my informants acknowledged that they invested in Bangladesh not only for financial reasons, but also for social recognition as homeowners or business owners, a status that was inaccessible to them in LA. Migration scholars identify similar investment patterns among other immigrant groups of low socioeconomic standing in the United States, whereby the immigrants find gratification using a transnational comparative optic[10] to elevate their own status through spending and investing in their origin communities.

Home Sweet Home

I first met Babu at Aladin restaurant in 2009, just a few months after I arrived in LA. Babu won the DV-1 lottery in 2007 when he was in the first year of his master's degree program at a university in Bangladesh. He migrated to the United States in 2008 without completing his degree because, as he told me, he had to enter the United States within a year of the visa issuance, or it would be revoked. He rented a shared studio apartment with another Bangladeshi and worked in a nearby KFC restaurant. I would meet him every Saturday afternoon at Aladin[11] for about two years until he moved to another apartment a few blocks away.

I supposed that, as a single male in his late twenties, Babu would be relatively enthusiastic about life in America and interested in continuing his studies, acquiring a driver's license, and exploring the region around LA. However, I found him self-contained. He worked only about thirty-four hours a week and did not take any ESL courses despite his complete lack of English and free time. He knew that a car would give him greater flexibility in finding jobs but did not try to get his driver's license. One reason he gave me was his disappointment in his life in LA. He told me that he had had very high hopes about living a better life in America, modeled on the TV series *Friends* and a few Hollywood movies. He also had some friends in LA who had told him good things about living there. But upon his arrival he found everything different—poor, dirty, and crowded. He did not like living without his family and not spending time with his friends. He always complained about how busy others around him were. He talked about how much he missed his mother and two brothers in Dhaka. Only one topic would animate him—the possibility of their joining him in LA after his naturalization.

In 2013, Babu still had not enrolled in an ESL course, but began to take driving lessons at one of two driving schools in LA run by Bangladeshi instructors. He got his driver's license almost effortlessly. Subsequently, he took another job at a liquor store, working sixty-two hours a week. Babu explained that his naturalization was nearing, so he needed to earn more money so that he could bring his mother and brothers. He would also need a car once his family joined him in LA. He asked me for help filling out his naturalization application. Given that he was single, had worked in only three jobs, and had lived in only two apartments during his entire stay in LA, his application was simple and straightforward. He submitted the application in January and went to visit his family in Bangladesh. He came back after a month, as he had received a letter assigning a fingerprinting date much earlier than he had anticipated. Although he had to come back quickly, he appeared very excited and happy. He had married a woman in Bangladesh, which his family had arranged for him. He had met his best friends and relatives and had enjoyed his visit very much.

In July, Babu called me to tell me that his naturalization interview was scheduled for the following month. I drove to his liquor store and picked him up after he finished his shift around 7 P.M. We went to the restaurant Deshi and took a table. Babu was exhausted after an eleven-hour shift. He told me that he opened the store at 8 A.M. and worked until 7 P.M., when the owner took over the store for rest of the night shift. This was his schedule for four days, including the weekends. He worked a little less—nine hours—on Tuesday and Wednesday, with Thursday off. I ordered Bengali sweets to celebrate the coming of his naturalization interview. He thanked me but seemed very worried about it. He told me that he was nervous about the interview. I tried to reassure him by saying that everyone was nervous about the interview and that no one among those we knew had failed it, so he should be fine. I recommended a few websites for preparation and a Korean NGO that offered mock interviews for naturalization applicants. I also recommended that he talk to a common acquaintance whose wife had recently taken the interview successfully. We spent about an hour there, and then I walked him up to his apartment.

Babu memorized all the information in a booklet provided by the U.S. Citizen and Immigration Services (USCIS). He also took several mock interviews and met with a few compatriots who had successfully taken the interview. He passed the interview without difficulty. On the day of his oath-taking, I drove him to the city hall in El Monte, about eighteen miles away from Little Bangladesh. He dressed up as he would for any celebratory event, like Eid or a marriage party. He was smiling all along. He called his mother and brothers several times while we drove. I walked with him up to the queue at the entrance to city hall. He had the flags of both the United States and Bangladesh with him but handed me the Bangladeshi flag when he entered the oath-taking event. I waited for about an hour outside until he came out with holding his U.S. citizenship certificate in one hand and waving the U.S. flag in the other hand. He almost ran to me and gave me a hug. He took a few moments, looked at me, and exclaimed, "Now this is my home!"

As the saying goes, home is where the heart is. To Babu, the naturalization ceremony marked the moment when he began to realize that the United States was his home. This had never occurred to him in his past five years of living in the country. He had an apartment, a job, and a few friends and acquaintances. Yet, he would not call America home until he became a U.S. citizen and attained the ability to bring his mother and brothers to share it with him. Here, we clearly see a departure from the discourses about migrant remittance that emphasize separation from the origin country. What we find in Babu's assertion about home is strikingly different. For him, home is where one lives with immediate family members, including parents, siblings and/or the spouse and children. Unable to sponsor his parents and brothers, Babu missed out on the experience of finding "home" during his many years living as a single man in LA. Additionally, knowing that his family would eventually join him once he sponsored their immigration perhaps made it seem pointless to invest in Bangladesh. Moreover, being a single male, Babu was not under pressure to earn prestige by investing in Bangladesh like his compatriots with family in LA. Thus, Babu did not try to maximize his earnings in part-time jobs to be able to save more and send money for anything other than family maintenance in Bangladesh.

Once he acquired citizenship and applied for the immigration of his family, Babu began preparing for the home he would have with them in LA. Thus, he started working longer hours to increase the income needed for his family and enrolled in driving classes. As Boccagni[12] argues, home is an experience that allows for realizing a sense of security, familiarity, and control. Babu had been unable to experience home in this sense and in several other ways. He could not bring his family to the United States and establish a home with familiar people (e.g., parents, siblings), objects (e.g., furniture, decorations, and things used to make a space one's own) and practices (e.g., habitual acts including eating, sleeping, leisurely activities, etc.). Only after he became a U.S. citizen did Babu realize that no one could stop him from bringing his family, and no one could deny his right to create a space with near-and-dear ones and familiar objects and to engage in habitual practices. Naturalization offered Babu the opportunity to create his home and feel belonging—what Wise[13] calls territorialization, conscious efforts to conquer a space as one's own.

Permanent Home, Partial Belonging

While feeling "at home" for Babu—like many other Bangladeshi immigrants—finally became a reality through his naturalization, there are additional factors contributing to immigrants' realization of home. Babu's first job was in a KFC with co-workers from Bangladesh and El Salvador. His neighborhood in Koreatown was almost exclusively populated by immigrants—Koreans, Latinx (mostly from Mexico, El Salvador, and Guatemala), Filipino/as, Bangladeshis, and other South Asians. However, living in the same neighborhood or working in the same workplace does not always lead to the kind of interethnic minority coalitions that migration scholars recognize in big immigrant cities. Kasinitz et al. give the example of immigrant minorities from Latin America and the Caribbean becoming part of the Puerto Rican and Black communities of New York City, with tangible benefits for the second generations.[14] While coexisting in neighborhoods, workplaces, and schools, my informants rarely engaged with immigrants from other ethnic backgrounds. Koreatown is well known for its nightlife and ethnic foods. However, Bangladeshis seldom visit a Korean, Latin American, or Filipino restaurant, perhaps because of their relatively low income and religious orientation: most Bangladeshis are Muslims, for whom alcohol and pork are prohibited. Instead, their social life appears to revolve around co-ethnic groceries/restaurants, ethnic organizations, and the Southern California Islamic Center. Like Bangladeshis in Japan, marriage and intimate relationships with other nationals are discouraged by a sense of failure to find a suitable Bangladeshi spouse among working-class immigrants, and by a repudiation of "being too American" among those in professional jobs. Two of my informants married to Filipina women confirmed these notions by sharing jocular comments they received from their friends about their marriages. One of my informants in a professional career lamented his daughter's marriage to her white partner because an implicit rejection among his relatives and close friends often manifested as awkward and led to uneasy conversation. This attitude toward marrying out of one's own ethnic group, however, is not unique to Bangladeshi Americans, as migration scholars recognize similar patterns of co-ethnic orientation among other immigrant minorities in LA.[15] During my fieldwork, I participated in a volunteer recruiting event by South Asian Network (SAN) and noticed that Bangladeshis, in comparison to Indians and Pakistanis, were reluctant to encourage their children to join SAN. The Bangladeshi immigrants' lack of interest in other immigrant groups and their cultures is also explicit, for instance, in their reluctance to visit the Korean or Mexican restaurants at their doorsteps. This may also signal their limited ability to spend on dining out.

Nearly all my informants reported significant changes in their lifestyle with the arrival of their families in the United States. Those entering the United States through family sponsored immigration visa migrated with their families; most DV-lottery winners entered the United States alone with aspirations of bringing their families later. Those with families immediately faced various economic and social challenges, whereas the single immigrants were relatively better off, with higher saving, and more flexibility allocating their time and socializing among co-ethnics. However, the tendency toward reuniting with the family would eventually eliminate these differences between those with family and singles and put everyone onto a similar path characterized by working in low-paid casual jobs, living in a poor co-ethnic neighborhood, and remaining dependent on government subsidies and informal community support networks.

As it had been for Babu, family unification inevitably increases the need for more money. Babu move out of a shared apartment and rented a two-bedroom apartment capable of accommodating his mother, a younger brother, and his soon-to-be wife. He also bought refurbished and used furniture and a used Toyota Camry. Once the family arrived, Babu's grocery bill increased significantly. The range of new and increased expenditures would consume almost all his monthly income. Still, Babu was much happier—throwing dinner parties at his apartment and attending such parties at his friends' places, going to community celebrations with the whole family, and taking the family to beaches and parks on his days off. When I last met Babu in 2016, his wife gave birth to their first child. Both his mother and his wife were able to find new friends among other Bangladeshi female immigrants in the neighborhood. As the pressure to earn more continued to grow while Babu's income from casual work stagnated, his wife completed a short course and took a part-time work as a front desk assistant in a nearby medical clinic. His younger brother enrolled in an ESL course at the local community college that offered stipends, while his mother started a home delivery business of Bangladeshi sweets to complement Babu's income.

When the family is settled in the United States, immigrants' lives then center around earning enough money and securing a comfortable livelihood. For the expenses slowly but steadily grow, with growing children and social commitments in LA in addition to back in the origin community. Shortly after their families arrive and settle in the United States, immigrants often realize they must maintain their connections with the origin country through relatives and friends, as well as by acquiring property. One of the reasons for this realization is that the individualism of American society will eventually separate adult children from their parents. Shahin (who migrated with family through the DV-1 lottery in 1999 and had two teenage children in high school) explained:

> My hairs are greying. Soon I will become old. My children are growing up in this country, where they will not take care of me and my wife. So I've made my plan. I'll buy two apartments in Dhaka city. After my retirement, my wife and I will go back and live in one apartment and will rent the other. Besides, I'll get a few hundred dollars from my Social Security savings here. This will also bring me some recognition. You know, if you do not have an apartment or home in Dhaka, no one respects you in Bangladesh. They will question what I have done after living so many years in America.

Shahin—and others like him—talked about his concern for life in old age. While first-generation Bangladeshi immigrants are able to raise their children in the United States, the splitting of the family due to the married children moving out and the meager stipend from Social Security savings often leads them to look back to their origins in Bangladesh. Shain contemplated that returning to Bangladesh would give him company and social recognition in addition to a more comfortable standard of living.

Almost all my informants—particularly those with teenage and grown-up children—acknowledged that generational succession would break apart their nuclear family. My working-class informants, including Shahin, emphasized the impact of separation from their children who grew up in America and their lack of an adequate income after retirement. While those in professional jobs and the middle class did not talk about their economic standing after retirement, they shared working-class immigrants' concerns about separation from their children and being lonely, which encouraged them, too, to look back to their origin in Bangladesh. As Tauhid elaborated in a long conversation,

> I'm an escapist. I left Bangladesh so that I could avail myself of opportunities in America, such as a better profession, assets, ability to send children to universities and professional careers, and a higher standard of living. I worked hard and accepted the American way of life. But I've not yet been able to embrace this wholeheartedly. I'm still a Bangladeshi at heart. I feel for Bangladesh, not for America. I do not want anything bad for America, but all my good wishes are for Bangladesh. This is because I've come out of Bangladesh. My root is there. After spending my whole life in America, I still think of Bangladesh, dream about Bangladesh. I still remember my friends in schools and university, recall what we did together, where we went to play, fight, etc. . . . I'm nearing my retirement. One of my daughters got married and moved to Florida with her husband. The other will graduate next year and most likely will move out, too. I wish our grandchildren would live with us, play with us all day when their parents are out at work. I wish we could spend time with our old fellows reminiscing about our common childhood memories. But the reality is that they [the children] will move out and we will stay at home alone. So I feel an urge to go back to my origin. . . . But I know I cannot go back to Bangladesh forever. First of all, my wife does not like this idea, because there are no reliable healthcare facilities, no close relatives, and also the problem with insecurity. Moreover, how can I permanently go back, leaving my children and grandchildren in America? But I want to go to Bangladesh and stay a few months so that I can spend time with my relatives, friends, and neighbors, and then come back to America for about half of the year. I guess I'll keep moving back and forth between America and Bangladesh until I die.

Tauhid's sense of home and belonging was unproblematic while he lived a middle-class suburban life with his wife and daughters in LA. With his daughters growing up and moving away and his own retirement coming up, Tauhid began to feel an emptiness in his home and to reflect on his sense of belonging, which he realized was divided between his home in the United States and his roots in Bangladesh. To feel "at home," he needed both.

Like Shahin and Tauhid, my informants reported that they perceived their roots in Bangladesh, which made them feel a need to reconnect to their roots in their origin communities once their children grew up and moved out. With all or most of their siblings and close relatives in the United States, these immigrants would turn to distant kin in their origin villages or towns through transnational practices, including remittance. This pattern was particularly common among my middle-class informants in professional jobs, as their children were more likely to graduate from college and enter professional jobs, often far away from LA. These immigrants reportedly sent money to build and/or renovate schools, mosques, and other charitable projects in their origin communities. Children growing up and moving away would reduce the financial burden on these immigrants, which allowed them to increase the amount and frequency of monetary help to distant kin and former neighbors in Bangladesh. Moreover, these first-generation immigrants would actively look for their childhood friends in Bangladesh and reconnect. Thus, in the opening vignette, Sharif spoke about creating a Facebook group with his childhood friends in Bangladesh and in different countries abroad and their plan to develop a gated housing community with modern facilities where he would stay a few months every year. These professional and middle-class immigrants sent substantial remittances to Bangladesh, which demonstrated their efforts to reconnect to their roots in the origin country and find belonging.

By contrast, the lower-middle-class and working-class immigrants explained their remittances in terms of their anticipated gains in income and social status through investing in Bangladesh. Their emphasis on gaining social status was conditioned by their membership and belonging in the origin community in both LA and Bangladesh, because social status comes from a recognition by others that one is a successful migrant. However, their investment ventures would often turn problematic due to eventual diminution in their belonging caused by their parents either joining them in the United States or passing away, and the parental family dissolving into the separate families of their siblings—a theme that I explore in detail in the following chapter. Dividing the family property and joint investments posed serious challenges to family solidarity among siblings and other close relatives. And the siblings, too, would migrate to the United States through these immigrants' sponsorship, leaving no one to manage property in Bangladesh. Thus, the investments the immigrants once saw as opportunities for achieving mobility in Bangladesh seemed unattractive and not worth the effort because of their weakening membership and social belonging to the origin community. Meanwhile, their children would grow up, perhaps graduate from universities, and often enter careers in the professional and semiprofessional sectors, freeing the immigrants from substantial financial burdens. The immigrants would also find new sources of status as successful parents and would demonstrate their children's achievements by offering expensive marriage ceremonies, sponsoring community events, donating to social and religious events, and so forth. However, like their better off professional counterparts, these immigrants would also come to realize a lack of belonging once they neared retirement and their children grew up and moved away. Thus, the idea of establishing a home in the United States would remain elusive, and all of these immigrants would send remittances to their origin communities in Bangladesh in search of belonging.

Conclusion

Bangladeshi immigrants in the United States send remittances to their relatives and neighbors in their origin communities, which has made the United States the third-largest source country of remittances for Bangladesh. While these immigrants hail from mostly middle- and upper-middle-class families, they experience downward social mobility in the United States, where the majority begin their new lives working in casual jobs and living in poor neighborhoods in gateway cities like LA. Despite some disappointment among these immigrants due to not finding the quality of life they expected in America, they continue to toil both economically and socially because they are motivated to permanently settle, become American citizens, and sponsor their family and immediate relatives to join them in the United States. They also commit to their responsibilities to their immediate family and relatives back home in Bangladesh by sending remittances. What distinguishes Bangladeshi migration to the United States from migration to Japan or other Asian countries is their permanent settlement with their family and relatives, and the possibility of upward social mobility. As my fieldwork shows, this significantly affected these immigrants' transnational engagement with their family and relatives in Bangladesh, including remittance.

Like Bangladeshi migrants to Japan and other destination countries, these immigrants identify themselves with their origin family and maintain their membership to the family and community in Bangladesh through sending remittances. Their narratives about remittance demonstrate some variation in terms of motivations and strategies, depending on their social position in the United States. What is interesting to note is that those in lower socioeconomic positions in the United States are the ones sending more remittances to Bangladesh than those who are relatively well-off in the United States. If all the immigrants were motivated by altruism in sending remittances, the trend would be reversed, and professional and middle-class Bangladeshi immigrants would send more remittances out of their larger savings. Similarly, if self-interest alone motivated these migrants to send remittances, the well-off immigrants would likely send more remittances like their counterparts in lower socioeconomic positions, but they do not.

Unsurprisingly, most Bangladeshi immigrants settle in the lower socioeconomic strata upon their arrival in the United States but see the prospects for improvement overtime by their hard work. Yet, those migrating with the family through the DV-1 lottery program or sponsorship from U.S.-citizen relatives face the most difficult barriers to upward mobility due to their greater family burdens in the United States compared to those who migrate alone. For while both married and the single immigrants obtain similar kinds of employment and incomes, their expenses in the United States are unequal as those with family spend almost all their income and those who are single are able to save much more. However, the single immigrants have greater family responsibilities as they left their entire families in Bangladesh and they must be provided for. Hence, these migrants send more money at more regular intervals in remittances. These single immigrants send remittances to their families and relatives in Bangladesh most diligently among all Bangladeshis in the United States. Once they bring their immediate family and relatives to the United States by sponsoring their immigration, they focus on establishing their homes and finding belonging in the United States. Gradually, they develop wide networks of friends among co-ethnic immigrants, which leads to their increasing engagement in the United States and declining involvement in the origin community. However, these immigrants realize that their small income and meager savings are not enough to achieve upward social mobility by moving into professional careers and pur-chasing houses in better neighborhoods that would both allow them to save on rent and enhance their social status. While they send their children to college and help them achieve occupational mobility, these immigrants see an oppor-tunity for themselves by investing in real estate in Bangladesh from their small savings, which allows them to earn both income and prestige. They also find other income-earning opportunities in Bangladesh by purchasing agricultural land and depositing money in savings accounts with high interest rates. Hence this group of immigrants are able to ensure upward mobility for their children in the United States, but not necessarily themselves, although it is possible for them to achieve upward mobility if they retire in Bangladesh.

For the immigrants settling in the U.S. professional and middle-class, the tra-jectory is different. They do not have to provide for their well-off family in Bangladesh. Instead, they can focus on higher education and learning skills that allow them to find a professional career. They settle with their families in middle-class neighborhoods and engage with co-ethnics and those from other ethnic groups. They report having limited engagement with their origin community in Bangladesh as they are able to achieve their American Dream with a professional career, their own house, and membership in the U.S. middle class relatively easily. Thus, their engagement with relatives and neighbors in the origin community through remittance is little, if any. However, these immigrants inevitably arrive at a stage in their lives when their grown-up children move out with their respective families and leave them behind. Their professional associations also end with their retirement, cutting them off from most of their long-term companionships in the United States. These immigrants interpret this as normal in the United States. While they accept such disintegration of the family they established in the United States, they crave the belonging they saw among previous generations of their families in the origin community. Hence, they turn back to their roots. They begin contacting their childhood friends and distant relatives still living in their origin communities in Bangladesh. And they reconnect with them through various kinds of remittance, including joint ventures and charity.

Thus, the remittances Bangladesh receives from the United States can be understood in terms of immigrants' sense of belonging to their family and origin community. All the immigrants reportedly send remittances so long as they see themselves as members of the receiving family and community in need of financial support. While many, especially in lower socioeconomic positions in the United States, send remittances for investment in Bangladesh to earn income, their concern for increased social status requires that they make such investments in their origin community to earn social recognition. This further supports the association between migrants' social belonging and remittance. Since individual belonging is embedded in family and community, they send remittances to the family and community in Bangladesh. This belonging, however, goes through a gradual development and erosion overtime as children grow up and form their own families, thereby disintegrating the origin family, and most immediate relatives migrate to the United States, thereby disintegrating ties to the origin community. This inevitably affects migrants' transnational belonging and engagements, which is discussed in the following chapter.

5

Going Global, Coming Home

● ●

Unlike in the previous chapters, which discuss the challenges migrants face establishing a home and finding belonging within the social and structural conditions of the destination country, this chapter looks at the transformations in migrants' families that shape their home-making and belonging. I begin with my experience at a family event to which I was invited in the United States.

I joined an annual picnic in Griffith Park, Los Angeles, organized by a community association and attended by more than three dozen families and a roughly equal number of single immigrants. Some adults were playing cricket and soccer in one corner of the park while others arranged food for lunch. Most women were sitting on chairs and a large carpet, and the children were running all around. The whole space was filled with lively conversation and activities. When the party began to wind down after lunch, I found Ashfaq, who helped organize the event, sitting alone looking over the crowd. He smiled and asked me to sit beside him.

I first met Ashfaq at Deshi in 2011, my first year in the field. A taxi driver and an organizer of an association whose members were mostly other Bangladeshi taxi drivers, he was actively involved in organizing community events such as the national day celebration, religious commemorations, and family days. He was well known for his commitment to fellow immigrants, especially families and younger generations; as he told me, he wanted to enable Bangladeshi immigrant families to introduce their children to the origin culture. His compatriots elected him several times to the executive committee of the largest community organization of Bangladeshis in California. He migrated to America in 1994 by winning the OP-1 lottery (a predecessor to the DV-1 lottery) and lived in the Little Bangladesh neighborhood with his wife and three children. After four years working in a gas station, he obtained a commercial driving license and began working for Yellow Cab. He still drove a cab, about ten hours a day, six days a week, and took Saturdays off—and breaks for community events when necessary. By following him at these events, I was able to build enough rapport that he would talk about his experience in America. I told him about my research from the beginning of my fieldwork. He seemed enthusiastic and volunteered as a key respondent. Knowing my interest, Ashfaq began:

> Our society [in Bangladesh] is a family based society. Our relation to the family is so close that we cannot do anything without involving the family. Ninety-nine percent of people [meaning Bangladeshi immigrants] who came to the U.S. received financial and all kinds of other support from their families. Just think about my example. When I won the OP lottery, I had a job. But I was not able to pay for the visa processing fee, let alone my air ticket and other expenses. So, I took help from my family and close relatives. My parents sold a piece of agricultural land to finance my visa processing and trip to Los Angeles. This created a sense of responsibility in me to provide for my family through remittances. In fact, whenever a member of a family migrates to America, he assumes a great responsibility to the family in Bangladesh.

Ashfaq had previously talked to me several times about his migration to America, always highlighting how his family's support was instrumental to his migration and how deeply he was indebted to them. Such reciprocation is recognized in both academic and public discourses about migrant remittance.[1] However, I asked if he had stopped sending money to his family in Bangladesh, given that he had been in America for almost two decades and his debt should have been repaid long ago. He replied:

> I still send money. There are various reasons. Some of my brothers and sisters are still living in Bangladesh [he had eleven siblings]. My other relatives and neighbors are there, too. They assume that they will get my financial support for expenses like building a mosque or madrassa [religious school] in the village. I also feel a sense of responsibility to them as I grew up and lived among them for many years before coming to America. Although I live here, I believe I should take responsibility for my community there.

Ashfaq's explanation of his remittance to his immediate family and relatives in Bangladesh may be regarded as both self-interested (reciprocating) and altruistic (sacrificing personal economic gains). Ashfaq and other immigrants saw themselves as members of their origin families and offered detailed accounts of their transnational engagements with them, including remittance. It is the migrants' recognition of this continued membership in the origin family and society—as opposed to the assumption of the migrants and the remittance-receiving family as separate entities—that motivates them to send remittances, as I detail in this chapter.

Economic migration from poor countries in the Global South, including Bangladesh, is recognized as a survival strategy for families experiencing resource constraints and uncertain economic prospects.[2] There is a long history of research on household coping strategies, especially in the context of population growth, rural development, and social change in agrarian societies.[3] As Bangladesh is one of the most densely populated countries in the world and has a weak economy, rural households cannot find agricultural employment for all members and consequently turn to informal economic activity and internal migration to cities and towns.[4] And the drivers of outmigration have increased with the adverse impacts of climate change.[5] Families often face various natural calamities as well as socioeconomic challenges, and sending members out of the rural residential village to cities and other parts of the country has long been a common survival strategy.[6] During the introduction of English colonial rule in Bengal in the late eighteenth century, rural families in some villages sent migrants to England and North America to earn additional income.[7] After 1850, Bengali men—particularly from the northeastern district of Sylhet—became a crucial workforce of the imperial merchant marine; many of them worked in the engine rooms of British merchant ships during the two world wars. Some began to settle in East London from the 1920s, and their numbers slowly increased until 1945.[8]

Sociologist Ketty Gardner[9] presents a vivid picture of how affluent rural households in the district of Sylhet adopted migration to the United Kingdom as a strategy to cope with increasing economic and sociocultural challenges. While poor households in rural areas tended to migrate internally, Gardner found that it was the relatively affluent families that sent their sons to work on the British ships and that many ended up settling permanently in England. She observed that the households in Sylhet were largely composed of independent farmers and liable to pay tax directly to the colonial administration, unlike those in other regions of Bengal where farmers were tenants to the local zamindars.[10] In the face of increasing tax burdens and land fragmentation, these households required additional income from outside their local and regional economies. Thus, they invested substantial amounts of money to send their young sons to work on the British ships and eventually migrate to England—sons who, in turn, would send remittance home. Finding this the most viable way to maintain and enhance social status in the village, most households adopted international migration as one of their primary coping strategies and for generations continued to send family members to England.

Similar socioeconomic processes occurred during the post-liberation years of the 1970s and gained momentum in the late 1980s and early 1990s. A new wave of migrants from Bangladesh began out of the pilgrimage to Mecca in the early 1970s, when a few Bangladeshis overstayed and took employment in Saudi Arabia. Their reputation for hard work, discipline, and productivity attracted the attention of Arab employers, who began to send delegations to Bangladesh to find more workers.[11] Noticing this as a potential source of foreign income, the government of newly independent Bangladesh took steps to encourage and facilitate migrant workers' entrance to the Middle East. It established the Bureau of Manpower, Employment and Training (BMET) and formulated laws and policies to regulate and license private recruiters, provided other services to them, and occasionally sent delegations to Middle Eastern countries in search of employment opportunities for Bangladeshi workers. The government encouraged similar migration to newly industrializing and oil-rich countries in the East, including Malaysia, Singapore, and Brunei, with the expectation of obtaining foreign currencies in remittances.

While the Bangladesh government has increasingly stepped in to facilitate overseas employment, its current share of labor migrants is only about 2 percent. About one-third of migrants (35 percent) are hired through private recruiters. The majority (63 percent) of foreign employment is procured by the migrants and their families.[12] It is important to note that these numbers do not include thousands of other Bangladeshis who migrate to developed countries in North America, Europe, and Australia through family sponsored immigration, higher education, and undocumented border crossings. Thus, for Bangladeshis, international migration is still a matter of the migrants and their families.

By the Family, for the Family

The family has played a central role in Bangladeshi migration from the very beginning. This is most obvious in countries such as Japan and the United States, where the Bangladesh government and commercial recruiters have not yet stepped in to regulate and facilitate migration.[13] As chapter 1 shows, family financing plays a pivotal role in migration to Japan; even the few students offered Monbusho scholarships consider the financial support of their families in their decisions.[14] Similarly, Bangladeshi migration to the United States is managed by families. As chapter 3 notes, the early cohorts of Bangladeshis entering the United States as students were entirely encouraged and helped by their families. Most present-day immigrants who entered the United States through the DV-1 lottery also depend heavily on family support for arranging their paperwork and financing their journey, as Ashfaq explains at the beginning of this chapter.[15]

The centrality of the family in these migrants' perception of who they are and how they belong is also evident in the way my informants talked about how their family's investment helped them develop their careers through higher education, employment, and migration. Migration to Japan is almost entirely a family affair; it is the family head who decides whether to send a son to work in Japan. Similarly, the involvement of the family in managing migration to the United States is so extensive that some of my informants called their own migration their "family migration." This salience of the family is also observed in the immigrants' practice of sponsoring nearly every eligible relative for U.S. immigration: a Bangladeshi legal services provider mentioned in chapter 3 commented that he did not know "any single person who did not apply for his relatives' immigration." Therefore, it is not surprising that Bangladeshis in both Japan and the United States identify with their origin family and maintain their family membership through various transnational engagements such as remittance.

In fact, Bangladeshis customarily identify themselves as part of a family. For example, no one addresses another by name, but rather by a real or fictive kinship title, such as brother, sister, uncle, or aunt. When someone meets a stranger, the second thing they ask after learning their name is where one comes from, information that is then used to establish some kind of fictive relationship based on place of origin. For instance, my informants often recognize total strangers among co-ethnics as *desi bhai*, meaning a brother from their origin district in Bangladesh. Confirming the sociocultural perspective, these immigrants continue to send money to the family in Bangladesh. Mubarak (a community leader who has lived in LA for twenty-eight years in Los Angeles and has a wife and three children) said:

> When one comes abroad, he helps his old parents and younger siblings by sending money and feels happy about it. All of us who have come here from Bangladesh have this experience of sharing resources. This has a lasting impact on our subconscious minds. Asking for monetary help may be a serious issue to those who are in America. If you ask for a dollar, someone may say, "What the hell, I'm to give a dollar!" But we will never ask why [we] should give. Instead, we will think [about] how much [we] should give.

Mubarak and several other U.S. informants recognized how their socialization had inculcated the practice of sharing resources as well as burdens, including financial responsibility to the family. Among those migrating to Japan, Rafiq explained his remittance in terms of a family tradition that he learned from his parents and other relatives, which he followed and expected his own children to continue. Interviewees also talked about an emotional bond to the family. Similarly, Jubeir (a professional migrant who has lived in Japan for thirty-two years and is Japanese citizen naturalized through his Japanese wife's sponsorship) explained, "I'm doing well here [in Japan], eating better foods, wearing better clothes, having a comfortable lifestyle. I feel my parents and siblings in Bangladesh also should have access to such things. Therefore, I send money to support them having a better life. This is purely out of my love for them, nothing else."

The idea that immigrants have a responsibility to help their families financially is almost universal among Bangladeshi immigrants.[16] They relate this responsibility to a person's moral standing and judge each other accordingly. Researchers identify similar findings among Bangladeshis in New York[17] and among other immigrant populations. For instance, studies recognize remittance as a filial duty for unmarried sons and daughters.[18] The recognition that migrants feel a moral obligation to send remittances to their families confirms their continuous membership and belonging in the family, which shapes their experiences of transnational engagements.

The norms of family assistance and sacrifice reinforce immigrants' moral obligation and responsibility, motivating them to "pay back" by sending remittances. This is not always an essential characteristic of individual migrants but can often originate from the migratory experience. For instance, Opu (who has lived in the United States for sixteen years and has a wife and two children) explained,

> I left Bangladesh when my father was in hospital. So, I began to send money from the time I received my first paycheck . . . $500, $1,000, and even $1,500 a month. Let me tell you first, whenever I sent money, I realized that it was my responsibility. But I realized it more after coming here. I saw that all my American colleagues had large amounts of student loans. But my father provided me with more than enough money to attend the university in Bangladesh. Even before university, he spent lots of extra money on my education. Moreover, I did not have to contribute to the family when I first got employed in Bangladesh. But when I came to America, I started realizing what my father had contributed for me to come to this position today. Looking at my colleagues' student loans, I saw an equation: that I did not have any loans just because my father gave me enough money. He did everything he could for me. Now it's my turn to do whatever I can for my parents.

Here we find that Opu was deeply grateful to his family and sent money regularly to fulfill his family responsibility. As he explained, his sense of responsibility grew stronger after his migration to the United States, which allowed him to realize how instrumental his family support was. A similar perception prevailed among migrants in Tokyo. As Sujon (a restaurant worker in Tokyo with a six-year student visa) said,

> I could not come here but for my father. Therefore, I send all my savings to him. I have opened a savings account on which he is a cosigner. I bought him a piece of land and a small commercial building. I also financed the migration of my younger brother so that he joins me in supporting our family. Together, we are now sending more money home so that my father is able to expand his business and purchase another plot of land in an expensive commercial area in the town.

The fact that immigrants often explain their remittance as reciprocation for their family's assistance points to the new economics of labor migration (NELM) assumption about self-interested remittance. For instance, Sujon's explanation about his remittance supports the idea of self-interested remittance. However, a closer look at the migrants' own words reveals the primacy of family belonging over personal rational calculation. The following excerpts from an interview with Karim (who has lived in LA for twenty-five years and lives with his wife and two children) vividly demonstrate this: "I saw a demand for money on my parents' faces while preparing to come to America. When I received my first paycheck of $600, I sent them $200. Since then, I have been sending them a certain portion of my income every month so that they could live more comfortably. In addition, I sent money for higher education of my two younger brothers and a sister."

So far, Karim's awareness of his family's expectations supports the NELM proposition. But, without my prodding, Karim also referred to a moral economy:

KARIM One of my uncles was having difficulty in arranging his daughter's marriage ceremony owing to his financial hardship. He did not have enough savings and would have to sell his only agricultural land. My father asked me to help him, and I sent him some money.

HM Why did you do that?

KARIM I personally felt it was my responsibility to help him as a close relative. I know that my relatives, like [those of] all other Bangladeshis here, have an expectation of me. Therefore, I sent him money. In fact, I always try to help my relatives. Any time they are in trouble, I try to help them financially as much as I can.

Like Karim, my informants explained remittance to their family in terms of both their responsibility to support the family financially and their moral obligation to reciprocate the assistance they received from the family. That is, a moral economy plays a decisive role in shaping their perspectives.[19] As E. P. Thompson[20] recognizes, a moral economy deploys existing cultural and social forces to create a basis for economic distribution in place of market forces such as rational utility calculation. The moral economy of remittance traces migrants' motivations to send remittance along multiple social and cultural axes, both explicit and implicit, in their narratives. The family organizes the actions of both migrant and non-migrant members regarding remittance. Of course, this does not mean that the family is egalitarian, or that it is dominated by the migrants because they are the main financial contributors. For, as James Scott[21] shows, traditional arrangements of distribution in the moral economy are not necessarily radically egalitarian and are, according to Edelman, "political constructions and outcomes of social struggles."[22] What I find useful for my study is the idea that migrants do not see themselves as separate from their origin families; they essentially feel that the family allows them to realize who they are and where they belong.

But how do migrants define family, which in turn shapes their sense of self and practices aimed at finding belonging? This is crucial, as the family is central in the mechanisms (in the classical Durkheimian sense) through which society shapes their transnational practices, including remittance.[23]

The Family, Remittance, and Belonging

Definitions of the family vary widely across cultures. But all the international migrants I spoke to say they send remittances "home," which my Bangladeshi respondents call *bari*. They used this word to mean two places: one where their parents lived and the other where they planned to build or purchase a new house/apartment. For the former, they would use the Bangla phrase *barir khoroch*, meaning household expenses; for the latter they used the Bangla phrase *bari kora*, meaning making a home. While the first refers to a place occupied by the migrant's most intimate, familiar, and reliable relatives—parents, spouse, children, and sometimes younger, dependent siblings—the latter refers to a future home involving deliberate processes of acquiring, transforming, and inhabiting a residence and raising a family. Migrants send remittance both to maintain their belonging to an existing home (the original home) and to make an aspirational home (the future home).

As chapter 2 shows, Bangladeshi migrants in Japan send remittances to their homes in Bangladesh. Almost all these migrants entered Japan as unmarried men in their twenties. Japan did not offer them opportunities to build a home where they would be able to live in a secure and familiar environment under their ownership and control. Even those who married Japanese women, acquired permanent residency, established homes, and raised their biracial children in Japan remained on the periphery of Japanese society and culture. They spent their free time with co-ethnic friends and on the telephone with relatives in Bangladesh. While they enjoyed economic and legal security, they felt socially and culturally isolated and longed for home, even when they built a family in Japan.

Jabber (a forty-eight-year-old migrant employed in a private company who lives in Tokyo with his Japanese wife and two children) explained that he often felt lonely at his home in Tokyo. Once during an interview, although it was already past 11 P.M., he did not seem ready to stop talking. I tried to remind him that his wife might be worried. He nodded, smiled, and said that she never would and was already asleep with the children. But he himself was always worried about his old father in Bangladesh:

> I'm going crazy to learn about the health of my ailing father. I feel for my
> siblings and their children, too, as I consider them members of my family
> in Bangladesh. I have deep feelings for all of them. I believe I must see
> them physically at least once a year. When I visit home, I sleep with my

eighty-year-old father in the same bed. I want to give him a feeling of comfort, as well as to get the same feeling for myself, like a child. I don't find this anywhere else.

Despite having economic and legal stability in Japan, Jabber was unable to find belonging and contentment. This was not only because of his social isolation and lack of belonging to Japanese society, but also because of his anticipation that he would face acute loneliness in his old age, which increased his longing for relatives and friends in his original home. He said:

About twenty years from now, I will retire. By that time my children will grow up and move out like their Japanese peers. My wife will also likely get involved with other Japanese old women. Where will I go? This makes me nostalgic about my childhood. I think I will go back to Bangladesh, to my birth village. I will find my old cousins and friends. I will spend time lazily chatting with them. I will have enough savings in my pension fund to depend on economically.

Jabber went on to describe how much money he had spent on building a new house beside his parental home in the village, how much he donated to reconstruction of a religious school and a mosque, and how much he spent on gifts for his siblings and their children during his annual visits—all contributing to the restoration and maintenance of membership and belonging to his origin family and community.

The permanent settlers among professional migrants in Japan tended to marry Bangladeshi women but raised their children in Japan. From the outside, this would appear a better arrangement than marrying a Japanese woman, since it allowed them to maintain Bengali culture and social practices in the home. But they, too, experienced a lack of belonging in Japan, having no access to Japanese social and cultural spheres. Their children would go to Japanese schools and find friends and colleagues among the Japanese, leaving their parents behind. As chapter 1 shows, my informants among the professionals would try remigrating to other traditional immigrant destinations (such as Australia, Canada, and the United States) or return to Bangladesh, where they would purchase new homes or apartments in posh residential areas in the capital city, with most of the consumer comforts they had gotten used to in Japan. While they maintained their membership in their origin family in Bangladesh, this small group of migrants did not see Bangladesh as a suitable place to establish their future homes. Thus, they looked to a third country where they would be allowed family immigration and citizenship. However, this would also fall short of enabling them to establish home and find belonging, as I show later with reference to my informants in the United States.

In my initial discussions with migrants about sending remittances, they often emphasized family relations, perhaps because we generally look at the family as a cohesive unit. There is a general social expectation that families will be characterized by love and mutual understanding, and casual conversations referring to the family tend to conform to this perception. However, in practice, families are fractured along gendered and generational lines,[24] and relationships may be fraught with egoistic competition and jealousy among members.[25] The untold and often purposely hidden stories are not easily accessible to outsiders, especially researchers. For instance, Stevanovic-Fenn[26] reported that her Bangladeshi informants would cordially invite her into their family apartments and happily talk about their remittance in the presence of several other family members. But any Bangladeshi would suspect such apparently candid narration as mere face-saving, for remittance is a major issue on which spouses often disagree in Bangladeshi immigrant families. Social background, domestic power structures, gender, and generational differences are central to understanding the real dynamics of remittance practices and motivations. As Stevanovic-Fenn recognizes, talking enthusiastically about remittance to one's family in Bangladesh allows one to claim the status of "good son." However, migrants are often subject to formidable social pressures from two mechanisms: *emotional exploitation* and *public shaming*. Often the mother, or another family member with whom the migrant is very close, will make repeated phone calls requesting money—a finding observed among migrants from other countries, too.[27] In other cases, if a migrant refuses to send remittances, people in their close social networks will begin to gossip and cause him to lose face in the community.[28]

Putting aside the assumption about migrants' being rational individuals, I focused my conversations with my informants on transitions within their parental families due to, for instance, the death of the father, separation of married siblings from the parental family, and so forth. I wanted to understand how their perception of belonging to the family transforms with intrafamily changes by looking at their changing patterns of remittance. Jamal (a fifty-one-year-old naturalized Japanese citizen who is employed in an IT job in Tokyo) explained:

> Now all my younger siblings have grown up and separated from my parents with their own families. So, I was able to reduce my remittance for family maintenance in Bangladesh substantially. But some of them were not happy about it. They accused my wife of influencing me to cut off remittance and did not treat her well. The situation got worse when I asked my mother to transfer the ownership of a residential plot from her name to my name. I gave her money to purchase that land many years ago. Now, some of my siblings thought they would get an equal share of that land.

Jamal did not go into detail about how this dispute over inheritance soured family relations, perhaps because it is against Bengali custom and etiquette to criticize family members in front of strangers. Reducing remittances after the parental family devolved into the siblings' separate families shows the transformation in Jamal's perception of self and his relation to the family: he no longer saw himself as part of the parental family in which everyone was a member. Instead, Jamal saw himself as well as others as members of separate families to which he had significantly less responsibility than his parental family. Jamal's subsequent remittance practices show his new perception of self and belonging to the recipient family: since Jamal does not see him as the sole breadwinner for the family of his parents, which evolved into the independent families of his siblings, he stopped sending remittances for family subsistence and other regular expenses. Moreover, he asked his mother to transfer the ownership of real estate purchased by his remittance to his name so that he did not have to share it with other family members. Åkesson [29] recognized similar changes in family belonging among Cape Verdean migrants in the United Kingdom. While such splitting of the parental family is due to the natural aging process of individuals and ensuing fragmentation resulting from marriage, this often involves conflicts of interest among family members, which cause emotionally charged and unpleasant reactions among members characterized by dissatisfaction, anger, fear, and so forth.

The development of migrants' identities away from their origin families and a gradual decline in their perception of belonging surfaced in their criticisms of remittance recipients. For instance, the migrants sometimes accused their family members in Bangladesh of cheating. I heard several stories among migrants in Tokyo about someone being cheated by their elder brother, or brother-in-law, whom the migrant had trusted to help manage his remittance. One story came from a migrant named Islam, who migrated to Japan in 1988 and had over-stayed his visa for eight years as an undocumented worker. He sent all his income to his elder brother, who built a six-story apartment building with the money. When Islam got arrested and deported to Bangladesh, he found that his brother had registered the building under his own name; the brother offered Islam only two apartments out of ten. Islam was thoroughly frustrated and disheartened but could do nothing about it. Another story concerned Ahmed, an undocumented migrant who lived near Osaka for six years. He sent all his income to his father in Sylhet, who bought a commercial plot near the local market and built a dozen shops that he rented out. When Ahmed returned home after his father's death, his five siblings had already divided the family property equally, including the shops he had purchased. Finding only two shops and a small piece of residential land allocated to him, Ahmed disputed the distribution to his siblings and other relatives but could not do anything. As a result, he cut off relations with his siblings.

Interestingly, all of my informants in Japan told me that they had heard stories of such behavior but did not personally know anyone who was a victim. So, the veracity of these stories remains questionable. Yet their circulation reveals something real—that while a migrant's perception of self and belonging to the origin family is clear, it is not static. In fact, migrants' understanding of who they are and how they are related to immediate family and relatives in Bangladesh keeps transforming, from being a member of the parental family to separation and gradual independence from those in the origin community. Such transformation corresponds with an increasing sense of self-interest and a decrease in mutual trust among members of the original family. This is perhaps why many of the early Bangladeshi migrants in Japan talked about "risks" in trusting their families with their remittances, particularly when they were visa-overstayers and could neither travel to Bangladesh nor open bank accounts in Japan.

Migration scholars have long recognized collective management of finances within the family in Bangladesh. For instance, Gardner[30] observed that Bangladeshi migrants in the United Kingdom often sent remittances to purchase property registered under their parents' names. Those who wanted to register property under their own names were strongly discouraged by a sense of being labeled as "selfish" and "ungrateful." Similarly, I have shown[31] that young and unmarried sons sent remittances to their parents and elder brothers if the parents were too old to work and had retired. My informants told me about purchasing agricultural land, residential apartments, and small businesses. The general practice was to register the property under the father's or the mother's name, which they explained in terms of their perception of being a member and the breadwinner of their parents' family. However, the eventual disintegration of the parental family and the migrant's belonging redirected to their own separate family poses a real problem: when the parents pass away, under family inheritance law in Bangladesh, the family property is distributed among all siblings, including sisters. Although some of my informants told me that their parents had transferred ownership to the migrant son's name or had given him a greater share of the family inheritance, the absence of legal provisions to ensure this remained a source of anxiety for migrants. I heard many stories in Japan about the recipients of remittance (among immediate family and relatives) in Bangladesh taking advantage of the migrant's absence. But I did not hear similar stories in the United States. This might be a result of family migration.

Previous chapters demonstrate that the contexts of reception in Japan and the United States shapes migrants' experiences of belonging by creating an unwelcoming environment in Japan and welcoming one in the United States. Highlighting the destination state's ability to exercise control over migrants, both at borders and inside the country, scholars have explored how this shapes migrants' transnational engagement with their families.[32] While the impact of the destination state's immigration policies on immigrants' incorporation and belonging has been well documented, less attention has been paid to the internal transformations in the origin family, how they anchor migrants, and in what ways migrants respond to family changes.

Instead of relying on the universal definition of the family, I paid particular attention to how migrants defined family and explained their relationship to it in conversations about their remittance. My informants consistently said they remit to their *paribar*, which translates in English to "family." This seemingly unproblematic use of the term paribar in fact represents a more complex social reality due to the range of meanings my informants attribute to the concept. As sociologist Shanti Rosario[33] observes, Bangladeshis use the term paribar to mean at least three distinct types of family organization in different contexts: first, the nuclear family consisting of the head of the family and his wife and children; second, the joint family consisting of the family head, his brothers, and their wives and children; and finally, the extended family, which includes more than two generations living under the guidance of one family head. In addition, one should distinguish between a paribar, in which members share a household and all resources in common, and a *gusthi* (lineage group), in which members share a blood relationship with a common male ancestor but no longer form a single household. People residing in different towns or abroad for reasons of employment are still considered members of their paribar until they have separated from the parental family by taking their share of the paternal land, for example. Moreover, the migrants do not necessarily engage with everybody in the family equally; rather, they deliberately emphasize some relations while overlooking others. Thus, an analysis of how they use the term paribar while talking about their remittance offers critical insight into transformations in family relations and, hence, the migrants' sense of self and belonging.

First and foremost, migrants referred to their parental family when talking about their remittances. For single male migrants, sending remittances to the family meant sending money to their parents and siblings still living with the parents in a family unit. This family, however, would eventually begin to disintegrate with the marriages and formations of separate nuclear families of the migrant and their siblings. The transition from a member of the parental family to the head of one's own family leads to a reorientation of family responsibility whereby the migrants' own families take priority over the family of their parents. This change in migrants' family belonging is marked by diminishing remittances to the parental/origin family. As Rajnish (who has been in LA for 12 years and lives with his wife, a child, and his parents) told me, "Since marriage, I do not send money as often as before. Now I send regularly only to my savings account. My brother also realizes this [that I have my own family] and does not ask for money like before. Moreover, my parents live here with me. So, I do not need to send money."

The migrants' regular remittance hinged on having parents in Bangladesh who used the monthly allowances for subsistence and was motivated by a sense of family responsibility. However, with the splitting of the parental family into separate sibling families, migrants' commitment to their parents remained unaffected, while their commitment to adult siblings was replaced by commitment to their own spouses and children. If a migrant had a spouse and children as well as parents in Bangladesh, he would send money regularly for their subsistence.

In general, all would live together in one family, and the migrant would send remittance for the entire household. Once the migrant's nuclear family started to live in separate sibling units—and eventually reunited in the United States— his commitment would be divided between parents in Bangladesh and his nuclear family in the United States, and remittance would be reduced substantially. If the spouse, their children, and his parents were in the United States, the migrant had no need to send money to Bangladesh for family subsistence. All my informants reported that they sent money to their parents, but none reported regularly sending remittance to siblings' families. Thus, the observed diminution in Bangladeshi remittance from the United States is directly related to their eroding sense of belonging to Bangladesh since their close kin are no longer there.

A closer look at the disintegration of the parental family and separation of the siblings into nuclear families also demonstrates how the evolution of family relationships complicates relational belonging and shapes migrants' sense of family obligation and remittance. Consider a joint investment by Hussain (a taxi-driver who has been in the United States for twenty-one years and lives with his wife and two children):

> I've invested in a big irrigation project and my two elder brothers manage it. They never share with me the profit from the project. And I do not ask for anything because they give enough money to my mother, which offsets my duty to send money for her living expenses. Besides, the project makes our family very influential in the village, as a few dozen farmers are totally dependent on it for their rice cultivation. So, whenever my brothers need any help from the neighbors, they find people ready.

This statement reveals a complicated and dynamic understanding of family belonging, which needs further explanation. Hussain's narrative includes several important aspects my informants often shared about their family relationships and remittance. First, Hussain recognized the change in the traditional practice of the elder son taking responsibility for his aged parents, which confirms migration scholars' findings about migrants assuming the role of the main financial provider for aged parents regardless of birth order. Second, Hussain and his elder brothers acknowledged that they no longer belonged to their parental/origin family and their primary obligation was toward their separate nuclear families. Thus, they entered an exchange of financial gain out of their joint irrigation project and divided the gains. His brothers managed and profited from the project and, because they contributed to their mother's expenses, Hussain was not concerned about gaining any profit himself. Third, Hussain recognized his belonging to the joint family of his brothers when talking about how their irrigation project enabled him and his brothers to command influence over their neighbors as a single family, which enhanced their social status in the village.

This confirms migration scholars' observations about migrants' sending remittances to establish joint investments with relatives. Yet what attracted my attention most was the way Hussain explained his belonging to his own nuclear family and his origin family. If anything, his story registers the fact that migrants' belonging to the family is not static but instead exists on a continuum that includes one's origin family, nuclear family, and joint family (consisting of the origin family and the nuclear families of siblings).

Joint investment with family members was common among my informants in LA. Out of 68 interviewees in my study, 43 reported purchasing housing plots in Dhaka or agricultural lands in their villages jointly with their parents and siblings. Bangladeshis in LA send remittances to such projects with the expectation of financial gain as well as increased family status and influence in the origin community. Unlike the case of Hussain's joint investment cited above, most joint investment projects end up souring family relations due to disputes over the distribution of gains, especially after the parents pass away. Aminul (who has lived in LA for twenty-one years and has a wife and three children) reported such an experience, which strained relationships with his siblings in Bangladesh. Aminul sent money to his family for nine years, with which his father bought 140 decimals (approximately 1.4 acres) of agricultural land in the village and a housing plot in Dhaka; he also used the money to renovate the family household. After his two younger brothers and three sisters grew up, got married, and formed their own separate families, Aminul returned to get married and take his share. He found that the homestead and agricultural lands had already been given to his two brothers and only the housing plot in Dhaka remained to be distributed among the six siblings. Thoroughly disappointed but failing to change the situation, Aminul simply stopped talking to his father until his mother mediated between them. While Aminul's case is an extreme example, 36 of my 43 informants involved in joint investment reported worsening family relations.

Ikuomola[34] observed that envy, distrust, and accusations of witch hunts destabilized cordial relationships between Nigerian migrants in Belgium, South Africa, Germany, and Italy and their family members. Similarly, my respondents told me how their remittance—particularly that sent to joint families—led to erosion of mutual trust and reliability, competition, and jealousy. In extreme cases, immigrants had to temporarily cut off communications with certain family members and relatives. The declining sense of belonging to the origin family is reflected in the drying up of remittances to joint projects. All 43 of my informants in LA who reported investing in joint projects with their brothers and sisters said they did this within the first few years of migrating, and none did it after they stayed eight years in the United States.

Nevertheless, I recognized a continued sense of belonging to the origin family and kin among my informants in LA. Their legal status as citizens and permanent residents allowed them to visit Bangladesh and sponsor their immediate family members for immigration to the United States, and both behaviors empowered migrants vis-à-vis their families in Bangladesh. Because these immigrants could visit Bangladesh in person to see how their remittance is spent, their relatives in Bangladesh saw it was in their interest to stay on good terms with the immigrant relative for future immigration sponsorship. Moreover, immigrants to the United States were better off than their counterparts in Japan as they could access government support in addition to the support from their co-ethnic community to ease their initial struggles. Finally, these immigrants could open bank accounts and save their income in both the United States and Bangladesh. Therefore, Bangladeshis in the United States were significantly less dependent than those in Japan on their families and relatives in Bangladesh. As chapter 3 explains, sheer economic profit motives encouraged immigrants to invest in individual projects in Bangladesh: purchasing land, depositing money in savings accounts, investing in the stock market, lending at high interest, and so forth. Such opportunities attracted immigrants from lower- and middle-income families in particular.

The fact that the migrants derive social status by acquiring houses in Dhaka or other assets in their origin communities also indicates their persistent belonging to Bangladesh. Among my informants, low-income immigrants were particularly keen on purchasing housing plots or apartment buildings in Dhaka and agricultural land in their villages. Historically, landownership in Bengali society is connected to upper-class status.[35] Scholars observe similar patterns among migrants from other countries who try to overcome the structural barriers they encounter in their destination country by sending remittance to their home country to achieve upward social mobility.[36] Several informants proudly told me about their purchase of land and apartments. Some migrants told me about other investment opportunities, such as purchasing land outside of their origin village or investing in the stock market. Given the fact that these immigrants choose to invest in landownership in their origin community rather than exploring more financially attractive investment destinations is indicative of their continued belonging to their place of origin. It is a place where they attempt to realize upward social mobility by demonstrating their successful immigration.

Transnationalism, Self, and Social Belonging

Besides an expectation of financial solvency after returning to the home country (detailed in chapter 2), or retirement in the destination country and gaining social prestige (detailed in chapter 4), migrants' remittances for investment in Bangladesh reveal a desire for cultural affinity. Shamsul (who has been in LA for twenty-three years in Los Angeles and lives with his wife, two sons, and a granddaughter) told me,

> Actually, no one leaves America, because of steady income, cheaper living, and good weather. Still, we have a strong desire to return to Bangladesh. This is

because we were born and brought up in Bangladesh. Standard of living is one thing and living a life is another. The living standard in America is undoubtedly high. But the culture here is different. Leisurely gossiping, prayer, and other such things—you cannot do these here as you would in Bangladesh.

Scholars studying transnational migration recognize a strong desire among migrants to return to their origin community in the home country.[37] Similarly, I noticed this longing for the origin community among my informants, as recorded in my fieldnotes:

I stepped up to a group of four taxi-drivers in front of Deshi [a Bangladeshi restaurant and grocery store]. They were debating about some ongoing political issues in Bangladesh. I asked them, "Why do you talk so much about Bangladeshi politics? You have got U.S. passports, and you are not going back, are you?" They all stopped and then spoke at once, saying that they would certainly return to Bangladesh. I asked, "People from all over the world are coming to America; why don't you want to stay here?" One of them explained, "America is heaven for immigrants. Everyone perseveres and enjoys their earnings here. But it is not our country. We always miss our childhood, our adolescence. No matter how much worse the situation is in Bangladesh, we like that."

Regardless of class, occupation, and income, all my respondents expressed their loneliness in the United States and a desire to return to Bangladesh. What I found most striking was that migrants saw Bangladesh as their final destination. Even after naturalizing as U.S. citizens and permanently settling with all their brothers and sisters in the United States, respondents would claim Bangladesh as their ultimate home. Irshad (who has been in LA for eighteen years and lives with his wife and two sons) told me,

I have my parents and many relatives—in fact, all from my side and my wife's side—in Los Angeles and the Valley region. So, I have enough social connections here. Still, I cannot help remembering Bangladesh, my days of childhood in schools, in the university. I have allowed my children to grow up like Americans, with the condition that they maintain a high GPA and be respectful to the elders. But I will take them to their roots in Bangladesh one day.

This statement clarifies a misconception that migrants' homes are only physical places. Irshad, by contrast, conceives of his and his children's roots in terms of his relationships with immediate family, relatives, and friends he grew up with. Bangladesh enters his talk merely as a geographical space where some of those original relations happened to reside. This indicates that Irshad—and many immigrants like him—felt his belonging divided between the United States and

Bangladesh, as his close relatives and those who complemented his sense of self and social belonging lived in both countries.

In addition to having many important relatives in Bangladesh, most of my informants in LA talked about how their intimate relationships—particularly, their relationships with children who were socialized to American individualism—reinforced their feelings of distance in the United States and longing for their origin community in Bangladesh. While attending social gatherings, I often noticed immigrant parents' concern that their adolescent children could not mingle enough with the first-generation migrants and their relatives in Bangladesh. While they were keen on getting their children into well-reputed schools and universities, and then into respected professional careers in the United States, they were also frustrated to see their children gradually becoming Americanized and leaving behind their Bangladeshi roots. This is not unique to Bangladeshi immigrants. Migration scholars have long recognized dissonant acculturation: the relational distance and generational conflicts that develop over time between migrant parents and their children who are raised in the destination country.[38] Research on Asian American migrants in the United States has found that the more integrated the second generation is, the greater the distance from their parents in child-rearing practices,[39] behavioral approaches to the parents,[40] mate selection and sexual practices,[41] and so forth. Similarly, a study of Muslim immigrants in Europe found that cultural and social integration through children's educational attainment hurt family relationships.[42]

I was not surprised, then, to find similar dissociative patterns of interaction among my interlocutors and their children. Several of my interviewees told me about how their children were growing up and growing apart,[43] recognizing and accepting this as a matter of fact. For instance, Sheikh (who has lived in LA for thirty-five years, and has a wife and two daughters) told me,

> We considered our parents as my own family. If my children eat, my parents will also eat. If my parents need medical care, I will certainly provide it. All my siblings treated our parents in this way. Once my mother was severely ill and the doctor suggested taking her to a nursing home. But I could not think of having her away from me for a single night. So, I provided whatever nursing she needed by myself at home. This is simply love. I saw my mother do it for my grandparents. It's our cultural tradition in Bangladesh. But my children do not have that feeling. My daughter says she will marry and leave us. It hurts me. But what can I do? It's a different society.

In addition to generational differences in caring and expressing love, my informants—especially those nearing retirement—shared their disappointment regarding the extent of independence their children exercised in mate selection, career choice, and socializing beyond their co-ethnic group. One of their common complaints about their adult children was that they addressed elders by their names instead of family titles like uncle, aunt, and grandma. While using names is an accepted practice in California, it is frowned upon among Bengalis as indicating a lack of respect. The second generation's practices of sleepovers at friends' houses, visiting night clubs and bars, and dating among other ethnic groups were other issues about which immigrant parents from all class levels worried about and frowned upon. Because there was no socio-cultural mechanism for parents to exercise control over their adult children, the parent-child relationship often grew uneasy and distant, which is a dramatic cultural shift. In Bangladesh, people depend on their children in old age,[44] a tradition enforced through the primacy of the family over the individual.[45] But many immigrants learned they could not rely on this tradition in America because their children had absorbed values of individualism. They grow up, find employment, and move away from the family, to wherever their jobs take them.[46] Children visit their parents only occasionally instead of living with them. This absence, together with their own nostalgia, generated migrants' sense of disconnection from American society, which compelled them to return to Bangladesh to find companions among relatives, neighbors, and friends. Consequently, they would begin to reconnect to their childhood friends and distant relatives in their origin communities and maintain their belonging through occasional visits and remittance.

While my informants explained the growing distance between their grown American-Bangladeshi children and themselves in relational terms, it has a spatial foundation, too. As Bennett[47] shows, the interrelationship of place and social life can be understood as an ontological necessity, whereby the perception of ourselves is inseparable from the places in which we live. Belonging is predicated on knowing and being known by other people, as well as on an in-depth knowledge of a place and its history, which leads to caring for the place. Arijit Sen[48] explores how everyday engagements with food, specifically fish harvested in the delta region of Bangladesh, trigger cultural memories that reinforce particular shopping practices and place identities among Bangladeshis in Chicago. I also observed patterns of place-making and identity formation among my informants in both LA and Tokyo. For instance, Bangladeshis in Tokyo have built a monument to commemorate Martyrs' Day and International Mother Language Day at Ikebukuro West Park with the help of the local city administration. The monument functions as the most important venue for Bangladeshi community events. Similarly, Bangladeshis in LA have successfully petitioned the city administration to recognize a certain place in Koreatown as "Little Bangladesh" and have transformed the area with new businesses and structural modifications of buildings that help to represent Bangladeshi ethnic identity.

Developing ethnic spaces (e.g., restaurants, grocery stores, ethnic schools, community organizations, etc.) is difficult in a destination country. My informants struggled to fit in and find belonging, but the difficulty varied depending on particular contexts in the receiving society. As chapter 1 shows, my respondents in Japan had a very difficult time forming their own community and finding belonging, owing to various legal, social, and cultural barriers. A telling example of this is the fading Bangladeshi dominance in the business of halal shops and *indo care* (Indian curry) restaurants in Tokyo, and its replacement mainly by Nepalese proprietors.[49] Similarly, I observed that the annual Bangla New Year celebration at Ikebukuro West Park drew fewer Bangladeshis in 2014 than in 2007 and 2008. This may be attributed to the legal and social barriers to establishing permanent residence and belonging in Japan, which I discuss in chapter 1. By contrast, my informants in the United States were generally accepted by the state and the minority community in permanently settling and establishing their new home. For instance, most of my working-class informants reportedly found jobs in workplaces owned and managed by members of other immigrant groups. They found rental housing in Koreatown (nearly all of which was owned by Koreans), while their professional and middle-class compatriots moved to suburbs in the San Fernando Valley among white Americans and multiple other ethnic groups. The official recognition of their ethnic neighborhood as Little Bangladesh and the immigrants' active role in local politics in LA are explicit signs of their success in permanent settlement and belonging.

To some extent, migrants could modify their physical environment, for example by reorganizing the bathroom and adding a water dispenser (bidet) to the toilet for cleaning up or installing additional cooking utensils and shelves for cooking desi-style food characterized by lots of spices, oil, and curry. However, respondents also experienced limits on incorporation, as their failed initiatives to expand their territorial boundary showed. Bangladeshis did not own the land, apartments, or stores in Little Bangladesh, and so could not reshape its architecture and landscape. For instance, a member of the mosque governing committee told me that the committee had established a mosque in a rented apartment but were prohibited from remodeling it as a traditional community mosque because of complicated approval procedures at the local city housing office. They also had to arrange for annual Eid prayers on a covered community basketball court. Traditionally, Bangladeshi Muslims arrange the Eid prayers in open spaces under the sky, and although there are two community parks near the Little Bangladesh, the city administration would not allow them to be used for Eid prayers and instead provided the covered community basketball court. Similarly, they did not have a specific place for their biggest community event of the year—Bangladesh Independence Day—and had to move the event to different venues each year as directed by the local city administration.

In day-to-day life, one of the most important deficiencies was the absence of tea stalls. In towns and village centers in Bangladesh, almost every street corner has a tea stall, providing both tea and a chance for *adda*: loud, meandering conversations with both neighbors and strangers, a daily leisure activity for most Bangladeshi males. As sociologist Habibul Khondker[50] observed among the incipient Bangladeshi middle-class community in Singapore, adda served as an expression of the presence of the Bengali community. Coffeeshops were available throughout LA, but these were unlikely venues for adda, owing to obvious differences in the environments of Bangladeshi tea stalls and U.S. coffeeshops and Bangladeshi migrants' limited income and strictly organized work schedules. The ethnic restaurants partly reproduced the atmosphere of tea stalls in Bangladesh by offering chai (tea with a lot milk and sugar), Bangla newspapers on the tables, loud Bangla music on the sound system, and Bangla channels on flat-screen TVs hanging on the walls. While single immigrants would frequently visit these ethnic restaurants, those with family and professionals living in outlying neighborhoods could get to restaurants only on weekends. Still, the craving for adda was so strong that I noticed Bangladeshis travelling over fifty miles from distant areas in the San Fernando Valley to spend time at the ethnic restaurants in Little Bangladesh.

I find Bourdieu's concepts of habitus and field useful for understanding my informants' desire to return to what they called their "roots." For Bourdieu, *habitus* is embodied dispositions we acquire in the early stages of life that are difficult to change or shake off, such as accent and taste; and *field* is a site of power, or "symbolic capital," which people inhabit more or less comfortably, depending on the "fit" with their embodied habitus. The relationship between the two indicates whether or not a person knows how to behave "correctly" in their culture or society at large. While Bourdieu himself wrote little about place, other scholars recognize the importance of field in his conceptualization. For instance, Savage et al.[51] use the idea of habitus to explore how globalization shapes our identity and sense of belonging and argue that belonging to a particular place is predicated upon moving to a social-cultural field that is appropriate for our habitus, which is, in turn, dependent upon economic, social, and cultural capital acquired throughout life. However, Gaventa[52] maintains that a field is not necessarily a space; rather, it involves various social and institutional arenas in which people express and reproduce their dispositions, and where they compete for the distribution of different kinds of capital. Thus, place is a tool through which people both accrue and display their symbolic capital.

Searching for places suitable for one's habitus is common, especially among migrants. They often create such places in their new countries if one is not already available, as Bangladeshi immigrants in Chicago did by establishing fish stores in an attempt to experience social belonging.[53] In line with this analysis, when someone migrates from Bangladesh to Tokyo or LA, they find it difficult to fit in, owing to unfamiliarity with many social and cultural elements in the new destination. This partly explains why my informants frequented crowded, visibly unhygienic ethnic restaurants in Little Bangladesh: these restaurants offered a place where they could fit in completely yet be seen as distinct, with high amounts of appropriate economic, social, and cultural capital.

The lack of power to reshape places and organize community events as they would have liked evoked migrants' foreign-ness in the United States, despite their permanent settlement and citizenship. While this sense of exclusion in Japan is readily understandable given the glaring marginalization of migrants, in general, my informants in LA found it hard to explain why they felt a lack of belonging and wanted to return to Bangladesh. Although they could earn economic capital through education and professional jobs or businesses, and social capital by expanding networks among their co-ethnics and potentially among co-workers in other ethnic groups, habitus (accent, eating habits, hobbies, leisure practices, and so forth) is hard to shake off. As Mirza (a fifty-eight-year-old owner of a financial business with a wife and two grown children) told me,

> The first-generation immigrants hold a strong desire to return to their origin country in their old age. Even if all their siblings migrate to the U.S., they keep their parental home in Bangladesh because of this desire to return. Look at what I did. All my brothers and sisters are settled in America. My father died many years ago. Still, I have not sold our parental home in Dhaka, nor even the telephone landline that my father installed in the early 1970s. I have created a Bangladeshi environment [meaning cultural atmosphere] at my home in the U.S. I think this is because I grew up in Bangladesh, am married to a Bangladeshi woman, and identify myself as a Bangladeshi [American]. My son tells me that I will never become American "because I always see you talk about Bangladesh, go to Bangladeshi events, or fly to Dhaka whenever you find an excuse." Well, I have been here for more than thirty years now. I have achieved success in America. But I cannot forget where I was born, and whom I grew up with.

A lack of feeling "at home" in their destination leads migrants to engage with their origin communities in Bangladesh, which is evident in their increasing transnational practices, including frequent phone calls, repeated visits to home, and remittances.

As I described in chapter 3, Bangladeshi immigrants in the United States were able to effectively utilize the rights they achieved (in the forms of citizenship and legal residence) to permanently settle in the country and create a space of their own. Furthermore, their legal status facilitated their access to various kinds of support from the state that not only helped them get settled with jobs, inexpensive housing, school, and healthcare, but also enhanced their capacity to engage in transnational practices including remittance. This challenges the assimilationist view that migrants belong through integration in the destination society and eventual erosion of ties to the origin country. Arguably, migrants might not choose to send remittances if the destination states allowed them to stay longer and settle permanently with their families. But my informants shared how they were unable to maintain a sufficient sense of belonging in the United States once their children were grown and thus sought renewed belonging by reconnecting to their origin in Bangladesh—an observation that challenges the conception of remittance decay emanating from the assimilationist perspective.[54]

Central to the transnationalism perspective is the idea that migrants simultaneously belong to both their country of origin and country of settlement, as Silke Meyer recognizes in her analysis of the remittance decay hypothesis. She observes that migrants' home—to which they assign belonging and send remittances—"can be in multiple places at the same time." [55] This is particularly true in contemporary sociopolitical contexts in most Western destination countries, which are characterized by the racialization and marginalization of immigrants and result in their growing sense of marginalization and exclusion[56] and transnational activities, such as sending remittances.[57] This confirms the idea that legal residence and citizenship do not automatically facilitate integration into the destination country. Thus, marginalization and structural exclusion (resulting from, for example, a racialized immigration system and labor market) present challenges to integration and may create a structural necessity for migrants to look back to their countries of origin. Yet, we should not assume that barriers to integration are the sole reason migrants to engage in transnational practices. This may be a condition that increases the likelihood that migrants will respond by actively participating in transnationalism.

Recognition of migrants' transitions over the life course show how their aspiration for a better life and their desire for connection to family, relatives, and home lead them to engage in transnationalism. Instead of acting in response to structural problems in the home country (i.e., the push factors) and opportunities in the destination country (i.e., the pull factors), they seek belonging in both the origin and destination societies and choose to engage with both simultaneously. This confirms that migrants do not only look for a better place/country to establish home but also want to be with their most intimate social relations who help them feel "at home." The ups and downs in their remittance flows demonstrate their sense of belonging to both the United States and Bangladesh.

Conclusion

Scholars have long observed that migration is a family affair[58] and families in Bangladesh have promoted the out-migration of (typically) young, unmarried men to work abroad and send money back home. While the state plays a vital role, in the origin country by encouraging international migration through various institutional supports, and in destination country by controlling or regulating international migration, Bangladeshi migration is primarily activated by the family unit. As the core institution of social reproduction, the family takes the initiative in encouraging and preparing its members to go abroad and find additional income for the family and the migrants.

The family socializes its member into the existing tradition of sharing family responsibilities and the norms and values in Bangladesh society. In the absence of legal provisions, society develops informal mechanisms to enforce traditions, which include emotional manipulation and public shaming. The family members who are most intimately connected to the migrant make claims for financial support by invoking emotional relations. All migrants in my study recognized their family's central role in their migration, further strengthening the family's claim for assistance. Public shaming works by judging individual migrants based on existing expectations of sons' taking financial responsibility for their families in adulthood. All my informants reported that assuming the role of breadwinner or becoming a lead income-earner for the family is "normal" for Bangladeshi migrants. Those performing up to this norm receive positive assessment and approval in the origin community, while those failing to live up to it are criticized and singled out as "bad sons." Immigrants depend significantly on their co-ethnic networks and the community for support in their daily life in the United States. Thus, losing face may lead to the loss of vital social connections. As a result, these immigrants try hard to keep their reputation untarnished by performing up to prevailing social expectations.

The effectiveness of informal mechanisms in eliciting migrant support for their families in Bangladesh depends on the strength of a migrant's belonging to their family, which tends to erode over time as the parental family naturally separates into nuclear sibling families. Migrants' sense of family responsibility then turns primarily toward their own family, making concern for their siblings' families secondary. While individuals are understanding of such changes and accept this as natural, migrants experience disputes in dividing family inheritance, especially assets acquired by the family through remittance. Moreover, family unification abroad causes declining remittance to extended relatives back home. Belonging to the origin (i.e., the parental) family naturally disintegrates with the emergence of siblings' own families and the death of parents, and it then reorients toward migrants' own families. If the migrant goes abroad alone with the prospect of his future family staying in Bangladesh, which was the case for most of my informants in Japan, he sends money for his own savings account and invests in his solely owned property in Bangladesh. If the migrant can take his family and the families of his siblings abroad, which was the case for my informants in the United States, his remittances for family maintenance in Bangladesh simply stop.

Migrants do not go abroad solely to find employment. They also look to settle permanently and raise a family in their destination country. Japan does not allow most Bangladeshi migrants to bring their families with them. While a few Bangladeshi migrants settle and obtain legal residency and citizenship, most eventually return to Bangladesh. Those naturalized as Japanese citizens also tend to leave Japan for another Western country due to several sociocultural barriers that marginalize them in Japan. In contrast, all Bangladeshis in the

United States migrate with their families and are allowed to sponsor the immigration of their siblings and other immediate relatives. This allowed my informants to develop their ethnic community and establish their own neighborhood (Little Bangladesh) in Los Angeles. However, a lack of opportunities for upward mobility for working-class migrants motivates them to earn additional income and social recognition by investing in Bangladesh. Those in the middle-class find belonging in the United States through professional careers, home ownership, and incorporation into the mainstream. However, they also turn to Bangladesh to reconnect with their "roots" when their career ends and their children grow up and move out. This shows how relational bonding within the family (shaped by natural progression in the family life-cycle) and the residential location (conditioned by immigration policies and practices of the destination country) together determine migrants' sense of a home to which they belong. When migrants see their home in their country of origin, they transnationally engage with that home by sending remittances.

Conclusion

•••••••••••••••••••••••

Why Do Migrants Send Remittances?

In our hyper-globalized world, about 3.6 percent of the world's total population lives outside of their origin country. For these migrants, a common practice is sending money to their homes, which is popularly called remittance. Regardless of where they go or what they do, these migrants send remittances to their families and relatives they left behind in their home country. Migrants originate from all types of countries, both rich and developed Western countries in Europe and North America and poorer countries in the Global South. As remittance data shows, they all send money to home in various forms. However, it is the money that migrants from poor countries send home that counts in academic and public narratives. For instance, despite France consistently being one of the top ten remittance-receiving countries, there is hardly any discussion of remittance to France. The current discussions of remittance are couched in a migration and development framework that seeks to explore the developmental potential of remittances, thereby leaving developed countries out of focus. Conceiving migrant remittance as an alternative funding source for conventional development for poor countries in the Global South is accomplished by experts and development organizations without incorporating migrants' perspectives about why they send remittances.

Looking at the sociocultural background of the migrants in their origin countries in the Global South, it is obvious why they send money home. Leaving home to work in faraway big cities or other worksites is a common livelihood strategy for most working-class people and professionals in these countries. Once a child grows up and takes on income-earning jobs, they begin to share the financial burden of the parental family. Some individuals find better income opportunities abroad and leave their homes, becoming income-earners of their origin family. They certainly think about their acts of sending money, consider why they should send money, how much, and to whom. While migrants' self-interest or altruism are recognized as the reasons they send remittances, this is hardly the case when one asks them about why they send remittances. Of course, there are elements of both altruism and self-interest in migrants' accounts of their remittance. However, developing an explanatory framework based on the dichotomous concepts of altruism and self-interest is hardly satisfactory. Understanding why migrants send remittances requires first understanding what they mean by remittance, which will allow recognition of their reasons for sending remittances. Thus, this begins by exploring the meaning migrants attach to the money they send home.

The amount and frequency of sending remittance depend on family pressure. Those from southern Bangladesh face greater pressures. For example, they will tell the migrants, "You earn abroad. So you must send money home. You come back and do something [productive, income-generating undertakings]. Because you cannot stay there forever." This idea is in their souls. You cannot imagine how much social pressure a man endures while living in Japan. He would often be compared with those of his peers who became doctors or engineers in Bangladesh. His relatives will say, "What have you accomplished by going abroad?" They must achieve success, which is lots of money. They have to send remittances, at any cost.

— Huda, single male, former Monbusho scholar, IT engineer,
fourteen years in Japan

I love Bangladesh more than I can say. But I did not send a single taka [Bangladeshi currency] out of my love for Bangladesh. If someone claims to have sent remittances for the country, he must be lying. You show me a single person who sent remittances outside of his family, outside of his relatives. Show me an example and I will withdraw my word. Every single person sends money to his parents, wife, or children. So he is not sending remittances to the country, but to his family. He sends money to that country because his family lives there. If he does not have anybody there, he will not send money. Period.

— Aslam, married with children, naturalized U.S. citizen
and community leader, eighteen years in LA

The first statement succinctly presents the overall perspective about migration and remittance among Bangladeshis in Japan and their families in Bangladesh. It shows that Bangladeshis migrate to Japan to earn money, perceive their stay abroad as temporary and return to Bangladesh as inevitable, and realize the need to both support the family and save income for their future. Huda, like many of my informants, explained this in terms of family expectations in their origin communities. In chapters 1 and 2 I noted that temporary migration to Japan is recognized as a socioeconomic strategy for the migrants and their families to amass wealth and gain upward mobility. By contrast, the second statement from a Bangladeshi immigrant in the United States criticized the idea of understanding remittance in terms of patriotism and love for the origin country, a common theme in discourses about migrants, who are applauded as "national heroes" for their altruism and economic contribution to the origin community and country.[1] Aslam claimed that although patriotism may be abundant in the hearts of Bangladeshi migrants, love of country does not factor into remittance behavior—only family factors in.

Academics and policymakers argue that migrants send remittances out of either altruism or self-interest. We engage in a normative assessment of the migrants as either altruistic or self-interested in a social context characterized by intimate relations between remittance senders and receivers. However, we do not ask the migrants about why they send remittances; instead we deduce migrants' motivations from how the remittance recipients spend the money. Such an assessment is untenable because it involves judging migrants' decisions based on the actions of others (i.e., spending/utilizing remittance) and because it fails to recognize important social and cultural factors that influence remittance-sending behavior. Even though remittance is an economic transaction, the migrants I studied spoke of a range of noneconomic factors to explain their remittance. In the statements above, Huda recognized social pressure from the origin family and community, while Aslam identified a sense of belonging to the family in the origin country.

Besides recognizing the motivations that the economic and sociocultural approaches identify in migrant remittance, I show throughout the book how migrants talk about their remittance in terms of belonging to family and community. Their belonging is predicated on their membership in the recipient family and community, to which they feel an obligation to provide financial support, as well as their (in)ability to reunite that family permanently in the destination country. Because migrant remittance is embedded in preexisting social relations centered in the family and origin community, it involves the classical sociological notions of altruism, reciprocity, and benevolence. But because it depends on international border-crossing, it also encounters the state apparatus, which regulates migrants' entry and stay as well as separation from or unification with the family. As a way of counterbalancing this external power, migrants engage in what is popularly known as transnationalism—establishing cross-border belonging through transnational families and communities, for which remittance serves as a central medium of communication and exchange.

Unlike most empirical quantitative studies of migrant remittance that examine how recipients in the origin country utilize remittances, I engaged with migrants in two destination countries to learn directly from them about their remittance behaviors. My findings show that the destination state's immigration policy, national and local labor markets, relations between citizens and foreigners, and intrafamily dynamics all shape migrants' perception of home, a pivotal perception for understanding their sense of belonging and associated remittance behaviors. Contrary to the notion of the lone traveler, migrants travel and stay abroad essentially as members of their families and communities and expend effort and resources to maintain their sense of belonging to home. This book discusses two dimensions of migrants' home: the spatial dimension, shaped by structural factors (e.g., state and local communities), and the relational dimension, evolving through natural progression in families' life cycles and through emotionally intense social interactions (both positive and negative) among individuals in families and communities. The former is highlighted in the dominant economic approaches to remittance, whereas the latter is central in social-cultural approaches. As I noted in the introduction, economic approaches miss instances of remittance in which there is no spatial separation between migrants and their families, while social-cultural approaches fail to address potential conflicts, deceit, and mistrust in family relations by assuming that remittance is inevitable. In this book, I show how conceptualizing migrant remittance as an expression of their belonging to home overcomes such limitations in the literature.

As my study shows, migrants' perception of themselves as members of a family unit who belong to a home is key to understanding their remittance. The customary practice of individuals living with extended family members in a home does not apply to migrants. Many Bangladeshis go abroad alone on a temporary basis, earn money, and send remittances to their family in Bangladesh, as my informants in Japan did. While their decision to go to Japan appears voluntary if not cooperatively conceived by a family unit, their decision to return home is largely determined by the Japanese immigration regime and, to a lesser extent, by their sociocultural marginalization. My study recognizes that many such migrants would have liked to prolong their stay, as their highly positive appraisal of life in Japan alluded to. Migrants of the professional class who were legally allowed to bring their spouses tried to settle permanently and raise family in Japan; however, despite opportunities for naturalization, they never felt fully accepted due to existing social and cultural barriers to integration. Therefore, Japan remained a temporary destination for them. This is reflected in remittance among Bangladeshi migrants in Japan: single migrants without documents (i.e., visa-overstayers) and those with liminal legality (i.e., self-funded students) send all their income and savings to their family in Bangladesh; those with proper legal status with their immediate family in Japan had less savings and thus remitted smaller amounts. Moreover, they were able to seek migration opportunities in more traditional receiving countries in the global West, which encouraged them to visit and spend money in those countries in anticipation of future migration, thus further reducing their capacity and propensity to send remittances to

Bangladesh. To this end, focusing on whether a migrant can settle in the destination country and raise family leads to another important question: If this is permitted, do they stop sending remittances? My study answers this question by looking at Bangladeshi immigrants in the United States.

Bangladeshi migration to the United States is characteristically permanent. Migrants arrive in the country with their families or bring their spouses directly after marriage; they also sponsor their parents, their siblings, and their siblings' families, in what is referred to as chain migration. In the case of Bangladeshi migrants in Japan, family separation motivates remittance, while those in the United States send remittances as long as they have family in Bangladesh. Both cases confirm the economic perspective, which predicts that migrant remittance practices are motivated by family separation and temporariness of stay. However, by continuing to send remittances to Bangladesh even after family unification and permanent settlement in the receiving country, Bangladeshi migrants to the United States complicate this narrative. Such remittance practices indicate that the full motivation for remittance cannot be explained by mere empirical observation. The reasons migrants share about why they send remittances are also inadequate, as they take their membership and belonging to the family as a given. As critical realism[2] suggests, understanding the reasons for migrant remittance requires interpreting the empirical evidence within a carefully constructed theoretical framework. This is where I use the idea of social belonging—the aspiration and strategies to maintain membership to home.

Migrants' sense of belonging is expressed in their narratives about who they are and why they do what they do. As my study recognizes, all migrants see themselves as members of their families to which they send remittance. Socialization into the values and norms relating to their roles in the family encourages them to send remittances as a natural act. However, individual selves and the family evolve along both spatial and relational lines. Family members often live in different countries and family roles transform, affecting a migrant's sense of self (as a migrant, citizen of a new country, returnee, visitor, etc.) and sense of belonging (as a son, father, brother, kin, etc.). In my study, spatial separation between migrants and their family members is primarily a result of the destination state's immigration policies, which allow only a select number of individuals to enter and stay for a certain time or permanently. This tends to affect migrants' willingness to cultivate a sense of belonging to their new destination. However, migrants' membership to the family is a given and therefore their belonging to the family is natural or spontaneous. The natural life cycle of the family, however, inevitably causes transformations in family belonging as migrants eventually form their own separate families and reorient to primary membership in their own family and often see old parents and unmarried siblings as dependent family members.

Bangladeshi migration to Japan and the United is a family affair in which migrants maintain their membership to the parental family back in Bangladesh throughout their stay abroad. A critical difference between the two migratory flows is whether or not there is the opportunity for family unification and permanent settlement. The social-cultural approach to remittance assumes that family unification in either the origin or the destination country will likely reduce remittance. If migrants are not allowed to bring family and settle permanently, they return home, which naturally stops remittance. If migrants can bring family and settle permanently, the natural outcome of family unification will be a growing sense of belonging in the destination country, leading to a decline in remittance. My informants in the United States confirmed this by reporting an increased sense of belonging in the country after family unification and immigration of their close relatives. However, they also reported a lack of belonging when their families struggled to find economic integration (an experience common to working-class migrants) and when their grown-up American-born children left home, as well when workplace relationships ended after retirement (an experience common to professional migrants). That immigrants (particularly those in the working class) continue to send remittances for economic gain and social status in Bangladesh reveals that they perceive themselves as members of their origin community in Bangladesh even after their immediate family and relatives join them in the United States. Working-class migrants' continued sense of belonging to their origin communities is further confirmed when they dream of retiring in Bangladesh, while migrants of the professional class take initiatives to reconnect to their "roots" after realizing their belonging in the United States devolves in their old age.

Remittance as Belonging

Anthropologist Michael Jackson[3] stresses that moving is a universal aspect of human life focused on a search for "the wherewithal of life"—something that may be "a matter of having wealth or health, fresh water or self-worth, love or lebensraum, food, family, or a future." This search ends only temporarily when one finds a balance between the search for opportunities in new places and a yearning for the comfort of the familiar, thereby striking a balance between being an actor and being acted upon, which Jackson calls "being at home in the world." Much like the migrants in Jackson's study, Bangladeshi migrants to both Japan and the United States search for better life, and their experiences involve the tension between movement in search of the wherewithal for life and a restful home.

As I described in chapters 2 and 3, Bangladeshi migration to Japan exemplifies the classic conception of economic migration wherein, because of unemployment and resource constraints in the origin country, the family sends a son, usually unmarried and young, to work abroad, earn money, and send remittance home. Researchers have observed that this family strategy for combatting economic hardship has existed since the colonial period in many parts of Bangladesh.

In a context characterized by increasing national economic struggles, as well as devastating natural disasters in Bangladesh, individuals and families saw an opportunity to migrate to Japan through the visa-waiver program for tourists from Bangladesh. These migrants (and their families) knew they would be working in Japan temporarily and would return home. Although the Japanese government's decision to offer port-of-entry visas to Bangladeshis initiated this migration, it was also its strict regulations that made it impossible for Bangladeshi migrants to prolong their stay or settle permanently. Japan revoked the visa-waiver program in 1990, three years after it began, and started to deport visa-overstayers. However, the knowledge about the availability of high-paying casual jobs continued to draw Bangladeshi aspirants who found an alternative way into the country: the language-student visa. The legality of "student" visas eased much of the segregation earlier migrants had faced, allowing new migrants to live in Tokyo and a few other big cities and work in part-time jobs. While they creatively circumvented the legal limit on work hours for students by finding multiple part-time jobs, they were still excluded from the formal job market and university education, and most had heard discouraging things about the difficulties of marriage to Japanese women. So, again, their home—the one they had grown up in (the family of orientation) and the one they aspired to build (the family of procreation)—remained in Bangladesh, where migrants would remit substantial amounts of money for family maintenance as well as invest in income-generating activities. Of all Bangladeshis in Japan, those who enter as university students and researchers with government scholarships report the most positive experiences, with support both from official sources and from volunteer organizations. In addition to receiving monthly stipends and subsidized transportation and medical insurance, they and their accompanying spouses can legally earn income, and many end up taking part-time jobs. But those in graduate degree programs face nearly insurmountable barriers to entering professional careers in Japan and find it an undesirable country to raise children in. As a result of the difficulty of finding belonging and establishing a home in Japan, most plan to move on to a more immigrant-welcoming country or to return to Bangladesh. The very small minority of students entering undergraduate programs learn native-level Japanese, enter professional careers relatively easily, and learn the local culture. Moreover, they easily qualify for naturalization and acquire Japanese citizenship. Yet they too experience social and cultural marginalization in daily life and look toward other immigrant countries or back to Bangladesh in search of home and belonging.

As the objective conditions for feeling at home remained unavailable to Bangladeshis in Japan, they sent substantial amounts of money to their parental families and relatives and to lay the foundation for a home of their own, someday, in Bangladesh. Hence, Japan emerged as the source country from which Bangladeshis received the largest amount per capita of remittances among all other destination countries of migration from Bangladesh. Remittances from Japan are utilized in real estate development, used-car businesses, and medical and dental clinics, all of which have a strong presence in Bangladesh. A notable exception to this pattern among Bangladeshis in Japan include those capable of further migrating to other immigrant-receiving countries in the West, such as the United States, the United Kingdom, Canada, Australia, and New Zealand. These migrants typically only sent small amounts of money necessary for the maintenance of their elderly parents and dependent siblings, and occasionally as gifts. Instead of sending remittances to save and invest in Bangladesh, these migrants saved their earnings to use in the country where they planned to permanently settle, further demonstrating the associations between the location of their home, sense of belonging, and direction of remittance.

Although the earnings are greater in Japan and immigration to the United States relies on luck, arduous processing, and less immediately lucrative future prospects, many Bangladeshis still aspire to migrate to the United States because it offers the possibility of permanent settlement with family and close relatives. As I discussed in chapter 3, Bangladeshi migration to the United States is most often initiated by the U.S. government through its DV-1 Program and cemented through its family unification policy. Winners of the visa lottery receive consultation from the U.S. Embassy in Bangladesh during visa processing and permanent residency, obtain the opportunity to work legally upon arrival, and receive other financial and social benefits. They automatically become eligible for naturalization after five years and can sponsor the immigration of their families and close relatives. Likewise, Bangladeshi ethnic neighborhoods in big cities across the United States, including Los Angeles, facilitate navigating the initial social and cultural barriers to establishing new homes. Thus, these migrants receive substantially better treatment from the destination state than their counterparts in Japan. This suggests that migrants settle permanently in the United States with ease, which should have resulted in a decline in remittance once they bring their entire parental family and close relatives to live permanently in the United States. However, this is not the pattern I found. Bangladeshis in the United States continue to send remittances, the amount of which grows every year, making it the source country from which Bangladesh receives the second-largest amount of remittances per capita. The United States is also the third-largest source country of remittances to Bangladesh after Saudi Arabia and Malaysia. A closer look at these immigrants' experience of settling in their new home and finding belonging in the United States explains why they continue to send remittances to Bangladesh.

Most DV-1 lottery winners migrate to the United States alone, leaving behind their parents and siblings in Bangladesh. Those who bring spouses and children—both lottery winners and family-sponsored chain immigrants— also often leave behind their parents and unmarried and dependent siblings. Both single migrants and families generally move into rented apartments in ethnic neighborhoods with other working-class immigrants, yet still long for customary facilities for leisure activities, like *adda* at tea stalls and communal events like prayer. Furthermore, in many cases and despite professional experience and education, most find only casual work at the beginning, and so their new social position is a step down from their original class background. Finally, they find limited opportunities for upward mobility into the middle class, although some do manage to send their children to prestigious schools and universities to study for professional careers. Anticipating little opportunity to enjoy their retirement, some first-generation migrants aspire to return to Bangladesh, and consequently send substantial remittances to invest in income-generating initiatives and rekindle belonging to their origin communities in Bangladesh.

Those who enter the United States as university students constitute the largest proportion of Bangladeshi American professionals. They generally come from educated, well-off families in Bangladesh and travel alone on student visas. After graduation, they enter professional careers and eventually become naturalized citizens. Then they get married—usually in Bangladesh—and bring their spouses and sometimes parents to the United States to settle permanently. They tend to live near their workplaces and in the suburbs of big cities. While their children go to mainstream schools with the children of their white and nonwhite professional neighbors, their social interactions mostly involve weekend family gatherings with co-ethnics or family drives to ethnic restaurants and events in the ethnic community. Unlike their working-class compatriots, the professionals achieve economic success and social prestige in the United States; but like the working-class migrants they experience a diminishing sense of belonging and realize a need for reconnecting to the origin community as their children grow up and move out to form their own families . Thus, these immigrants begin to send remittances to charitable causes and reconnect to their childhood friends back home to find belonging. They may also invest in second homes in Bangladesh, but as an emotional indulgence rather than an actual practice. For most of these immigrants do not actually return to Bangladesh and stay in the United States due to having their immediate family members in the country. Still, they seriously consider returning to their origin communities, which confirms the idea that they look for belonging in Bangladesh that they see devolving in the United States as they get older.

My study observes that Bangladeshis never feel at home in Japan and therefore maintain their belonging to the origin family and community in Bangladesh, with a few migrating to a third country. But those in the United States are able to bring their families and settle permanently, thereby establishing their new home in the United States. Common sense suggests, given the legal, social, cultural supports available to them, that they will eventually be incorporated into the sociocultural fabric of immigrant America. However, consequential limitations on their feeling at home in the United States encourage them to look back to their origins in Bangladesh, which is reflected in changing remittance patterns. Thus, my study recognizes a high propensity to send remittances in their early days among Bangladeshi Americans, when all or some members of the family still remain in Bangladesh; a relative decline in remittance upon family unification in the United States; and a resurgence in the proportion and frequency of remittance as they migrants approach mid-career and retirement. This pattern differs starkly from that of Japan, where migrants' belonging is always minimal and remittance remains high throughout their stay. As scholars[4] of transnationalism recognize among several other immigrant groups, home for Bangladeshi migrants in America is transnational—here in the United States, but also there in Bangladesh.

Migrants' belonging is anchored to their sense of home. Home is where migrants feel a sense of belonging and is constituted of intimate relations in a community characterized by receptive legal, social, and cultural conditions. Home is where individuals feel safe, owing to recognition of their rights; comfortable, owing to a familiar ("homey") atmosphere; and at ease, through interactions with family, relatives, and neighbors. Home allows migrants to experience both their "being" and "becoming." To summarize, home is where migrants find belonging, and their cross-border interactions, including remittance, confirm their efforts of maintaining the home they have and the home they aspire to.

Globalization and Migration: Belonging, Home, and Identity

This book shows that Bangladeshi migrants in Japan and the United States send remittances because of their belonging to the families and communities from which they acquire their identity and with whom they construe their home. It also demonstrates how globalization offers new opportunities for them and their families to attain betterment but at the same time limits the extent to which they can take advantage of such opportunities. Remittance functions as a resource with which migrants aspire to create a home and establish a sense of belonging to that home. By means of remittance, migrants negotiate with the family and community as well as the state in realizing their desired home and, where possible, improving it.

In talking about migration and identity in the contemporary globalized world, sociologist Zygmunt Bauman[5] states that identity is "solely in the process of continuous renegotiation." He emphasizes the "non-finality" or inconclusiveness of individuals' identities due to the continuously changing conditions of life as well as to sets of opportunities and threats. Among such identity-morphing contingencies, we may count the inauguration of the visa-waiver program in Japan and the launching of the DV-1 Program in the United States, and their subsequent closure to Bangladeshis on the one hand and transformations in migrants' relationship to and within the family on the other hand. Migrants seek to belong to a home that they share with immediate family members and a community of relatives and associates. The home is place bound and conditioned primarily by one's citizenship and class status (as chapters 2 and 4 show), but it also has a relational dimension (highlighted in chapter 5). Once the location of the home is settled, migrants inevitably negotiate and renegotiate the relationships that allow them to feel at home. The remigration of some Bangladeshis from Japan to traditional target countries of immigration and from the United States back to Bangladesh demonstrates that the relationships constituting home are more important than the location of the home. It is relationships that confer identity and belonging. Hence, remittance is a relational act and an expression of migrants' belonging.

By assuming that remittance is motivated by migrants' altruism or self-interest, we inadvertently simplify the complex and emotionally loaded interactions between migrants and their remittance receivers as market transactions aimed at maximizing self-interest. We thus convert relatively permanent social relations and interactions in the family context into arm's-length economic transactions that dissolve immediately after the act is done. Whereas arm's-length transactions are likely to have transient consequences, the comparable consequences of remittance transactions tend to be long-lasting, emotionally intense, and socially comprehensive, involving many more individuals than the two parties directly engaged in the transaction. This is because remittance is guided by moral expectations of reciprocity, benevolence, and caring, among many other possible social and cultural factors mediating the relationships between senders and recipients.

Understanding remittance as motivated by the migrant's altruism or self-interest posits that they gain satisfaction either from sacrificing their personal interest for their loved ones' benefit or from accomplishing personal goals. In both cases, the migrant appears to have acted on their own motives and to have achieved positive outcomes. In real life, migrants' experiences of remittance are remarkably different, as this book shows. Oftentimes, migrants send remittances against their own will under considerable social pressure, and occasionally the outcome is negative. And even when remittance is truly voluntary, its motives can range far beyond the expectation of self-approval, whether founded on sacrifice or on acquisition. As chapters 2 and 4 note, through remittance, migrants want to make sure that the family they left behind feels their presence while they are away from home, to allow their parents to feel pride and to be seen by others as good sons and daughters by conforming to prevailing norms. Underlying all these subjectivities is the conviction and the desire to belong to the family. Without this sense of belonging, all the moral components fall apart, norms and values become irrelevant, and submission to any social pressure becomes unnecessary.

Despite its ordinary and unproblematic appearance, closer attention to remittance identifies migrants' compliance and defiance, happiness and sorrows, and accomplishments and frustrations. Migrants engage in sending (and in a few situations, not sending) remittance not only because they have calculated their own economic interest, or because they cannot avoid cultural prescriptions and proscriptions. As this book shows, migrants fully consider economic interests and cultural norms concerning monetary transactions. Yet, the interactions embedding remittance behaviors reveal the migrant as neither *homo economicus*—an individual preoccupied with rational utility calculation—nor *homo socius*—an individual thoroughly socialized into following cultural scripts. Migrants are individuals with desires embedded within particular sociocultural settings characterized by limits and possibilities. Recognizing the centrality of the individual's desire in migration, Collins[6] defines migration as "an expression of transformation, an actualisation of deterritorialising and reterritorialising processes both in individual subjects and the places they inhabit through migration." As inherently social beings, migrants engage in these processes within the context of family and community, where remittance functions as one of the pivotal resources. Migrants do aspire to increase financial benefits with remittance, but they also adhere to the prevailing normative standards of their society. Whereas their economic motive shows their desire to improve their material conditions, their culturally patterned actions demonstrate their desire to belong to the family and community from which they derive their identity and belonging. Thus, they approach remittances as a kind of "relational accounting."[7] That is, migrants send remittances as members of families and communities and as aspirants looking to improve the material conditions of the intimate social unit from which they derive their identity. At the same time, remittance behaviors change over time as the original family unit evolves and as migrants experience belonging or rejection in their destination country.

This book is replete with evidence of both utility calculations and moral considerations, but it tells more nuanced and complicated stories that go beyond either economic or cultural determinism. Empirical investigations into migrant remittance needs to revise the ontological assumption that migrants act as separate individuals and reframe the discussion about their culturally conditioned individuality by incorporating both moral and rational considerations. Thus, we should ask not "Why do migrants send remittances?" but "Who sends remittance to whom?" For our commonsensical understanding of remittance as a natural act of migration success is, in fact, conditioned by a lack of belonging in the destination country and consequent search for belonging in the origin country. Remittance originates out of a relational vacuum in the migrants' sense of belonging at the destination. Spatial distance from the home country does not by itself cause remittance if the migrants are able to establish their home in the new destination and find belonging there, or if they no longer look to relations in the origin country to find belonging.

Acknowledgments

This book is a result of my decades-long learning of the meaning migrant remittance has for migrants, their families, and the countries they come to. This is also a reflection of my understanding of remittance as I began to see myself as a migrant when I left my home country to study abroad. My early days in Japan were lonely due to leaving family, friends, and a familiar life behind in Bangladesh, which was further compounded by the challenges of adapting to the demanding higher educational culture at Sophia University. Jafar's halal store at Shinokubo in Tokyo City offered me much-needed respite in a physically and psychologically draining life. I would spend hours every other day at that small store on a chair beside the cash counter, watching Bangladeshi customers dropping by on their way to work or from work to home, buying their daily necessities. Most of the time, the store owner Jafar bhai, or his cashier Mizan bhai, would talk to me about their experiences, including their journeys from Bangladesh to Japan and about other migrants they got to know. Over time, I became friends with some regular customers, who would ask me to have coffee or snacks outside. The stories these migrants shared about remittance centered around their families. I am deeply grateful to them for inciting my interest in studying migrant remittance.

It was Professor David Wank at Sophia University who inspired me to undertake an ethnographic field study on migrant remittance. Hearing some of the stories I learned from Bangladeshi migrants, he suggested that I conduct an ethnographic study among them. Courses on globalization, the state's role in shaping people's experience, and global ethnography at Sophia University prepared my theoretical and methodological foundation, which I further developed at the University of California, Los Angeles under the mentorship of Professor Min Zhou and Professor Ruben Hernandez-Leon. I express my gratitude to Professor Ruben for his invaluable assistance and mentorship during the initial stages of the graduate program. I am immensely grateful to Professor Min for her empathetic mentorship and caring support, without which I would not have been able to successfully complete my dissertation project and overcome the significant obstacles in my academic journey. In addition, I am greatly indebted to Professor James Farrer and Professor Koichi Nakano at Sophia University, and to Professor Roger Waldinger, Professor Leisy Abrego, Professor Ching Kwan Lee, Professor Rebeca Emigh, Professor Cesar Ayala, Professor Andreas Wimmer, and Professor Stefan Timmermans for their invaluable support at various stages in my graduate studies at UCLA.

I feel fortunate to have had people who cared for me and offered unconditional support throughout my research and fieldwork. Transitioning to the graduate program at UCLA was a life-changing experience, which involved balancing the high demands of the academic program and regular life. I would not have been able to survive with my limited knowledge of conversational English and even more limited knowledge of an American PhD program had not my dear friends Caitlin Patler and Elina Shih extended their unconditional support and guidance. I also want to express my gratitude to my friends Julia Tomassetti, Eijiroh Isa, Yool Choi, Shabnam Shenasi Azari, and Mirna Trencoso for sharing the pain and motivation to continue that formed the foundation of the research I present in this book.

The idea of my study originated in Tokyo in 2008 and traveled with me to Los Angeles. During this decade-long journey, I received generous support from various institutions in the form of fellowships and travel grants. I would like to express my gratitude to the Terasaki Center for Japanese Studies for awarding me the Herbert and Helen Kawahara Fellowship and to the Asia Institute graduate fellowship for allowing me to conduct summer fieldwork in Tokyo and Los Angeles. I am also deeply indebted to the Hosei International Fund fellowship and Professor Chieko Kamibayashi at Hosei University, Tokyo, for supporting my last year of fieldwork in Tokyo with a wonderful office and pertinent supervision in addition to financial support.

Fieldwork was the center of my research for this book. While my professor and friends in the graduate program of sociology at UCLA helped prepare my academic understanding and skills necessary for this study, it was my interlocutors who facilitated my entry into the field in Tokyo and Los Angeles. One of the biggest challenges for any ethnographer is gaining access to the field. My initial optimism about getting easy access to Bangladeshi migrants and immigrants in both places proved wrong as I started asking people about their remittances. Financial issues within one's family context are deemed too personal to share with someone outside of the family. Moreover, these migrants are judged by others based on their financial contributions to their families and relatives in Bangladesh. Thus, my Bangladeshi roots and ethnicity originally discouraged participants from talking with me about what they considered personal issues. I needed assistance from several people to overcome this hurdle. In Los Angeles, these people included Alam bhai, Babu bhai, Bacchu bhai, Bulbul bhai, Hashem bhai, Huda bhai, Juwel bhai, Kabir bhai, Momin bhai, Nazmul bhai, Pintu bhai, Tuhin bhai, and several others. I express my heartiest gratitude to them for their assistance in relocating to the Bangladeshi immigrant neighborhood in Los Angeles and getting to know other Bangladeshis from whom I drew interviewees. My three-year stay in the community was possible due to their cordial acceptance and help in every way possible to overcome my challenges in getting by and doing my fieldwork.

My fieldwork in Tokyo involved the additional challenge of finding Bangladeshi migrants in their daily routine activities. There was no identifiable Bangladeshi immigrant community in Tokyo like its counterpart in Los Angeles. Therefore, I had to take additional measures to find potential interviewees and travel across Tokyo to observe community events on various occasions. Abdul Mannan bhai, Asaduzzaman bhai, Masud bhai, Robin bhai, Sumon bhai, Juwel bhai, Emdad Haq, Imran, Shahadat, Sujan and many others invited me to stay at their residences, took me to attend community events, introduced me to other Bangladeshis, and guided me to various locations to find Bangladeshi migrants. I would also like to give credit to the cadet college fraternity in Tokyo, which was a great source of social and emotional support throughout my stay in Tokyo. I must also mention the owners and employees of the halal shops for their invaluable support.

I worked on this book from the time I began my fieldwork until Rutgers University Press accepted the final draft. I extend my gratitude to the organizers and panel participants at the annual conferences of the International Sociological Association, the American Sociological Association, the Canadian Sociological Association, and the Pacific Sociological Association for allowing me to present sections of my book and get valuable scholarly feedback. I also presented the final revision of my central argument at the Faculty Colloquium at Northwestern University in Qatar where I received critical feedback and appreciation from my colleagues that boosted my confidence significantly. I would like to thank Professor Zachary Wright for inviting me to the colloquium and offering professional mentorship during the final stage of my manuscript preparation. I also want to acknowledge and thank Professor Anto Mohsin, James Hoddap, and Sami Hermaz for their tremendous emotional and professional support during my writing. Additionally, I am thankful to Professor Habibul Haque Khondker and Professor Md Saidul Islam—two prominent sociologists of Bangladeshi origin—for their ongoing encouragement and support from the beginning of my PhD studies until now. An abridged version of chapters 3 and 4 appeared in the *International Migration* journal entitled "Beyond Economics: The Family, Belonging, and Remittances among the Bangladeshi Migrants in Los Angeles." Some material from chapters 1 and 2 also appeared in the *Current Sociology* journal, entitled "'It's My Money': Social Class and the Perception of Remittance among Bangladeshi Migrants in Japan."

If conducting the fieldwork and writing the manuscript of this book were challenging, finding a press for it was no less difficult. I felt incredibly lucky that my manuscript drew the attention of Jasper Chang, an acquisitions editor at Rutgers University Press. While Jasper put my manuscript through the review process, it was his predecessor, Carah Naseem, who completed the review process and got me the book contract. Carah was very responsive and supportive of my book and pushed it through the review process in a timely manner. I express my sincere gratitude to both Jasper and Carah for their support and the anonymous reviewers for their thoughtful and constructive feedback that helped improve the final manuscript significantly.

It does not take anyone much to understand how critical our families are to whatever we aspire to and achieve. I am immensely indebted to my loving wife, Sumiya Fatima Mahmud, and our daughter, Afreen Fatima Mahmud, for standing by me throughout the exhaustive processes of fieldwork and preparing this manuscript. While my mother, Azizunnahar, stays thousands of miles away, she continues to inspire me to work hard. I cannot thank them enough for their sacrifices for me and the unconditional emotional support they offer me. I am eternally grateful to them.

Notes

Introduction

1 This and all other names in this book are pseudonyms, used to conceal the true identity of my interlocutors.

2 A Bangladeshi restaurant-cum-grocery-store catering to Bangladeshi immigrants.

3 An area in Koreatown, Los Angeles, officially recognized as a Bangladeshi neighborhood.

4 A form of casual conversation on random topics with friends as well as strangers; one of the most common forms of leisurely activity.

5 U.S. family unification policy allows every naturalized citizen to sponsor immigration of their parents, spouse, and siblings immediately after they become a U.S. citizen.

6 As Bangladesh is a country with one of the heaviest rainy seasons and is crisscrossed by hundreds of rivers and cannels, water is always plentiful and almost valueless to Bangladeshis. Thus "spending money like water" is a common phrase used in colloquial Bangla to refer to a person who is profligate.

7 In fact, an amendment to Japanese immigration laws in 2012 allowed Mian, and many other professional migrants like him, to acquire Japanese permanent residence and eventually citizenship.

8 Migrants and their families in their communities of origin often measure their success in terms of material possessions acquired with remittances. For more on this see Ali, S. (2007), "Go West young man": The culture of migration among Muslims in Hyderabad, India, *Journal of Ethnic and Migration Studies*, *33*(1), 37–58; Cohen, J. H. (2011), Migration, remittances, and household strategies, *Annual Review of Anthropology*, *40*, 103–114.

9 Bangladesh Bank (2023). Wage earners' remittance inflows: Top 30 countries received, https://www.bb.org.bd/econdata/remittance/top_30_country.pdf (accessed March 22, 2024).

10 Bangladesh Bank fiscal year begins in July and ends in June in the following year.

11 Belanger, D., & Rahman, M. (2013), Migrating against all the odds: International labour migration of Bangladeshi women, *Current Sociology*, *61*(3), 356–373; Oishi, N. (2005), *Women in motion: Globalization, state policies, and labor migration in Asia*, Stanford University Press.

12 Bureau of Manpower, Employment and Training (BMET) (2018), *Overseas employment and remittances (1976–2018)*. For later reports, see http://www.old.bmet .gov.bd/BMET/stattisticalDataAction.

13 Knights, M. (1996), Bangladeshi immigrants in Italy: From geopolitics to micropolitics, *Transactions of the Institute of British Geographers*, 105–123; Mapril, J. (2011), The patron and the madman: Migration, success and the (in)visibility of failure among Bangladeshis in Portugal, *Social Anthropology*, *19*, 288–296; Mapril, J. (2014), The dreams of middle class: Consumption, life-course and migration between Bangladesh and Portugal, *Modern Asian Studies*, *48*, 693–719; Morad, M., & Puppa, F. D. (2019), Bangladeshi migrant associations in Italy: Transnational engagement, community formation and regional unity, *Ethnic and Racial Studies*, *42*, 1788–1807; Zeitlyn, B. (2012), The Sylheti bari and the Londoni flat, *Space and Culture*, *15*(4), 317–329.

14 U.S. Embassy Dhaka (2023), More than 13,000 Bangladeshis—an all-time high—are currently studying in the United States in a record-setting year.

15 Ethnic shops selling ethnic foodstuffs, including halal food products for Muslims.

16 Gardner, K. (2002), *Age, narrative and migration: The life course and life histories of Bengali elders in London*, Berg Publishers.

17 Datta, K., et al. (2008), *Mobile masculinities: Men, migration and low paid work in London*, Queen Mary University and Economic and Social Research Council.

18 Connell, R. W. (2005), Hegemonic masculinity: Rethink the concept, *Gender and Society*, *19*(6), 829–859.

19 Pande, A. (2017), Mobile masculinities: Migrant Bangladeshi men in South Africa, *Gender and Society*, *31*(3), 383–406.

20 Mahmood, R. A. (1994), Adaptation to a new world: Experience of Bangladeshis in Japan, *International Migration*, *32*(4), 513–532; Mahmud, H. (2014), "It's my money": Social class and the perception of remittances among Bangladeshi migrants in Japan, *Current Sociology*, *62*(3), 418–430.

21 For example, the guestworker program in Europe and the *bracero* program in the United States after World War II, as well as the contemporary *kafaala* system in the Middle East.

22 Mahmud, H. (2013), Enemy or ally: Migrants, intermediaries and the state in Bangladeshi migration to Japan and the United States, *Migration and Development*, *2*(1), 1–15.

23 Haines, D. W., Minami, M., & Yamashita, S. (2007), Transnational migration in East Asia: Japan in comparative focus, *International Migration Review*, *41*(4), 963–967; Higuchi, N. (2007), Remittances, investments and social mobility among Bangladeshi and Iranian returnees from Japan, *Proceedings for the 8th Asia and Pacific Migration Research Network Conference on Migration, Development and Poverty Reduction*, Asia Pacific Migration Research Network; Mahmud, "It's my money"; Oishi, N. (2012), The limits of immigration policies: The challenges of highly skilled migration in Japan, *American Behavioral Scientist*, *56*(8), 1080–1100.

24 Mahmud, "It's my money."

25 Mahmud, H. (2021), Beyond economics: The family, belonging and remittances among the Bangladeshi migrants in Los Angeles, *International Migration*, https:// doi.org/10.1111/imig.12809.

26 I use this statistic to reflect the size of the immigrant community during my fieldwork. Given the trend of continuous growth, the community will likely be much larger when this book is published.

27 Due to most Bangladeshis entering Japan through undocumented channels, a reliable figure of their total number is unavailable. Mahmood (1994) estimated this number as somewhere between 50,000 and 150,000.

28 Liu-Farrer, G. (2009), Educationally channeled international labor mobility: Contemporary student migration from China to Japan, *International Migration Review*, *43*(1), 178–204; Mahmud, "It's my money."

29 Mahmud, Beyond economics.

30 For more on migrant home and belonging, see Espiritu, E. L. (2003), *Home bound: Filipino American lives across cultures, communities, and countries*, University of California Press; Levitt, P. (2001), *The transnational villagers*, University of California Press; Wise, J. M. (2000), Home: Territory and identity, *Cultural Studies*, *14*(2), 295–310.

31 Glytsos, N. P. (1997), Remitting behaviour of "temporary" and "permanent" migrants: The case of Greeks in Germany and Australia, *Labor*, *11*(3), 409–435; Goza, F., & Ryabov, I. (2012), Remittance activity among Brazilians in the US and Canada, *International Migration*, *50*(4), 157–185.

32 Blue, S. A. (2004), State policy, economic crisis, gender, and family ties: Determinants of family remittances to Cuba, *Economic Geography*, *80*(1), 63–82; Burawoy, M. (1976), The functions and reproduction of migrant labor: Comparative material from Southern Africa and the United States, *American Journal of Sociology*, *81*(5), 1050–1087; Hollifield, J. (2004), The emerging migration state, *International Migration Review*, *38*(3), 885–912.

33 Åkesson, L. (2011), Remittances and relationships: Exchange in Cape Verdean transnational families, *Ethnos*, *76*(3), 326–347; Rindfuss, R. R., et al. (2012), Migrant remittances and the web of family obligations: Ongoing support among spatially extended kin in north-east Thailand, 1984–94, *Population Studies: A Journal of Demography*, *66*(1), 87–104.

34 Deneulin, S. (2006), Individual well-being, migration remittances and the common good, *The European Journal of Development Research*, *18*(1), 45–58.

35 Arestoff, F., Kuhn-Le Braz, M., & El Mouhoub, M. (2016), Remittance behaviour of forced migrants in post-Apartheid South Africa, *The Journal of Development Studies*, *52*(6), 824–837.

36 Arun, T., & Ulku, H. (2011), Determinants of remittances: The case of the South Asian community in Manchester, *Journal of Development Studies*, *47*(6), 894–912.

37 Meyer, S. (2020), "Home is where I spend my money": Testing the remittance decay hypothesis with ethnographic data from an Austrian-Turkish community, *Social Inclusion*, *8*(1), 275–284, http://dx.doi.org/10.17645/si.v8i1.2435.

38 Mahmud, Beyond economics.

39 For more on the NELM perspective, see Lucas, R.E.B., & Stark, O. (1985), Motivations to remit: Evidence from Botswana, *The Journal of Political Economy*, *93*(5), 901–918; Taylor, E. J. (1999), The new economics of labour migration and the role of remittances in the migration process, *International Migration*, *37*(1), 63–88.

40 Mahmud, H. (2020), From individual motivations to social determinants: Towards a sociology of migrants' remittances, *International Social Science Journal*, https://doi.org/10.1111/issj.12247.

41 Wakefield, J. C. (1993), Is altruism part of human nature? Toward a theoretical foundation for the helping professions, *Social Service Review*, *67*(3), 406–458.

42 Goldring, L. (2004), Family and collective remittances to Mexico: A multi-dimensional typology, *Development and Change*, *35*(4), 799–840.

43 Stevanovic-Fenn, N. (2012), *Remittances and the moral economies of Bangladeshi New York immigrants in light of the economic crisis.* [Doctoral dissertation, Columbia University], Columbia Academic Commons.

44 Shen, Y. (2016), Filial daughters? Agency and subjectivity of rural migrant women in Shanghai, *The China Quarterly, 226,* 519–537; Thai, H. C. (2006), Money and masculinity among Vietnamese low wage immigrants in transnational families, *International Journal of Sociology of the Family, 32*(2), 247–271.

45 Carling, J. (2008), The determinants of migrant remittances, *Oxford Review of Economic Policy, 24*(3), 581–598.

46 Thompson, E. P. (1991), *The making of the English working class,* Penguin Books.

47 Lacroix, T. (2013), Collective remittances and integration: North African and North Indian comparative perspectives, *Journal of Ethnic and Migration Studies, 39*(6), 1019–1035.

48 Åkesson, L. (2009), Remittances and inequality in Cape Verde: The impact of changing family organization, *Global Networks, 9*(3), 381–398; Singh, S., Robertson, S., & Cabraal, A. (2012), Transnational family money: Remittances, gifts and inheritance, *Journal of Intercultural Studies, 33*(5): 475–492.

49 Thai, Money and masculinity; Yeoh, B.S.A., et al. (2013), Between two families: The social meaning of remittances for Vietnamese marriage migrants in Singapore, *Global Networks, 13*(4), 441–458.

50 Peter, K. (2010), Transnational family ties, remittance motives, and social death among Congolese migrants: A socio-anthropological analysis, *Journal of Comparative Family Studies, 41*(2), 225–243.

51 Ali, "Go West, young man"; Thai, H. C. (2014), *Insufficient funds: The culture of money in low-wage transnational families,* Stanford University Press; Zhou, M., & Li, R. (2018), Remittances for collective consumption and social status compensation: Variations on transnational practices among Chinese international migrants, *International Migration Review, 52*(1), 4–42.

52 Duquette-Rury, L. (2014), Collective remittances and transnational coproduction: The 3 × 1 program for migrants and household access to public goods in Mexico, *Studies in Comparative International Development, 49*(1), 112–139.

53 Paerregaard, K. (2015), *Return to sender: The moral economy of Peru's migrant remittances,* University of California Press.

54 Adams, J. R. (2009), The determinants of international remittances in developing countries, *World Development, 37*(1), 93–103.

55 The NELM perspective.

56 Austin, D. M. (1994), Altruism, *Social Service Review, 68*(3), 437–440.

57 Migrant households do not necessarily constitute a unit but are usually fractured along gender and generational lines (King, et al., 2013). Moreover, migrants' marital status and the presence of children, parents, and siblings in the household of origin affect intra-household exchanges (Rindfuss et al., 2012). Male and female migrants approach remittance differently, further supporting arguments that migrant households do not act cohesively in using remittance (Abrego, 2014; McKenzie & Menjívar, 2011; Thai, 2014). Lastly, the meaning and determination of primary loyalty hinders precisely identifying the household as a "decision-making unit," since distant kin or non-kin members are sometimes found to share the family budget (Wall & Gouveia, 2014).

58 Mahmud, "It's my money."

59 Lacroix, T. (2014), Conceptualizing transnational engagements: A structure and agency perspective on (hometown) transnationalism, *The International Migration Review, 48*(3), 661.

60 Dilip, R. (n.d.),What are remittances? *Finance and Development*, p. 76, https://www .imf.org/external/pubs/ft/fandd/basics/pdf/ratha-remittances.pdf.

61 Ahsan Ullah, A.K.M. (2011), Dynamics of remittance practices and development: Bangladeshi overseas migrants, *Development in Practice*, *21*(8), 1153–1167; De Bruyn, T., Kuddus, U. (2005), *Dynamics of remittance utilization in Bangladesh*, International Organization for Migration (IOM) Research Series, vol. 18; Rashid, S. R. (2016), *Uncertain tomorrows: Livelihoods, capital and risk in labour migration from Bangladesh*, University Press Limited.

62 Dreby, J. (2010), *Divided by borders: Mexican migrants and their children*, University of California Press; Levitt, *Transnational villagers*; Parreñas, R. S. (2001), *Servants of globalization: Migration and domestic work*, Stanford University Press; Thai, *Insufficient funds.*

63 Abrego, L. (2014), *Sacrificing families: Navigating laws, labor, and love across borders*, Stanford University Press.

64 Åkesson, Remittances and inequality; Singh, S. (2006), Towards a sociology of money and family in the Indian diaspora, *Contributions to Indian Sociology*, *40*(4), 376–98; Thai, *Insufficient funds.*

65 Duquette-Rury, Collective remittances and transnational coproduction.

66 Strasser, E., et al. (2009), Doing family, *The History of the Family*, *14*(2), 165–176.

67 Jacobs, K., & Malpas, J. (2013), Material objects, identity and the home: Towards a relational housing research agenda, *Housing, Theory and Society*, *30*(3), 285.

68 Rubinstein, R. L., & Madeiros, K. D. (2005), Home, self and identity, in G. D. Rowles & Habib Chaudhury (Eds.), *Home and identity in late life: International perspectives* (pp. 47–62), Springer Publishing.

69 Hall, S. (2015), Cultural identity and diaspora, in P. Williams & L. Chrisman (Eds.), *Colonial discourse and post-colonial theory* (pp. 392–403), Routledge.

70 Easthope, H. (2009), Fixed identities in a mobile world? The relationship between mobility, place, and identity, *Identities: Global Studies in Culture and Power*, *16*(1), 61–82; La Barbera, M. C. (2015), Identity and migration: An introduction, in *Identity and migration in Europe: Multidisciplinary perspectives* (pp. 1–13), Springer Publishing; Lipski, J. (2014), Roderick's and Peregrine's protean identities, in *Quest of the self: Masquerade and travel in the eighteenth-century novel* (pp. 105–133), Brill.

71 Chapman, T. (2001), There is no place like home, *Theory, Culture and Society*, *18*(6), 135–146.

72 Fathi, M. (2022), "My life is on hold": Examining home, belonging and temporality among migrant men in Ireland, *Gender, Place & Culture*, *29*(8), 1097–1120.

73 Kakhkharov, J., & Ahunov, M. (2020), Squandering remittances income in conspicuous consumption? in A. Akimov & G. Kazakevitch (Eds.), *30 years since the fall of the Berlin Wall*, Palgrave Studies in Economic History, Palgrave Macmillan; Chacko, E. (2020), Conspicuous consumption and philanthropy connections between Punjabi immigrants from the Doaba Region and their hometowns, *Economics and Business*, 152–68.

74 Afaha, J. S. (2013), Migration, remittance and development in origin countries: Evidence from Nigeria, *African Population Studies*, *27*(1); Arif, I., et al. (2019), The role of remittances in the development of higher education: Evidence from top remittance receiving countries, *Social Indicators Research*, *141*(3), 1233–1243; Dhakal, S., & Oli, S. (2020), The impact of remittance on consumption and investment: A case of province five of Nepal, *Quest Journal of Management and Social Sciences*, *2*(1), 35–49.

75 Boccagni, P. (2022), Homing: A category for research on space appropriation and "home-oriented" mobilities, *Mobilities*, *17*(4), 585–601.

76 Wise, Home: Territory and identity, 299.
77 Harper, R. A., & Zubida, H. (2018), Being seen: Visibility, families and dynamic remittance practices, *Migration and Development*, *7*(1), 8.
78 Espiritu, *Home bound*, 2.
79 Castañeda, E. (2018), *A place to call home: Immigrant exclusion and urban belonging in New York, Paris, and Barcelona*, Stanford University Press.
80 Walton, G. M., & Cohen, G. L. (2007), A question of belonging: Race, social fit, and achievement, *Journal of Personality and Social Psychology*, *92*(1), 82.
81 Thai, *Insufficient funds*.
82 Soehl, T., & Waldinger, R. (2012), Inheriting the homeland? Intergenerational transmission of cross-border ties in migrant families, *American Journal of Sociology*, *118*(3), 778–813.
83 Åkesson, Remittances and relationships; Arun & Ulku, Determinants of remittances; Hunte, C. K. (2004), Workers' remittances, remittance decay and financial deepening in developing countries, *The American Economist*, *48*(2), 82–94; Makina, D., & A. Masenge (2015), The time pattern of remittances and the decay hypothesis: Evidence from migrants in South Africa, *Migration Letters*, *12*(1), 79–90.
84 Lacroix, Collective remittances and integration.
85 Erdal, M. B. (2012), Who is the money for? Remittances within and beyond the household in Pakistan, *Asian and Pacific Migration Journal*, *21*(4), 437–457.
86 Waite, L., & Cook, J. (2011), Belonging among diasporic African communities in the UK: Plurilocal homes and simultaneity of place attachments, *Emotion, Space and Society*, *4*(4), 238–248.
87 Meyer (2020), "Home is where I spend my money," 282.
88 Creese, G. (2019), "Where are you from?" Racialization, belonging and identity among second-generation African-Canadians, *Ethnic and Racial Studies*, *42*(9), 1476–1494; Erel, U. (2011), Complex belongings: Racialization and migration in a small English city, *Ethnic and Racial Studies*, *34*(12), 2048–2068; Korteweg, A. C. (2017), The failures of "immigrant integration": The gendered racialized production of non-belonging, *Migration Studies*, *5*(3), 428–444; Onasch, E. A. (2017), Lessons on the boundaries of belonging: Racialization and symbolic boundary drawing in the French civic integration program, *Social Problems*, *64*(4), 577–593; Ossipow, L., Counilh, A., and Chimienti, M. (2019), Racialization in Switzerland: Experiences of children of refugees from Kurdish, Tamil and Vietnamese backgrounds, *Comparative Migration Studies*, *7*(19), https://doi.org/10.1186/s40878-019-0117-7.
89 Mahmud, "It's my money."
90 Thompson, *English working class*.
91 Götz, N. (2015), "Moral economy": Its conceptual history and analytical prospects, *Journal of Global Ethics*, *11*(2), 147–162.
92 Brette, O. (2017), The vested interests and the evolving moral economy of the common people, *Journal of Economic Issues*, *51*(2), 503–510.
93 Zelizer, V. A. (1994), *The social meaning of money*, Basic Books; Zelizer (1996), Payments and social ties, *Sociological Forum*, *11*, 481–495.
94 Zelizer, V. A. (2000), The purchase of intimacy, *Law & Social Inquiry*, *25*, 842.
95 Aldous, J., & Klein, D. (1991), Sentiment and services: Models of intergenerational relationships in midlife, *Journal of Marriage and the Family*, *53*, 595–608.
96 A number of empirical studies on transnational migration also recognize how various moral customs and traditions shape interactions between migrants and their immediate families and relatives. See, for example, Abrego, L. J. (2009), Economic well-being in Salvadoran transnational families: How gender affects remittance

practices, *Journal of Marriage and Family*, *71*(4), 1070–1085; Abrego, *Sacrificing families*; Parreñas, R. S. (2001), *Servants of globalization*; Mahmud, "It's my money"; Sana, M., & Massey, D. S. (2005), Household composition, family migration, and community context: Migrant remittances in four countries, *Social Science Quarterly*, *86*(2), 509–528; Stodolska, M., & Santos, C. A. (2006), You must think of *familia*: The everyday lives of Mexican migrants in destination communities, *Social and Cultural Geographer*, *7*(4), 627–647; Thai, *Insufficient funds*; Vanwey, L. K. (2004), Altruistic and contractual remittances between male and female migrants and households in rural Thailand, *Demography*, *41*(4), 739–756; Wong, M. (2006), The gendered politics of remittance in Ghanaian transnational families, *Economic geography*, *82*(4), 355–381.

97 For examples among other migrant groups, see Åkesson, Remittances and inequality.

98 Huennekes, J. (2018), Emotional remittances in the transnational lives of Rohingya families living in Malaysia, *Journal of Refugee Studies*, *31*(3), 353–370; Kunz, R., Maisenbacher, J., & Paudel, L. N. (2020), The financialization of remittances: Governing through emotions, *Review of International Political Economy*, *28*(6), 1607–1631; McKenzie, S., & Menjívar, C. (2011), The meanings of migration, remittances and gifts: Views of Honduran women who stay, *Global Networks*, *11*(1), 63–81; Montes, V. (2013), The role of emotions in the construction of masculinity: Guatemalan migrant men, transnational migration, and family relations, *Gender and Society*, *27*(4), 469–490.

99 Peter, Transnational family ties; Zelizer, V. (2010), *Economic lives: How culture shapes the economy*, Princeton University Press.

100 "Each script specifies, at a variable level of detail, the transaction's constituent roles, actions, and statuses, and the relations between these elements. People engage scripts in flexible ways to make sense of and direct specific and recurring remittance transactions." Carling, J. (2014), Scripting remittances: Making sense of money transfers in transnational relationships, *International Migration Review*, *48*, S221.

101 For example, in a study of remittances to Honduras, McKenzie and Menjívar (2011) found that migrant husbands viewed their remittances as an act of caring for the family, whereas their wives considered the remittances as an act of obligation by their husbands. Similarly, Thai (2014) observes that male Vietnamese immigrants in the United States perceive their remittances as a means to demonstrate economic success, whereas their female counterparts view remittances as resources to improve the well-being of their families left behind in Vietnam.

102 Levitt, *Transnational villagers*; Smith, M. P., & Guarnizo, L. (1998), *Transnationalism from below*, University of California Press.

103 Abdin, Z. U., & Erdal, M. B. (2016), Remittance-sending among Pakistani taxi-drivers in Barcelona and Oslo: Implications of migration-trajectories and the protracted electricity crisis in Pakistan, *Migration and Development*, *5*(3): 378–393; Abrego, *Sacrificing families*; Åkesson, Remittances and relationships; Carling, J. (2008), The human dynamics of migrant transnationalism, *Ethnic and Racial Studies*, *31*(8), 1452–1477; Dreby, *Divided by borders*; Gardner, K. (1995), *Global migrants, local lives: Travel and transformation in rural Bangladesh*, Clarendon Press; Johnson, P., and Stoll, K. (2008), Remittance patterns of Southern Sudanese refugee men: Enacting the global breadwinner role, *Family Relations*, *57*, 431–443; Landolt, P. (2001), Salvadoran economic transnationalism: Embedded strategies for household maintenance, immigrant incorporation, and entrepreneurial expansion, *Global Networks*, *1*(3), 217–242; Levitt, *Transnational villagers*; Lindley A. (2009),

The early-morning phonecall: Remittances from a refugee diaspora perspective, *Journal of Ethnic and Migration Studies*, *35*(8), 1315–1334; Mazzucato, V. (2008), The double engagement: Transnationalism and integration. Ghanaian migrants' lives between Ghana and the Netherlands, *Journal of Ethnic and Migration Studies*, *34*(2), 199–216; Paerregaard, *Return to sender*; Parreñas, *Servants of globalization*; Smith, R. C. (2006), *Mexican New York: Transnational lives of new immigrants*, University of California Press; Singh, S., & Robertson, S. (2012), Transnational family money: Remittances, gifts and inheritance, *Journal of Intercultural Studies*, *33*(5), 475–492; Spener, D. (2009), *Clandestine crossings: Migrants and coyotes on the Texas–Mexico border*, Cornell University Press; Thai, *Insufficient funds*.

104 Werbner, P. S. (1990), *The migration process: Capital, gifts and offerings among British Pakistanis*, Berg Publishers.
105 Gardner, *Global migrants, local lives*.
106 Thai, *Insufficient funds*.
107 Waldinger, R. (2015), *The cross-border connection: Immigrants, emigrants, and their homelands*, Harvard University Press.
108 Burawoy, Functions and reproduction of migrant labor.

Chapter 1   A Rush to the East

1 Gardner, K. (1995), *Global migrants, local lives: Travel and transformation in rural Bangladesh*, Clarendon Press.
2 Clark, R. L., et al. (2010), Population decline, labor force stability, and the future of the Japanese economy, *European Journal of Population*, *26*(2), 207–227.
3 Goodman, R. (2004), [Review of the books *Brokered homeland: Japanese Brazilian migrants in Japan*, by J. Hotaka Roth, and *Strangers in the ethnic homeland: Japanese Brazilian return migration in transnational perspective*, by T. Tsuda], *The Journal of Japanese Studies*, *30*(2), 465–471.
4 Higuchi, N. (2007), Remittances, investments and social mobility among Bangladeshi and Iranian returnees from Japan, in *Proceedings for the 8th Asia and Pacific Migration Research Network Conference on Migration, Development and Poverty Reduction* (pp. 145–158), Asia Pacific Migration Research Network; Okabe, M. (2011), The "outside-in"—An overview of Japanese immigration policy from the perspective of international relations, in E. Guild & S. Mantu (Eds.), *Constructing and imagining labour migration: Perspectives of control from five continents* (pp. 189–204), Ashgate.
5 Mahmood, R. A. (1994), Adaptation to a new world: Experience of Bangladeshis in Japan, *International Migration*, *32*(4), 513–532. However, the community leaders and long-term Bangladeshi migrants reported a much higher number, over 100,000.
6 Higuchi, Remittances, investments and social mobility.
7 Mahmood, Adaptation to a new world.
8 Fee, L. K., & Rahman, M. (2006), International labor recruitment: Channeling Bangladeshi migrants to East and Southeast Asia, *Asia-Pacific Population Journal*, *21*(1), 85–107; Mahmud, H. (2013), Enemy or ally: Migrants, intermediaries and the state in Bangladeshi migration to Japan and the United States, *Migration and Development*, *2*(1), 1–15.
9 Mahmood, R. A. (1995), Data on migration from Bangladesh, *Asian and Pacific Migration Journal*, *4*(4), 531–541.
10 Hotaka Roth, J. (2002), *Brokered homeland: Japanese Brazilian migrants in Japan*, Cornell University Press; Tsuda, T. (2003), *Strangers in the ethnic homeland:*

Japanese Brazilian return migration in transnational perspective, Columbia University Press.

11 Tsuda, *Strangers in the ethnic homeland*.

12 Liu-Farrer, G. (2011), *Labour migration from China to Japan: International students, transnational migrants*, Nissan Institute, Routledge Japanese Studies, Book 77.

13 Mahmud, Enemy or ally.

14 Massey, D. S., et al. (1993), Theories of international migration: A review and appraisal, *Population and Development Review, 19*(3), 431–466.

15 Mahmud, Enemy or ally.

16 Elrick, T., & Lewandowska, E. (2008), Matching and making labour demand and supply: Agents in Polish migrant networks of domestic elderly care in Germany and Italy, *Journal of Ethnic and Migration Studies, 34*, 717–734; Spaan, E. (1994), Taikongs and calos: The role of middlemen and brokers in Javanese international migration, *International Migration Review, 28*(1), 93–113.

17 Embassy of Japan in Bangladesh, (2019), *Statistical information on Bangladeshi students*, retrieved June 21, 2023, from https://www.bd.emb-japan.go.jp/itpr_en /statisticalinfo.html.

18 Bangladesh Bank, *Wage earners remittance inflows*, retrieved June 21, 2023, from https://www.bb.org.bd/en/index.php/econdata/wagermidtl.

19 Mahmud, H. (2016), Impact of the destination state on migrants' remittances: A study of remitting among Bangladeshi migrants in the USA, the UAE and Japan, *Migration and Development, 5*(1), 79–98.

20 Mahmood, Adaptation to a new world; Mahmood, Data on migration from Bangladesh.

21 Massey, D. S., et al. (1994), An evaluation of international migration theory: The North American case, *Population and Development Review, 20*(4), 699–751; Lucas, R.E.B., & Stark, O. (1985), Motivations to remit: Evidence from Botswana, *The Journal of Political Economy, 93*(5), 901–918.

22 Burawoy, M. (1976), The functions and reproduction of migrant labor: Comparative material from Southern Africa and the United States, *American Journal of Sociology, 81*(5), 1050–1087.

23 Walzer, M. (1983), *Spheres of justice: A defense of pluralism and equality*, Basic Books.

24 Babar, Z. (2014), The cost of belonging: Citizenship construction in the state of Qatar, *The Middle East Journal, 68*(3): 403–420; Vora, N., & Koch, N. (2015), Everyday inclusions: Rethinking ethnocracy, *kafala*, and belonging in the Arabian Peninsula, *Studies in Ethnicity and Nationalism, 15*(3), 540–552.

25 Fernandez, B. (2013), Traffickers, brokers, employment agents, and social networks: The regulation of intermediaries in the migration of Ethiopian domestic workers to the Middle East, *International Migration Review, 47*(4), 814–843; Pande, A. (2017), Mobile masculinities: Migrant Bangladeshi men in South Africa, *Gender and Society, 31*(3), 383–406; Jureidini, R. (2010), Trafficking and contract migrant workers in the Middle East, *International Migration, 48*, 142–163.

26 Liu-Farrer, *Labour Migration from China to Japan*; Mahmood, R. A. (1991), International migration for employment: Experiences of Bangladeshi returned migrants from Japan, *The Bulletin of the Department of Sociology, Meisei Univ., 13*, 69–83.

27 Rodrik, D. (2011), *The globalization paradox: Democracy and the future of the world economy*, W. W Norton & Co.

28 Friedman, T. L. (2000), *The Lexus and the olive tree: Understanding globalization*, Farrar, Straus and Giroux.

29 Soysal, Y. N. (1994), *Limits of citizenship: Migrants and postnational membership in Europe*, University of Chicago Press.

30 Batalova, J. (2022, July 21), *Top statistics on global migration and migrants*, Migration Policy Institute, https://www.migrationpolicy.org/article/top-statistics-global-migration-migrants.

31 Zolberg, A. (1999), Matters of state: Theorizing immigration policy, in C. Hirschman, P. Kasinitz, & J. Dewind (Eds.), *The handbook of international migration: The American Experience* (pp. 71–93), Russell Sage Foundation.

32 Seol, D.-H., & Skrentny, J. D. (2009), Why is there so little migrant settlement in East Asia? *International Migration Review*, *43*, 578–620; Shipper, A. W. (2002), The political construction of foreign workers in Japan, *Critical Asian Studies*, *34*(1), 41–68; Tseng, Y., & Wang, H. (2011), Governing migrant workers at a distance: Managing the temporary status of guestworkers in Taiwan, *International Migration*, *51*(4), 1–19.

33 Castles, S. (2011), Migration, crisis, and the global labour market, *Globalizations*, 8(3), 311–324; Munck, R. (2008), Globalisation, governance and migration: An introduction, *Third World Quarterly*, *29*, 1227–1246; Neumayer, E. (2006), Unequal access to foreign spaces: How states use visa restrictions to regulate mobility in a globalized world, *Transactions of the Institute of British Geographers*, *31*, 72–84.

34 Brownell, P. B. (2010), Wage differences between temporary and permanent immigrants, *International Migration Review*, *44*, 593–614; Markova, E., & Reilly, B. (2007), Bulgarian migrant remittances and legal status: Some micro-level evidence from Madrid, *South-Eastern Europe Journal of Economics*, *5*, 55–69; Steinhardt, M. F., & Wedemeier, J. (2012), The labor market performance of naturalized immigrants in Switzerland—New findings from the Swiss labor force survey, *Journal of International Migration and Integration*, *13*, 223–242.

35 Kossoudji, S. A., & Cobb-Clark, D. A. (2002), Coming out of the shadows: Learning about legal status and wages from the legalized population, *Journal of Labor Economics*, *20*, 598–628.

36 DeVoretz, D. J., & Pivnenko, S. (2005), The economic causes and consequences of Canadian citizenship, *Journal of International Migration and Integration*, *6*, 435–468.

37 Mahmood, Adaptation to a new world; Mahmud, Enemy or ally.

38 Mahmud, Enemy or ally.

39 Hernandez-Leon, R. (2008), *Metropolitan migrants: The migration of urban Mexicans to the United States*, University of California Press; Okabe, M. (2011), The "outside-in"—an overview of Japanese immigration policy from the perspective of international relations, in E. Guild & S. Mantu (Eds.), *Constructing and imagining labour migration: Perspectives of control from five continents* (pp. 189–204), Ashgate.

40 Hollifield, J. F. (2004), The emerging migration state, *International Migration Review*, *38*(3), 885–912.

41 Mahmud, H. (2016), Impact of the destination state on migrants' remittances: A study of remitting among Bangladeshi migrants in the USA, the UAE and Japan, *Migration and Development*, *5*(1), 79–98.

42 Vera-Sanso, P. (2005), "They don't need it, and I can't give it": Filial support in South India, in P. Kreager & E. Schröder-Butterfill, (Eds.), *Ageing without children: European and Asian perspectives on elderly access to support networks* (pp. 77–105), Berghahn Books.

43 Belanger, D., & Rahman, M. (2013), Migrating against all the odds: International labour migration of Bangladeshi women. *Current Sociology*, *61*(3), 356–373;

Dannecker, P. (2005), Transnational migration and the transformation of gender relations: The case of Bangladeshi labour migrants, *Current Sociology*, *53*(4), 655–674; Oishi, N. (2005), *Women in motion: Globalization, state policies, and labor migration in Asia*, Stanford University Press.

44 Hotaka Roth, *Brokered homeland*; Tsuda, *Strangers in the ethnic homeland*.

45 It should be noted that the number of Bangladeshi men married to Japanese women was very small, perhaps less than a few hundred, as one community leader told me.

46 Casual conversation.

47 Burgess, C. (2004), (Re)constructing identities: International marriage migrants as potential agents of social change in a globalising Japan, *Asian Studies Review*, *28*(3), 223–242; Piper, N. (2003), Wife or worker? Worker or wife? Marriage and cross-border migration in contemporary Japan, *Population, Space and Place*, *9*(6), 457–469.

48 Piper, N., & Roces, M. (2003), *Wife or worker: Asian women and migration*, Rowman & Littlefield.

49 Rahman, M. M., Giedraitis, V. R., & Akhtar, T. M. (2013), The social sanction of divorce: Who ultimately pays the social costs of its adverse effects? *Sociology and Anthropology*, *1*(1), 26–33; Khaleque, A. (2011), An overview of the effects of divorce on culture and society within Bangladesh, in R. E. Emery (Ed.), *Cultural sociology of divorce: An encyclopedia*, SAGE Publications.

50 Abrego, L. (2014), *Sacrificing families: Navigating laws, labor, and love across borders*, Stanford University Press; Castañeda, E. (2018), *A place to call home: Immigrant exclusion and urban belonging in New York, Paris, and Barcelona*, Stanford University Press; Paul, A. M. (2015), Negotiating migration, performing gender, *Social Forces*, *94*(1), 271–293; Smith, R. C. (2006), *Mexican New York: Transnational lives of new immigrants*, University of California Press; Thai, H. C. (2014), *Insufficient funds: The culture of money in low-wage transnational families*, Stanford University Press; Vora, N. (2013), *Impossible citizens: Dubai's Indian diaspora*, Duke University Press.

51 Charsley, K. (2005), Vulnerable brides and transnational *Ghar Damads*: Gender, risk and "adjustment" among Pakistani marriage migrants to Britain, *Indian Journal of Gender Studies*, *12*(2&3), 381–406; Chopra, R. (2014), Dependent husbands: Reflections on marginal masculinities, in U. Skoda, K. B. Nielsen, & M. Q. Fibiger (Eds.), *Navigating social exclusion and inclusion in contemporary India and beyond: Structures, agents, practices* (pp. 41–54), Anthem Press; Ellickson, J. (1972), Islamic institutions: Perception and practice in a village in Bangladesh, *Contributions to Indian Sociology*, *6*(1), 1–27.

52 Mahmud, H. (2014), "It's my money": Social class and the perception of remittances among Bangladeshi migrants in Japan, *Current Sociology*, *62*(3), 418–430.

53 The Japanese phrase *benkyo wa kankeinai* is apt here. Roughly translated, it means "I don't care."

54 Parreñas, R. S. (2010), Homeward bound: The circular migration of entertainers between Japan and the Philippines, *Global Networks*, *10*(3), 301–323.

55 Shipper, Political construction of foreign workers.

56 Manzenreiter, W. (2017), Living under more than one sun: The Nikkei diaspora in the Americas, *Contemporary Japan*, *29*(2), 193–213.

57 Hotaka Roth, *Brokered homeland*; Tsuda, *Strangers in the ethnic homeland*.

58 Tsuda, *Strangers in the ethnic homeland*.

59 Tsuda, T. (2010), Ethnic return migration and the nation-state: Encouraging the diaspora to return "home," *Nations and Nationalism*, *16*(4), 616–636.

60 Sasaki, K. (2013), To return or not to return: The changing meaning of mobility among Japanese Brazilians, 1908–2010, in B. Xiang, B.S.A. Yeoh, and M. Toyota (Eds.), *Return: Nationalizing transnational mobility in Asia* (pp. 21–38), Duke University Press.

Chapter 2   Narratives of Remittance from Japan

1 Alpes, M. J. (2014), Imagining a future in "bush": Migration aspirations at times of crisis in Anglophone Cameroon, *Identities*, 21(3), 259–274; Carling, J. R. (2002), Migration in the age of involuntary immobility: Theoretical reflections and Cape Verdean experiences, *Journal of Ethnic and Migration Studies*, 28(1), 5–42; Castles, S., De Haas, H., & Miller, M. J. (2014), *The age of migration: International population movements in the modern world*, Guilford Press; Creighton, M. J. (2013), The role of aspirations in domestic and international migration, *The Social Science Journal*, 50(1), 79–88; Crivello, G. (2015), "There's no future here": The time and place of children's migration aspirations in Peru, *Geoforum*, 62, 38–46; De Haas, H. (2010), The internal dynamics of migration processes: A theoretical inquiry, *Journal of Ethnic and Migration Studies*, 36(10), 1587–1617.

2 Collins, F. L. (2018), Desire as a theory for migration studies: Temporality, assemblage and becoming in the narratives of migrants, *Journal of Ethnic and Migration Studies*, 44(6), 964–980.

3 Mahmud, H. (2014), "It's my money": Social class and the perception of remittances among Bangladeshi migrants in Japan, *Current Sociology*, 62(3), 412–430; Shipper (2002), The political construction of foreign workers in Japan, *Critical Asian Studies*, 34(1), 41–68.

4 Cortazzi, M. (2001), *Narrative analysis in ethnography*, in P. Atkinson, A. Coffey, S. Delamont, J. Lofland, & L. Lofland (Eds), *Handbook of ethnography* (pp. 384–394), SAGE Publications; Riessman, C. K. (1993), *Narrative analysis*, Vol. 30 of SAGE Qualitative Research Methods Series, SAGE Publications.

5 While all Bangladeshi migrants shared the belief that sons should financially support their parents, this does not mean that all sons would send remittance. I observed a few migrants who did not send money to their parents and offered various reasons for doing so.

6 Amin and others like him would use informal channels called *hundi* to send money home.

7 Mahmud, Social class and perception of remittances.

8 Liu-Farrer, G. (2009), Educationally channeled international labor mobility: Contemporary student migration from China to Japan, *International Migration Review*, 43(1), 178–204.

9 I have discussed this in detail in Mahmud, Social class and perception of remittances. and Mahmud (2017), Social determinants of remitting practices among Bangladeshi migrants in Japan, *Sociological Perspectives*, 60(1), 95–112.

10 Gouldner, A. (1960), The norm of reciprocity: A preliminary consideration, *American Sociological Review*, 25(2), 161–178.

11 Ali, S. (2007), "Go West young man": The culture of migration among Muslims in Hyderabad, India, *Journal of Ethnic and Migration Studies*, 33(1), 37–58.

12 See, for example, Siddiqui, T. (2003, June), *Migration as a livelihood strategy of the poor: The Bangladesh case* [Paper presentation], Regional Conference on Migration, Development & Pro-Poor Policy Choices in Asia 2003, Dhaka, Bangladesh; Rashid, S. R. (2016), *Uncertain tomorrows: Livelihoods, capital and risk in labour migration from Bangladesh*, University Press Limited; Sikder, M.J.U., & V. Higgins. (2017),

Remittances and social resilience of migrant households in rural Bangladesh, *Migration and Development*, *6*(2), 253–275.

13 For more about Japanese immigration policy in different contexts, see Mahmud, Social class and perception of remittances; Hotaka Roth, J. (2002), *Brokered homeland: Japanese Brazilian migrants in Japan*, Cornell University Press.

14 Rahman, M. M., & Yeoh, B. S. (2008), The social organization of *hundi*: Channelling migrant remittances from East and South-East Asia to Bangladesh, *Asian Population Studies*, *4*(1), 5–29; Sharma, D. (2006), Historical traces of *hundi*, sociocultural understanding, and criminal abuses of *hawala*, *International Criminal Justice Review*, *16*(2), 99–121.

15 Liu-Farrer, Educationally channeled international labor mobility; Liu-Farrer, (2011), *Labor migration from China to Japan: International students, transnational migrants*, Nissan Institute, Routledge Japanese Studies Book 77.

16 The normal practice in Bangladesh is that the family chooses a wife for the son. See Ballard, R. (1982), South Asian families, in R. Rapoport & M. Fogarty (Eds.), *Families in Britain* (pp. 1–18), Routledge and Kegan Paul.

17 Mahmud, Social class and perception of remittances.

18 Mahmud, Social class and perception of remittances.

19 Puppa, F. D., & King, R. (2019), The new "twice migrants": Motivations, experiences and disillusionments of Italian-Bangladeshis relocating to London, *Journal of Ethnic and Migration Studies*, *45*(11), 1936–1952.

20 Singh, S., Cabraal A., & Robertson, S. (2010), Remittance as a medium of relationships and belonging, in A. Babacan & S. Singh (Eds.), *Migration, belonging and the nation state* (pp. 85–104), Cambridge Scholars Publishing.

21 Paul, A. M. (2017), *Multinational maids: Stepwise migration in a global labor market*, Cambridge University Press.

22 Haines, D. W., Minami, M., & Yamashita, S. (2007), Transnational migration in East Asia: Japan in comparative focus, *International Migration Review*, *41*(4), 963–967.

23 Thai, H. C. (2012), The dual roles of transnational daughters and transnational wives: Monetary intentions, expectations and dilemmas, *Global Networks, 12*(2), 216–232.

24 Ali, S. (2007), "Go West young man"; Cohen, J. C. (2004), *The culture of migration in Southern Mexico*, University of Texas Press; Cohen, J. C., & Sirkeci, I. (2011), *Cultures of migration: The global nature of contemporary mobility*, University of Texas Press; Kandel, W., & Massey, D. S. (2002), The culture of Mexican migration: A theoretical and empirical analysis, *Social Forces*, *80*(3), 981–1004.

25 Burawoy, M. (1976), The functions and reproduction of migrant labor: Comparative material from Southern Africa and the United States, *American Journal of Sociology*, *81*(5), 1050–1087; Glytsos, N. P. (1997), Remitting behaviour of "temporary" and "permanent" migrants: The case of Greeks in Germany and Australia, *Labor*, *11*(3), 409–435; Pinger, P. (2010), Come Back or Stay? Spend Here or There? Return and remittances: The case of Moldova, *International Migration*, *48*(5), 142–173.

26 Thränhardt, D. (1999), Closed doors, back doors, side doors: Japan's nonimmigration policy in comparative perspective, *Journal of Comparative Policy Analysis: Research and Practice*, *1*(2), 203–223.

Chapter 3   The American Dream

1 Winning the DV-1 lottery does not guarantee everyone a U.S. visa. Only about half of the winners will finally get their immigration visa, which puts all the winners under severe pressure to complete their visa application quickly and flawlessly.

2 Rodriguez, C. E. (2018), *America, as seen on TV: How television shapes immigrant expectations around the globe*, New York University Press.

3 Pesando, L. M., et al. (2020), The internetization of international migration, *Population and Development Review*, *47*(1), 70–111.

4 Bald, V. (2013), *Bengali Harlem and the lost histories of South Asian America*, Harvard University Press.

5 Bald, *Bengali Harlem*, 198.

6 Hossain, N. (2017), *The aid lab: Understanding Bangladesh's unexpected success*, Oxford University Press; Kibria, N. (2011, August 9), *Working Hard for the money: Bangladesh faces challenges of large-scale labor migration*, Migration Policy Institute, https://www.migrationpolicy.org/article/working-hard-money-bangladesh-faces -challenges-large-scale-labor-migration.

7 Sawada, Y., Mahmud, M., & Kitano, N. (2018), *Economic and social development of Bangladesh*, Springer International Publishing.

8 Aswad, B. C., & Bilge, B. (1996), *Family and gender among American Muslims: Issues facing Middle Eastern immigrants and their descendants*, Temple University Press, 159.

9 Vaughan, J., & Huennekens, P. (2018, January), *Bangladesh: A case study in chain migration*, Center for Immigration Studies, https://cis.org/Report/Bangladesh -Case-Study-Chain-Migration.

10 Alamgir, M. (2023, May 11), Number of students studying abroad triples over 16 years. *University World News*, https://www.universityworldnews.com/post.php ?story=20230511115449218.

11 Bal, E. (2014), Yearning for faraway places: The construction of migration desires among young and educated Bangladeshis in Dhaka, *Identities*, *21*(3), 275–289.

12 Alamgir, M. (2018, August 31), Bangladeshi students heading for univs abroad on rise, *Daily New Age*, https://www.newagebd.net/article/49482/bangladeshi -students-heading-for-univs-abroad-on-rise.

13 Alamgir, Bangladeshi students heading for univs abroad.

14 Qayum, N. (2017, October 5), *Chasing the Dubai dream in Italy: Bangladeshi migration to Europe*, Migration Policy Institute, https://www.migrationpolicy.org /article/chasing-dubai-dream-italy-bangladeshi-migration-europe.

15 Chiang, S.-Y., & Leung, H. H. (2011), Making a home in US rural towns: The significations of home for Chinese immigrants' work, family, and settlement in local communities, *Community, Work & Family*, *14*(4), 469–486.

16 Massey, D. S. (1987), Understanding Mexican migration to the United States, *The American Journal of Sociology*, *92*(60), 1372–1403.

17 Logan, J. R., Alba, R. D., & Zhang, W. (2002), Immigrant enclaves and ethnic communities in New York and Los Angeles, *American Sociological Review*, *67*(2), 299–322.

18 Alba, R., & Logan, J. R. (1992), Assimilation and stratification in the homeowner-ship patterns of racial and ethnic groups, *International Migration Review*, 26, 1314–1341.

19 For instance, the high rate of homeownership among Chinese immigrants in California is because of peer pressure about owning a home as proof of settlement. See Painter, G., Yang, L. H., & Yu, Z. (2003), Heterogeneity in Asian American home-ownership: The impact of household endowments and immigrant status, *Urban Studies*, *40*(3), 505–530; Myers, D., & Lee, S. W. (1998), Temporal analysis of residential assimilation, *International Migration Review*, *32*(3), 593–625.

20 The idea of assimilation can be traced back to the 1920s Chicago School. It was conceptualized with a general optimism that immigrants would move upwards socially and outwards spatially, and would blend in culturally over time. For more on this, see Park, R., & Burgess, E. (1921), *Introduction to the science of sociology*, University of Chicago Press; Park, R. E. (1950), *Race and culture*, Free Press.

21 Alba, R., & Nee, V. (2003), *Remaking the American mainstream: Assimilation and contemporary immigration*, Harvard University Press.

22 Gordon, M. (1964), *Assimilation in American life: The role of race, religion and national origins*, Oxford University Press; Glazer, N., & Moynihan, D. (1970), *Beyond the melting pot: The Negroes, Puerto Ricans, Jews, Italians and Irish of New York City*, MIT Press; Alba, R., & Nee, V. (1997), Rethinking assimilation theory for a new era of immigration, *International Migration Review, 31*, 826–874; Portes, A., & Zhou, M. (1993), The new second generation: Segmented assimilation and its variants, *Annals of the American Academy of Political and Social Sciences, 530*, 74–96.

23 Portes & Zhou, The new second generation; Portes, A., & Rumbaut, R. (1996), *Immigrant America: A portrait*, University of California Press.

24 Schiller, N. G., Basch, L., & Blanc, C. S. (1995), From immigrant to transmigrant: Theorizing transnational migration, *Anthropological Quarterly, 68*(1), 48–63; Levitt, P. (2001), *The transnational villagers*, University of California Press; Smith, R. (2006), *Mexican New York: Transnational lives of new immigrants*, University of California Press.

25 Brubaker, R. (2001), The return of assimilation? Changing perspectives on immigration and its sequels in France, Germany, and the United States, *Ethnic and Racial Studies, 24*(4), 531–548.

26 Grzymala-Kazlowska, A. (2018), From connecting to social anchoring: Adaptation and "settlement" of Polish migrants in the UK, *Journal of Ethnic and Migration Studies, 44*(2), 252–269.

27 Toruńczyk-Ruiz, S., & Brunarska, Z. (2020), Through attachment to settlement: Social and psychological determinants of migrants' intentions to stay, *Journal of Ethnic and Migration Studies, 46*(15), 3191–3209.

28 De Haas, H., & Fokkema, T. (2011), The effects of integration and transnational ties on international return migration intentions, *Demographic Research, 25*, 755–782; Zhao, Y. (2002), Causes and consequences of return migration: Recent evidence from China, *Journal of Comparative Economics, 30*(2), 376–394.

29 De Vroome, T., & Van Tubergen, F. (2014), Settlement intentions of recently arrived immigrants and refugees in the Netherlands, *Journal of Immigrant & Refugee Studies, 12*(1), 47–66; Di Saint Pierre, F., Martinovic, B., & De Vroome, T. (2015), Return wishes of refugees in the Netherlands: The role of integration, host national identification and perceived discrimination, *Journal of Ethnic and Migration Studies, 41*(11), 1836–1857.

30 One of the oldest and largest ethnic stores/restaurants in LA.

31 Swadesh profile page, Yelp, retrieved July 5, 2014, from http://www.yelp.com/biz/swadesh-los-angeles?osq=Bangladeshi+Restaurant.

32 Redstone Akresh, I. (2006), Occupational mobility among legal immigrants to the United States, *International Migration Review, 40*(4), 854–884; Gans, H. J. (2009), First generation decline: Downward mobility among refugees and immigrants, *Ethnic and Racial Studies, 32*(9), 1658–1670; Salami, B., & Nelson, S. (2014), The downward occupational mobility of internationally educated nurses to domestic workers, *Nursing Enquiry, 21*(2), 153–161.

33 Beydoun, K. A. (2018), *American Islamophobia: Understanding the roots and rise of fear*, University of California Press; Love, E. (2017), Islamophobia and racism in America, in *Islamophobia and Racism in America* (pp. 83–116), New York University Press; Sabharwal, M., Becerra, A., & Oh, S. (2022), From the Chinese Exclusion Act to the COVID-19 Pandemic: A historical analysis of "otherness" experienced by Asian Americans in the United States, *Public Integrity, 24*(6), 535–549.

34 Giridharadas, A. (2014), *The true American: Murder and mercy in Texas*, W. W. Norton & Co.; Human Rights Watch & ACLU, (2022, August 8), *Racial discrimination in the United States*, https://www.hrw.org/report/2022/08/08/racial-discrimination-united-states/human-rights-watch/aclu-joint-submission; Al Jazeera, (2022, September 11), *Decades after 9/11, Muslims battle Islamophobia in US*, https://www.aljazeera.com/news/2022/9/11/decades-after-9-11-muslims-battle-islamophobia-in.

35 Lee, J., & Zhou, M. (2014), From unassimilable to exceptional: The rise of Asian Americans and "stereotype promise," *New Diversities, 16*(1), 7–22; Lee, J., & Zhou, M. (2017), Why class matters less for Asian-American academic achievement, *Journal of Ethnic and Migration Studies, 43*(14), 2316–2330.

36 Banerjee, P., & Rincón, L. (2019), Trouble in tech paradise, *Contexts, 18*(2), 24–29; Obinna, D. N. (2014), The challenges of American legal permanent residency for family- and employment-based petitioners, *Migration and Development, 3*(2), 272–284.

37 Axelsson, L., Malmberg, B., & Zhang, Q. (2017), On waiting, work-time and imagined futures: Theorising temporal precariousness among Chinese chefs in Sweden's restaurant industry, *Geoforum, 78*, 169–178.

38 The threshold is 15,000 immigrants per year over three successive years in 2009, 2010, and 2011.

Chapter 4 Narratives of Remittance from the United States

1 Sana, M. (2005), Buying membership in the transnational community: Migrant remittances, social status, and assimilation, *Population Research Policy Review, 24*, 231–261; Ali, S. (2007), "Go West young man": The culture of migration among Muslims in Hyderabad, India, *Journal of Ethnic and Migration Studies, 33*(1), 37–58.

2 Sociologist Max Weber is credited for introducing the ideal type as a method of investigation and explanation. Ideal types are determined by taking into account the real environment, but they also include choosing components that make the most sense individually or as a group. For instance, Weber's use of the ideal bureaucracy incorporates those elements of actual bureaucratic institutions that make sense as a cohesive means-end sequence. For more detail, see Hekman, S. J. (1983), Weber's ideal type: A contemporary reassessment, *Polity, 16*(1), 119–137.

3 Cho, E. Y. (2017), Revisiting ethnic niches: A comparative analysis of the labor market experiences of Asian and Latino undocumented young adults, *RSF: The Russell Sage Foundation Journal of the Social Sciences, 3*(4), 97–115; Waldinger, R. (1994), The making of an immigrant niche, *International Migration Review, 28*(1), 3–30.

4 Patel, V. V., Rajpathak, S., & Karasz, A. (2012), Bangladeshi immigrants in New York City: A community based health needs assessment of a hard to reach population, *Journal of Immigrant and Minority Health, 14*(5), 767–773.

5 Bangladesh Bank remittances data, https://www.bb.org.bd/en/index.php/econdata/wagermidtl.

6 Mahmud, H. (2016), Impact of the destination state on migrants' remittances: A study of remitting among Bangladeshi migrants in the USA, the UAE and Japan, *Migration and Development*, *5*(1), 79–98.

7 For details, see Mahmud, H. (2013), Enemy or ally: Migrants, intermediaries and the state in Bangladeshi migration to Japan and the United States, *Migration and Development*, *2*(1), 1–15.

8 Arther, W. B., & McNicoll, G. (1978), An analytical survey of population and development in Bangladesh, *Population and Development Review*, *4*(1), 23–80; Indra, D. M., & Buchignani, N. (1997), Rural landlessness, extended entitlements and inter-household relations in South Asia: A Bangladesh case, *The Journal of Peasant Studies*, *24*, 25–64; Kabir, Z. N., Szebehely, M., & Tishelman, C. (2002), Support in old age in the changing society of Bangladesh, *Ageing and Society*, *22*, 615–636.

9 Portes, A., & Zhou, M. (1993), The new second generation: Segmented assimilation and its variants, *The Annals of the American Academy of Political and Social Science*, *530*(1), 74–96; Alba, R., & Nee, V. (2003), *Remaking the American mainstream: Assimilation and contemporary immigration*, Harvard University Press.

10 Zhou, M., & Li, R. (2018), Remittances for collective consumption and social status compensation: Variations on transnational practices among Chinese international migrants, *International Migration Review*, *52*(1), 4–42; Thai, H. C. (2014), *Insufficient funds: The culture of money in low-wage transnational families*, Stanford University Press.

11 One of the ethnic restaurants in Little Bangladesh.

12 Boccagni, P. (2017), *Migration and the search for home: Mapping domestic space in migrants' everyday lives*, Palgrave.

13 Wise, J. M. (2000), Home: Territory and identity, *Cultural Studies*, *14*(2), 299.

14 Kasinitz, P., Mollenkopf, J., & Waters, M. C. (2002), Becoming American/ becoming New Yorkers: Immigrant incorporation in a majority minority city, *International Migration Review*, *36*(4), 1020–1036.

15 Zhou, M. (2009), How neighbourhoods matter for immigrant children: The formation of educational resources in Chinatown, Koreatown and Pico Union, Los Angeles, *Journal of Ethnic and Migration Studies*, *35*(7), 1153–1179.

Chapter 5 Going Global, Coming Home

1 Åkesson, L. (2011), Remittances and relationships: Exchange in Cape Verdean transnational families, *Ethnos*, *76*(3), 326–347; Mazzucato, V. (2011), Reverse remittances in the migration–development nexus: Two-way flows between Ghana and the Netherlands, *Population, Space and Place*, *17*(5), 454–468; Erdal, M. B. (2014), The social dynamics of remittance-receiving in Pakistan: Agency and opportunity among non-migrants in a transnational social field, in G. J. Ran & L. S. Liu (Eds.), *Migrant remittances in South Asia: Social, economic and political implications* (pp. 115–134), Springer; Ran, G. J., & Liu, L. S. (2023), Re-constructing reverse family remittances: The case of new Chinese immigrant families in New Zealand, *Journal of Ethnic and Migration Studies*, *49*(1), 313–331.

2 Afsar, R. (2003, June 22–24), *Internal migration and the development nexus: The case of Bangladesh* [Paper presentation], Regional Conference on Migration, Development & Pro-Poor Policy Choices in Asia 2003, Dhaka, Bangladesh; Ibrahim, F. N., & Ruppert, H. (1991), The role of rural-rural migration as a survival strategy in the Sahelian Zone of the Sudan—A case-study in Burush, N Darfur, *GeoJournal*, *25*(1),

31–38; Konseiga, A. (2007), Household migration decision as survival strategy: The case of Burkina Faso, *Journal of African Economies*, *16*(2), 198–223; Siddiqiu, T. (2003, June), *Migration as a livelihood strategy for the poor: The Bangladesh case* [Paper presentation], Regional Conference on Migration, Development & Pro-Poor Policy Choices in Asia 2003, Dhaka, Bangladesh; Sikder, J. U., Higgins, V., & Ballis, P. H. (2017), *Remittance income and social resilience among migrant households in rural Bangladesh*, Palgrave Macmillan; Rashid, S. R. (2016), *Uncertain tomorrows: Livelihoods, capital and risk in labour migration from Bangladesh*, University Press Limited.

3 Grigg, D. B. (1980), *Population growth and agrarian change*, Cambridge University Press; Guest, P. (1989), *Labor allocation and rural development: Migration in four Javanese villages*, Westview Press; Wood, C. H. (1981), Structural changes and household strategies: A conceptual framework for the study of rural migration, *Human Organization*, *40*(4), 338–344.

4 Afsar, *Internal migration and the development nexus*; Chaudhury, R. H., & Curlin, G. C. (1975), Dynamics of migration in a rural area of Bangladesh, *Bangladesh Development Studies*, *3*(2), 181–230.

5 Bernzen, A., Jenkins, J. C., & Braun, B. (2019), Climate change-induced migration in coastal Bangladesh? A critical assessment of migration drivers in rural households under economic and environmental stress, *Geosciences*, *9*(1), 51, https://doi.org/10.3390/geosciences9010051; Carrico, A. R., & Donato, K. (2019), Extreme weather and migration: Evidence from Bangladesh, *Population & Environment*, *41*(1), 1–31; Islam, M. R. (2018), Climate change, natural disasters and socioeconomic livelihood vulnerabilities: Migration decision among the Char Land people in Bangladesh, *Social Indicators Research*, *136*(2), 575–593.

6 Gray, C., & Mueller, V. (2012), Natural disasters and population mobility in Bangladesh, *Proceedings of the National Academy of Sciences of the United States of America*, *109*(16), 6000–6005; Kabir, M. E., et al. (2018), Seasonal drought thresholds and internal migration for adaptation: Lessons from Northern Bangladesh, in M. Hossain, R. Hales, & T. Sarker (Eds.), *Pathways to a sustainable economy* (pp. 167–189), Springer.

7 Bald, V. (2013), *Bengali Harlem and the lost histories of South Asian America*, Harvard University Press.

8 Alexander, C., Chatterji, J., & Jalais, A. (2015), *The Bengal diaspora: Rethinking Muslim migration*, Routledge Contemporary South Asia Series.

9 Gardner, K. (1995), *Global migrants, local lives: Travel and transformation in rural Bangladesh*, Clarendon Press.

10 The British colonial government received revenue from the landlords known as zamindars, who gathered rent from the peasants.

11 World Bank, (1981), *Labor migration from Bangladesh to the Middle East*, World Bank Staff Working Paper No. 454, https://documents1.worldbank.org/curated/en/750081468768650896/pdf/multi-page.pdf.

12 International Organization for Migration (IOM), (2019), *Bangladesh Annual Migration Report 2017*, Dhaka, Bangladesh, https://publications.iom.int/system/files/pdf/annual_migration_report_2017.pdf.

13 Mahmud, H. (2013), Enemy or ally: Migrants, intermediaries and the state in Bangladeshi migration to Japan and the United States, *Migration and Development*, *2*(1), 1–15.

14 See Mahmud, H. (2014), "It's my money": Social class and the perception of remittances among Bangladeshi migrants in Japan, *Current Sociology*, *62*(3), 412–430.

15 Mahmud, Enemy or ally.

16 Ahsan Ullah, A.K.M. (2011), Dynamics of remittance practices and development: Bangladeshi overseas migrants, *Development in Practice*, *21*(8), 1153–1167; Gardner, *Global migrants, local lives*; Mahmud, Social class and perception of remittances; Mahmud, H. (2017), Social determinants of remitting practices among Bangladeshi migrants in Japan, *Sociological Perspectives*, *60*(1), 95–112; Rashid, *Uncertain tomorrows*; Stevanovic-Fenn, N. (2012), *Remittances and the moral economies of Bangladeshi New York immigrants in light of the economic crisis* [Doctoral dissertation], Columbia University.

17 Stevanovic-Fenn (2012) observes that among Bangladeshi immigrants in New York, a person who does not send money to the family in Bangladesh is regarded as a bad person and loses their reputation in the community; this informal public shaming enforces the cultural norm.

18 King, R., Castaldo, A., & Vullnetari, J. (2011), Gendered relations and filial duties along the Greek-Albanian remittance corridor, *Economic Geography*, *87*(4), 393–419; Yeoh, B.S.A., et al. (2013), Between two families: The social meaning of remittances for Vietnamese marriage migrants in Singapore, *Global Networks*, *13*(4), 441–458.

19 Åkesson, L. (2009), Remittances and inequality in Cape Verde: The impact of changing family organization, *Global Networks*, *9*(3), 381–398; Lindley, A. (2009), The early-morning phonecall: Remittances from a refugee diaspora perspective, *Journal of Ethnic and Migration Studies*, *35*(8), 1315–1334; Yeoh, et al., Between two families; Thai, H. C. (2014), *Insufficient funds: The culture of money in low-wage transnational families*, Stanford University Press.

20 Thompson, E. P. (1991), *The making of the English working class*, Penguin Books.

21 Scott, J. C. (1976), *The moral economy of the peasant: Subsistence and rebellion in Southeast Asia*, Yale University Press.

22 Edelman, M. (2005), Bringing the moral economy back in . . . to the study of 21st-century transnational peasant movements, *American Anthropologist*, *107*(3), 332.

23 Åkesson, Remittances and inequality in Cape Verde; Mahmud, Social determinants of remitting practices.

24 King, R., & Vullnetari, J. (2009), The intersections of gender and generation in Albanian migration, remittances and transnational care, *Geografiska Annaler: Series B, Human Geography*, *91*(1), 19–38; Baldassar, L., et al. (2014), Transnational families, in J. Treas, J. Scott, & M. Richards (Eds.), *The Wiley Blackwell companion to the sociology of families* (pp. 155–175), Wiley; Isotalo, R. (2008), Transnational family dynamics, second generation and the ties that flex: Palestinian migrants between the United States and the West Bank, *Hawwa*, *6*(1), 102–123.

25 Ikuomola, A. D. (2015), Unintended consequences of remittance: Nigerian migrants and intra-household conflicts, *SAGE Open*, https://doi.org/10.1177/2158244015605353.

26 Stevanovic-Fenn, *Remittances and moral economies*.

27 Lindley, The early-morning phonecall.

28 Mahmud, Social class and perception of remittances; Peter, K. B. (2010), Transnational family ties, remittance motives, and social death among Congolese migrants: A socio-anthropological analysis, *Journal of Comparative Family Studies*, *41*(2), 225–243.

29 Åkesson, L., Remittances and relationships.

30 Gardner, *Global migrants, local lives*.

31 Mahmud, Social class and perception of remittances.

32 Abrego, L. (2014), *Sacrificing families: Navigating laws, labor, and love across borders*, Stanford University Press; Dreby, J. (2010), *Divided by borders: Mexican migrants and their children*, University of California Press.

33 Rozario, S. (2007), Outside the moral economy? Single female migrants and the changing Bangladeshi family, *The Australian Journal of Anthropology, 18*(2), 154–171.

34 Ikuomola, Unintended consequences of remittance.

35 Gardner, K. (2008), Keeping connected: Security, place and social capital in a Londoni village in Sylhet, *Journal of the Royal Anthropological Institute, 14*, 447–495.

36 Zhou, M., & Li, R. (2018), Remittances for collective consumption and social status compensation: Variations on transnational practices among Chinese international migrants, *International Migration Review, 52*(1), 4–42; Thai, *Insufficient funds.*

37 Basch, L., Schiller, N. G., & Blanc, C. S. (Eds.), (2005), *Nations unbound: Transnational projects, postcolonial predicaments, and deterritorialized nation-states*, Routledge; Levitt, P. (2001), *The transnational villagers*, University of California Press; Kibria, N. (2011, August 9), *Working hard for the money: Bangladesh faces challenges of large-scale labor migration*, Migration Policy Institute, https://www.migrationpolicy.org/article/working-hard-money-bangladesh-faces-challenges-large-scale-labor-migration; Smith, R. (2006), *Mexican New York: Transnational lives of new immigrants*, University of California Press.

38 Bernzen et al., Climate change-induced migration; Foner, N., & Dreby, J. (2011), Relations between the generations in immigrant families, *Annual Review of Sociology, 37*, 545–564; Rumbaut, R. G., & Portes, A. (2001), *Ethnicities: Children of immigrants in America*, University of California Press.

39 Espiritu, Y. (2009), Emotions, sex, and money: The lives of Filipino children of immigrants, in N. Foner (Ed.), *Across generations: Immigrant families in America* (pp. 47–71), New York University Press.

40 Zhou, M. (2007), Conflict, coping, and reconciliation: Intergenerational relations in Chinese immigrant families, in N. Foner (Ed.), *Across generations: Immigrant families in America* (pp. 21–46). New York University Press.

41 Kibria, N. (2009), "Marry into a good family": Transnational reproduction and intergenerational relations in Bangladeshi American families, in N. Foner (Ed.), *Across generations: Immigrant families in America* (pp. 98–113), New York University Press.

42 Kalmijn, M. (2019), Contact and conflict between adult children and their parents in immigrant families: Is integration problematic for family relationships? *Journal of Ethnic & Migration Studies, 45*(9), 1419–1438.

43 Zhou, M. (1997), Growing Up American: The challenge confronting immigrant children and children of immigrants, *Annual Review of Sociology, 23*, 63–95.

44 Nugent, J. (1985), The old-age security motive for fertility, *Population and Development Review, 11*(1), 75–97.

45 Choudhury, A. (1995), Families in Bangladesh, *Journal of Comparative Family Studies, 26*(1), 27–41.

46 Morshed, M. M. (2018), *Parenting, identity and culture in an era of migration and globalization: How Bangladeshi parents navigate and negotiate child-rearing practices in the USA* [Doctoral dissertation], University of Massachusetts Amherst.

47 Bennett, J. M. (2013), *Doing belonging: A sociological study of belonging in place as the outcome of social practices* [Doctoral dissertation], The University of Manchester.

48 Sen, A. (2016), Food, place, and memory: Bangladeshi fish stores on Devon Avenue, Chicago, *Food and Foodways, 24*(1–2), 67–88.

49 Kharel, D. (2016), From *Lahures* to global cooks: Network migration from the western hills of Nepal to Japan, *Social Science Japan Journal, 19*(2), 173–192.

50 Khondker, H. H. (2008), Bengali-speaking families in Singapore: Home, nation and the world, *International Migration*, 46(4), 177–198.

51 Savage, M., Bagnall, G., & Longhurst, B. (2005), *Globalization and belonging*, SAGE Publications.

52 Gaventa, J. (2003), Power after Lukes: An overview of theories of power since Lukes and their application to development, *Institute of Development Studies*, 8(11).

53 Sen, Food, place, and memory.

54 Favell, A. (2015), *Immigration, integration and mobility: New agendas in migration studies*, ECPR Press.

55 Meyer, S. (2020), "Home is where I spend my money": Testing the remittance decay hypothesis with ethnographic data from an Austrian-Turkish community, *Social Inclusion*, 8(1), p. 282.

56 Creese, G. (2019), "Where are you from?" Racialization, belonging and identity among second-generation African-Canadians, *Ethnic and Racial Studies*, 42(9), 1476–1494; Erel, U. (2011), Complex belongings: Racialization and migration in a small English city, *Ethnic and Racial Studies*, 34(12), 2048–2068; Korteweg, A. C. (2017), The failures of "immigrant integration": The gendered racialized production of non-belonging, *Migration Studies*, 5(3), 428–444; Onasch, E. A. (2017), Lessons on the boundaries of belonging: Racialization and symbolic boundary drawing in the French civic integration program, *Social Problems*, 64(4), 577–593; Ossipow, L., Counilh, A., & Chimienti, M. (2019), Racialization in Switzerland: Experiences of children of refugees from Kurdish, Tamil and Vietnamese backgrounds, *Comparative Migration Studies*, 7(1), article no. 19, https://doi.org/10.1186/s40878-019-0117-7.

57 Mahmud, Social class and perception of remittances; Mahmud, Enemy or ally.

58 Bun, C. K. (1997), A family affair: Migration, dispersal, and the emergent identity of the Chinese cosmopolitan, *Diaspora: A Journal of Transnational Studies*, 6(2), 195–213. This article shows that the patrilineal Chinese family decides on some members' migration to strengthen the family with resources and resilience. For other examples of this phenomenon, see Hugo, G. (1995), International labor migration and the family: Some observations from Indonesia, *Asian and Pacific Migration Journal*, 4(2–3), 273–301; Scott, S., & Cartledge, K. H. (2009), Migrant assimilation in Europe: A transnational family affair, *International Migration Review*, 43(1), 60–89; Eurenius, A. M. (2020), A family affair: Evidence of chain migration during the mass emigration from the county of Halland in Sweden to the United States in the 1890s, *Population Studies*, 74(1), 103–118.

Conclusion

1 Rodriguez, R. M. (2010), *Migrants for export: How the Philippine state brokers labor to the world*, University of Minnesota Press.

2 Gorski, P. S. (2013), What is critical realism? And why should you care? *Contemporary Sociology*, 42(5), 658–670; Iosifides, T. (2016), *Qualitative methods in migration studies: A critical realist perspective*, Routledge.

3 Jackson, M. (2013), *The wherewithal of life: Ethics, migration, and the question of well-being*, University of California Press, 3.

4 Levitt, P. (2004, October 1), *Transnational migrants: When "home" means more than one country*, Migration Policy Institute, https://www.migrationpolicy.org/article/transnational-migrants-when-home-means-more-one-country; Moskal, M. (2015), "When I think home I think family here and there": Translocal and social

ideas of home in narratives of migrant children and young people, *Geoforum*, *58*, 143–152.

5 Bauman, Z. (2001), Identity in the globalising world, *Social Anthropology*, *9*(2), 431.

6 Collins, F. L. (2018), Desire as a theory for migration studies: Temporality, assemblage and becoming in the narratives of migrants, *Journal of Ethnic and Migration Studies*, *44*(6), 968.

7 Wherry, F. F. (2017), How relational accounting matters, in N. Bandelj, F. F. Wherry, & V. A. Zelizer (Eds.), *Money talks: Explaining how money really works* (pp. 57–69), Princeton University Press.

References

Abdin, Z. U., & M. B. Erdal. (2016). Remittance-sending among Pakistani taxi-drivers in Barcelona and Oslo: Implications of migration-trajectories and the protracted electricity crisis in Pakistan. *Migration and Development, 5*(3), 378–393.

Abrego, L. J. (2009). Economic well-being in Salvadoran transnational families: How gender affects remittance practices. *Journal of Marriage and Family, 71*(4), 1070–1085.

Abrego, L. (2014.) *Sacrificing families: Navigating laws, labor, and love across borders.* Stanford University Press.

Adams, J. R. (2009). The determinants of international remittances in developing countries. *World Development, 37*(1), 93–103.

Afaha, J. S. (2013). Migration, remittance and development in origin countries: Evidence from Nigeria. *African Population Studies, 27*(1).

Afsar, R. (2003, June 22–24). *Internal migration and the development nexus: The case of Bangladesh* [Paper presentation]. Regional Conference on Migration, Development and Pro-Poor Policy Choices in Asia 2003, Dhaka, Bangladesh.

Ahsan Ullah, A.K.M. (2011). Dynamics of remittance practices and development: Bangladeshi overseas migrants. *Development in Practice, 21*(8), 1153–1167.

Åkesson, L. (2009). Remittances and inequality in Cape Verde: The impact of changing family organization. *Global Networks, 9*(3), 381–398.

Åkesson, L. (2011). Remittances and relationships: Exchange in Cape Verdean transnational families. *Ethnos, 76*(3), 326–347.

Alamgir, M. (2023, May 11). Number of students studying abroad triples over 16 years. *University World News,* https://www.universityworldnews.com/post.php?story=20230511115449218.

Alba, R., & Logan, J. R. (1992). Assimilation and stratification in the homeownership patterns of racial and ethnic groups. *International Migration Review, 26,* 1314–1341.

Alba, R., & Nee, V. (1997). Rethinking assimilation theory for a new era of immigration. *International Migration Review, 31,* 826–874.

Alba, R., & Nee, V. (2003). *Remaking the American mainstream: Assimilation and contemporary immigration.* Harvard University Press.

Aldous, J., & Klein, D. (1991). Sentiment and services: Models of intergenerational relationships in midlife. *Journal of Marriage and the Family, 53*, 595–608.

Alexander, C. J., Chatterji, J., & Jalais, A. (2015). *The Bengal diaspora: Rethinking Muslim migration*. Routledge.

Ali, S. (2007). "Go west young man": The culture of migration among Muslims in Hyderabad, India. *Journal of Ethnic and Migration Studies, 33*(1), 37–58.

Al Jazeera. (2022, September 11). *Decades after 9/11, Muslims battle Islamophobia in US*. https://www.aljazeera.com/news/2022/9/11/decades-after-9-11-muslims-battle -islamophobia-in.

Alpes, M. J. (2014). Imagining a future in "bush": Migration aspirations at times of crisis in Anglophone Cameroon. *Identities, 21*(3), 259–274.

Arestoff, F., Kuhn-Le Braz, M, & Mouhoud, E. M. (2016). Remittances behaviour of forced migrants in post-Apartheid South Africa. *The Journal of Development Studies, 52*(6), 824–837.

Arif, I., Raza, S. A., Friemann, A., & Suleman, M. T. (2019). The role of remittances in the development of higher education: Evidence from top remittance receiving countries. *Social Indicators Research, 141*(3), 1233–1243.

Arther, W. B., & G. McNicoll. (1978). An analytical survey of population and development in Bangladesh. *Population and Development Review, 4*(1), 23–80.

Arun, T., & Ulku, H. (2011). Determinants of remittances: The case of the South Asian community in Manchester. *Journal of Development Studies, 47*(6), 894–912.

Aswad, B. C., & Bilge, B. (1996), *Family and gender among American Muslims: Issues facing Middle Eastern immigrants and their descendants*. Temple University Press.

Austin, D. M. (1994). Altruism. *Social Service Review, 68*(3), 437–440.

Axelsson, L., Malmberg, B., & Zhang, Q. (2017). On waiting, work-time and imagined futures: Theorising temporal precariousness among Chinese chefs in Sweden's restaurant industry. *Geoforum, 78*, 169–178.

Babar, Z. (2014). The cost of belonging: Citizenship construction in the state of Qatar. *The Middle East Journal, 68*(3), 403–420.

Bal, E. (2014). Yearning for faraway places: The construction of migration desires among young and educated Bangladeshis in Dhaka. *Identities, 21*(3), 275–289.

Bald, V. (2013). *Bengali Harlem and the lost histories of South Asian America*. Harvard University Press.

Baldassar, L., Kilkey, M., Merla, L., & Wilding, R. (2014). Transnational families. In J. Treas, J. Scott, & M. Richards (Eds.), *The Wiley Blackwell companion to the sociology of families* (pp. 155–175). Wiley.

Ballard, R. (1982). South Asian families. In R. N. Rapoport, M. P. Fogarty, & R. Rapoport (Eds.), *Families in Britain* (pp. 1–18). Routledge and Kegan Paul.

Banerjee, P., & Rincón, L. (2019). Trouble in tech paradise. *Contexts, 18*(2), 24–29.

Bangladesh Bank. *Wage earners remittance inflows*. Retrieved June 21, 2023, from https:// www.bb.org.bd/en/index.php/econdata/wagermidtl.

Basch, L., Schiller, N. G., & Blanc, C. S. (Eds.). (2005). *Nations unbound: Transnational projects, postcolonial predicaments, and deterritorialized nation-states*. Routledge.

Batalova, J. (2022, July 21). *Top statistics on global migration and migrants*. Migration Policy Institute. https://www.migrationpolicy.org/article/top-statistics-global -migration-migrants.

Bauman, Z. (2001). Identity in the globalising world. *Social Anthropology, 9*(2), 121–129.

Belanger, D., & M. Rahman. (2013). Migrating against all the odds: International labour migration of Bangladeshi women. *Current Sociology, 61*(3), 356–373.

Bennett, J. M. (2013). *Doing belonging: A sociological study of belonging in place as the outcome of social practices*. Doctoral dissertation, The University of Manchester.

Bernzen, A., Jenkins, J. C., & Braun, B. (2019). Climate change-induced migration in coastal Bangladesh? A critical assessment of migration drivers in rural households under economic and environmental stress. *Geosciences, 9*(1), 51. https://doi.org/10.3390/geosciences9010051.

Beydoun, K. A. (2018). *American Islamophobia: Understanding the roots and rise of fear*. University of California Press.

Blue, S. A. (2004). State policy, economic crisis, gender, and family ties: Determinants of family remittances to Cuba. *Economic Geography, 80*(1), 63–82.

Boccagni, P. (2017). *Migration and the search for home: Mapping domestic space in migrants' everyday lives*. Palgrave MacMillan.

Boccagni, P. (2022). Homing: A category for research on space appropriation and "home-oriented" mobilities. *Mobilities, 17*(4), 585–601.

Brette, O. (2017). The vested interests and the evolving moral economy of the common people. *Journal of Economic Issues, 51*(2), 503–510.

Brownell, P. B. (2010). Wage differences between temporary and permanent immigrants. *International Migration Review, 44*, 593–614.

Brubaker, R. (2001). The return of assimilation? Changing perspectives on immigration and its sequels in France, Germany, and the United States. *Ethnic and Racial Studies, 24*(4), 531–548.

Bun, C. K. (1997). A family affair: Migration, dispersal, and the emergent identity of the Chinese cosmopolitan. *Diaspora: A Journal of Transnational Studies, 6*(2), 195–213.

Burawoy, M. (1976). The functions and reproduction of migrant labor: Comparative material from Southern Africa and the United States. *American Journal of Sociology, 81*(5), 1050–1087.

Bureau of Manpower, Employment and Training (BMET). (2018). *Overseas employment and remittances (1976–2018)*. http://www.old.bmet.gov.bd/BMET/stattisticalDataAction.

Burgess, C. (2004). (Re)constructing identities: International marriage migrants as potential agents of social change in a globalising Japan. *Asian Studies Review, 28*(3), 223–242.

Carling, J. (2002). Migration in the age of involuntary immobility: Theoretical reflections and Cape Verdean experiences. *Journal of Ethnic and Migration Studies, 28*(1), 5–42.

Carling, J. (2008). The determinants of migrant remittances. *Oxford Review of Economic Policy, 24*(3), 581–598.

Carling, J. (2008). The human dynamics of migrant transnationalism. *Ethnic and Racial Studies, 31*(8), 1452–1477.

Carling, J. (2014). Scripting remittances: Making sense of money transfers in transnational relationships. *International Migration Review, 48*, S218–S262.

Carrico, A. R., & Donato, K. (2019). Extreme weather and migration: Evidence from Bangladesh. *Population & Environment, 41*(1), 1–31.

Castañeda, E. (2018). *A place to call home: Immigrant exclusion and urban belonging in New York, Paris, and Barcelona*. Stanford University Press.

Castles, S. (2011). Migration, crisis, and the global labour market. *Globalizations, 8*(3), 311–324.

Castles, S., De Haas, H., & Miller, M. J. (2014). *The age of migration: International population movements in the modern world*. Guilford Press.

Chacko, E. (2020). Conspicuous consumption and philanthropy connections between Punjabi immigrants from the Doaba Region and their hometowns. *Economics and Business, 1,* 52–68.

Chapman, Tony. (2001). There is no place like home. *Theory, Culture and Society, 18*(6), 135–146.

Charsley, K. (2005). Vulnerable brides and transnational *ghar damads*: Gender, risk and "adjustment" among Pakistani marriage migrants to Britain. *Indian Journal of Gender Studies, 12*(2–3), 381–406.

Chaudhury, R. H., & Curlin, G. C. (1975). Dynamics of migration in a rural area of Bangladesh. *Bangladesh Development Studies, 3*(2), 181–230.

Chiang, S.-Y., & Leung, H. H. (2011). Making a home in US rural towns: The significations of home for Chinese immigrants' work, family, and settlement in local communities. *Community, Work & Family, 14*(4), 469–486.

Cho, E. Y. (2017). Revisiting ethnic niches: A comparative analysis of the labor market experiences of Asian and Latino undocumented young adults. *RSF: The Russell Sage Foundation Journal of the Social Sciences, 3*(4), 97–115.

Chopra, R. (2014). Dependent husbands: Reflections on marginal masculinities. In U. Skoda, K. B. Nielsen, & M. Q. Fibiger, *Navigating Social Exclusion and Inclusion in Contemporary India and Beyond: Structures, Agents, Practices* (pp. 41–54). Anthem Press.

Choudhury, A. (1995). Families in Bangladesh. *Journal of Comparative Family Studies, 26*(1), 27–41.

Clark, R. L., Ogawa, N., Kondo, M., & Matsukura, R. (2010). Population decline, labor force stability, and the future of the Japanese economy. *European Journal of Population, 26*(2), 207–227.

Cohen, J. C. (2004). *The culture of migration in Southern Mexico.* University of Texas Press.

Cohen, J. C., & Sirkeci, I. (2011). *Cultures of migration: The global nature of contemporary mobility.* University of Texas Press.

Cohen, J. H. (2011). Migration, remittances, and household strategies. *Annual Review of Anthropology, 40,* 103–114.

Collins, F. L. (2018). Desire as a theory for migration studies: Temporality, assemblage and becoming in the narratives of migrants. *Journal of Ethnic and Migration Studies, 44*(6), 964–980.

Connell, R. W. (2005). Hegemonic masculinity: Rethink the concept. *Gender and Society, 19*(6), 829–859.

Cortazzi, M. (2001). Narrative analysis in ethnography. In P. Atkinson, A. Coffey, S. Delamont, J. Lofland, & L. Lofland (Eds.), *Handbook of ethnography* (pp. 384–394). SAGE Publications.

Creese, G. (2019). "Where are you from?" Racialization, belonging and identity among second generation African-Canadians. *Ethnic and Racial Studies, 42*(9), 1476–1494.

Creighton, M. J. (2013). The role of aspirations in domestic and international migration. *The Social Science Journal, 50*(1), 79–88.

Crivello, G. (2015). "There's no future here": The time and place of children's migration aspirations in Peru. *Geoforum, 62,* 38–46.

Dannecker, P. (2005). Transnational migration and the transformation of gender relations: The case of Bangladeshi labour migrants. *Current Sociology, 53*(4), 655–674.

Datta, K., McIlwaine, C., Herbert, J., Evans, Y., May, J., & Wills, J. (2008). Mobile masculinities: Men, migration and low-paid work in London. *Geography, 10*(8), 853–873.

De Bruyn, T., & Kuddus, U. (2005). *Dynamics of remittance utilization in Bangladesh* (IOM Research Series, Vol. 18). International Organization for Migration.

De Haas, H. (2010). The internal dynamics of migration processes: A theoretical inquiry. *Journal of Ethnic and Migration Studies, 36*(10), 1587–1617.

De Haas, H., & Fokkema, T. (2011). The effects of integration and transnational ties on international return migration intentions. *Demographic Research, 25,* 755–782.

Deneulin, S. (2006). Individual well-being, migration remittances and the common good. *The European Journal of Development Research, 18*(1), 45–58.

DeVoretz, D. J., & Pivnenko, S. (2005). The economic causes and consequences of Canadian citizenship. *Journal of International Migration and Integration, 6,* 435–468.

De Vroome, T., & Van Tubergen, F. (2014). Settlement intentions of recently arrived immigrants and refugees in the Netherlands. *Journal of Immigrant & Refugee Studies, 12*(1), 47–66.

Dhakal, S., & Oli, S. (2020). The impact of remittance on consumption and investment: A case of Province Five of Nepal. *Quest Journal of Management and Social Sciences, 2*(1), 35–49.

Dilip Ratha, (n.d.). *What are remittances?* https://www.imf.org/external/pubs/ft/fandd/basics/pdf/ratha-remittances.pdf.

Di Saint Pierre, F., Martinovic, B., & De Vroome, T. (2015). Return wishes of refugees in the Netherlands: The role of integration, host national identification and perceived discrimination. *Journal of Ethnic and Migration Studies, 41*(11), 1836–1857.

Dreby, J. (2010). *Divided by borders: Mexican migrants and their children.* University of California Press.

Duquette-Rury, L. (2014). Collective remittances and transnational coproduction: The 3 × 1 Program for migrants and household access to public goods in Mexico. *Studies in Comparative International Development, 49*(1), 112–139.

Easthope, H. (2009). Fixed identities in a mobile world? The relationship between mobility, place, and identity. *Identities: Global Studies in Culture and Power, 16*(1), 61–82.

Edelman, M. (2005). Bringing the moral economy back in . . . to the study of 21st-century transnational peasant movements. *American Anthropologist, 107*(3), 331–345.

Ellickson, J. (1972). Islamic institutions: Perception and practice in a village in Bangladesh. *Contributions to Indian Sociology, 6*(1), 1–27.

Elrick, T., & Lewandowska, E. (2008). Matching and making labour demand and supply: Agents in Polish migrant networks of domestic elderly care in Germany and Italy. *Journal of Ethnic and Migration Studies, 34,* 717–734.

Embassy of Japan in Bangladesh. (2019). *Statistical information on Bangladeshi students.* Retrieved June 21, 2023, from https://www.bd.emb-japan.go.jp/itpr_en/statisticalinfo.html.

Erdal, M. B. (2017). Who is the money for? Remittances within and beyond the household in Pakistan. *Asian and Pacific Migration Journal, 21*(4), 437–457.

Erdal, M. B. (2014). The social dynamics of remittance-receiving in Pakistan: Agency and opportunity among non-migrants in a transnational social field. In G. J. Ran & L. S. Liu (Eds.), *Migrant Remittances in South Asia: Social, economic and political implications* (pp. 115–134). Springer.

Erel, U. (2011). Complex belongings: Racialization and migration in a small English city. *Ethnic and Racial Studies, 34*(12), 2048–2068.

Espiritu, E. L. (2003). *Home bound: Filipino American lives across cultures, communities, and countries.* University of California Press.

Espiritu, Y. (2009). Emotions, sex, and money: The lives of Filipino children of immigrants. In N. Foner (Ed.), *Across generations: Immigrant families in America* (pp. 47–71). New York University Press.

Eurenius, A. M. (2020). A family affair: Evidence of chain migration during the mass emigration from the county of Halland in Sweden to the United States in the 1890s. *Population Studies, 74*(1), 103–118.

Fathi, M. (2022). "My life is on hold": Examining home, belonging and temporality among migrant men in Ireland. *Gender, Place & Culture, 29*(8), 1097–1120.

Favell, A. (2015). *Immigration, integration and mobility.* ECPR Press.

Fee, L. K., & Rahman, M. (2006). International labor recruitment: Channeling Bangladeshi migrants to East and Southeast Asia. *Asia-Pacific Population Journal, 21*(1), 85–107.

Fernandez, B. (2013). Traffickers, brokers, employment agents, and social networks: The regulation of intermediaries in the migration of Ethiopian domestic Workers to the Middle East. *International Migration Review, 47*(4), 814–843.

Foner, N., & Dreby, J. (2011). Relations between the generations in immigrant families. *Annual Review of Sociology, 37*, 545–564.

Friedman, T. L. (2000). *The Lexus and the olive tree: Understanding globalization.* Farrar, Straus and Giroux.

Gans, H. J. (2009). First generation decline: Downward mobility among refugees and immigrants. *Ethnic and Racial Studies, 32*(9), 1658–1670.

Gardner, K. (1995). *Global migrants, local lives: Travel and transformation in rural Bangladesh.* Clarendon Press.

Gardner, K. (2002). *Age, narrative and migration: The life course and life histories of Bengali elders in London.* Routledge.

Gardner, K. (2008). Keeping connected: Security, place and social capital in a Londoni village in Sylhet. *Journal of the Royal Anthropological Institute (JRAI), 14*, 447–495.

Gaventa, J. (2003). *Power after Lukes: An overview of theories of power since Lukes and their application to development.* Institute of Development Studies. *8*(11).

Giridharadas, A. (2014). *The true American: Murder and mercy in Texas.* W. W. Norton & Co.

Glazer, N., & Moynihan, D. (1970). *Beyond the melting pot: The Negroes, Puerto Ricans, Jews, Italians and Irish of New York City.* MIT Press.

Glytsos, N. P. (1997). Remitting behaviour of "temporary" and "permanent" migrants: The case of Greeks in Germany and Australia. *Labor, 11*(3), 409–435.

Goldring, L. (2004). Family and collective remittances to Mexico: A multi-dimensional typology. *Development and Change, 35*(4), 799–840.

Goodman, R. (2004), [Review of *Brokered homeland: Japanese Brazilian migrants in Japan*, by J. Hotaka Roth, and *Strangers in the ethnic homeland: Japanese Brazilian return migration in transnational perspective*, by T. Tsuda]. *The Journal of Japanese Studies, 30*(2), 465–471.

Gordon, M. (1964.) *Assimilation in American life: The role of race, religion and national origins.* Oxford University Press.

Gorski, P. S. (2013). What is critical realism? And why should you care? *Contemporary Sociology, 42*(5), 658–670.

Götz, N. (2015). "Moral economy": Its conceptual history and analytical prospects. *Journal of Global Ethics, 11*(2), 147–162.

Gouldner, A. (1960). The norm of reciprocity: A preliminary consideration. *American Sociological Review, 25*(2), 161–178.

Goza, F., & Ryabov, I. (2012). Remittance activity among Brazilians in the US and Canada. *International Migration, 50*(4), 157–185.

Gray, C., & Mueller, V. (2012). Natural disasters and population mobility in Bangladesh. *Proceedings of the National Academy of Sciences of the United States of America, 109*(16), 6000–6005.

Grigg, D. B. (1980). *Population growth and agrarian change.* Cambridge University Press.

Grzymala-Kazlowska, A. (2018). From connecting to social anchoring: Adaptation and "settlement" of Polish migrants in the UK. *Journal of Ethnic and Migration Studies, 44*(2), 252–269.

Guest, P. (1989). *Labor allocation and rural development: Migration in four Javanese villages.* Westview Press.

Haines, D. W., Minami, M., & Yamashita, S. (2007). Transnational migration in East Asia: Japan in comparative focus. *International Migration Review, 41*(4), 963–967.

Hall, S. (2015). Cultural identity and diaspora. In P. Williams & L. Chrisman (Eds.), *Colonial discourse and post-colonial theory* (pp. 392–403). Routledge.

Harper, R. A., & Zubida, H. (2018). Being seen: Visibility, families and dynamic remittances practices. *Migration and Development, 7*(1), 5–25.

Hekman, S. J. (1983). Weber's ideal type: A contemporary reassessment. *Polity, 16*(1), 119–137.

Hernandez-Leon, R. (2008). *Metropolitan migrants: The migration of urban Mexicans to the United States.* University of California Press.

Higuchi, N. (2007). Remittances, investments and social mobility among Bangladeshi and Iranian returnees from Japan. *Proceedings for the 8th Asia and Pacific Migration Research Network Conference on Migration, Development and Poverty Reduction.*

Hollifield, J. (2004). The emerging migration state. *International Migration Review, 38*(3), 885–912.

Hossain, N. (2017). *The Aid Lab: Understanding Bangladesh's unexpected success.* Oxford University Press.

Hotaka Roth, J. (2002). *Brokered homeland: Japanese Brazilian migrants in Japan.* Cornell University Press.

Huennekes, J. (2018). Emotional remittances in the transnational lives of Rohingya families living in Malaysia. *Journal of Refugee Studies, 31*(3), 353–370.

Hugo, G. (1995). International labor migration and the family: Some observations from Indonesia. *Asian and Pacific Migration Journal, 4*(2–3), 273–301.

Human Rights Watch & ACLU. (2022, August 8). *Racial discrimination in the United States.* https://www.hrw.org/report/2022/08/08/racial-discrimination-united-states/human-rights-watch/aclu-joint-submission.

Hunte, C. K. (2004). Workers' remittances, remittance decay and financial deepening in developing countries. *The American Economist, 48*(2), 82–94.

Ibrahim, F. N., & Ruppert, H. (1991). The role of rural-rural migration as a survival strategy in the Sahelian Zone of the Sudan—A case-study in Burush, N Darfur. *GeoJournal, 25*(1), 31–38.

Ikuomola, A. D. (2015). Unintended consequences of remittance: Nigerian migrants and intra-household conflicts. *SAGE Open.* https://doi.org/10.1177/2158244015605353.

Indra, D. M., & Buchignani, N. (1997). Rural landlessness, extended entitlements and inter-household relations in South Asia: A Bangladesh case. *The Journal of Peasant Studies, 24*(3), 25–64.

International Organization for Migration (IOM). (2019). *Bangladesh Annual Migration Report 2017.* Dhaka, Bangladesh. https://publications.iom.int/system/files/pdf/annual_migration_report_2017.pdf.

Iosifides, T. (2016). *Qualitative methods in migration studies: A critical realist perspective.* Routledge.

Islam, M. R. (2018). Climate change, natural disasters and socioeconomic livelihood vulnerabilities: Migration decision among the Char Land people in Bangladesh. *Social Indicators Research, 136*(2), 575–593.

Isotalo, R. (2008). Transnational family dynamics, Second generation and the ties that flex: Palestinian migrants between the United States and the West Bank. *Hawwa, 6*(1), 102–123.

Jackson, M. (2013). *The wherewithal of life: Ethics, migration, and the question of well-being.* University of California Press.

Jacobs, K., & Malpas, J. (2013). Material objects, identity and the home: Towards a relational housing research agenda. *Housing, Theory and Society, 30*(3), 281–292.

Johnson, P., & Stoll, K. (2008). Remittance patterns of Southern Sudanese refugee men: Enacting the global breadwinner role. *Family Relations, 57,* 431–443.

Jureidini, R. (2010). Trafficking and contract migrant workers in the Middle East. *International Migration, 48,* 142–163.

Kabir, M. E., Davey, P., Serrao-Neumann, S., & Hossain, M. (2018). Seasonal drought thresholds and internal migration for adaptation: Lessons from Northern Bangladesh. In M. Hossain, R. Hales, & T. Sarker (Eds.), *Pathways to a Sustainable Economy* (pp. 167–189). Springer.

Kabir, Z. N., Szebehely, M., & Tishelman, C. (2002). Support in old age in the changing society of Bangladesh. *Ageing and Society, 22,* 615–636.

Kakhkharov, J., & Ahunov, M. (2020). Squandering remittances income in conspicuous consumption? In A. Akimov & G. Kazakevitch (Eds.), *30 years since the fall of the Berlin Wall* (pp. 271–288). Palgrave Studies in Economic History.

Kalmijn, M. (2019). Contact and conflict between adult children and their parents in immigrant families: Is integration problematic for family relationships? *Journal of Ethnic & Migration Studies, 45*(9), 1419–1438.

Kandel, W., & D. S. Massey. (2002). The culture of Mexican migration: A theoretical and empirical analysis. *Social Forces, 80*(3), 981–1004.

Kasinitz, P., Mollenkopf, J., & Waters, M. C. (2002). Becoming American/becoming New Yorkers: Immigrant incorporation in a majority minority city. *International Migration Review, 36*(4), 1020–1036.

Khaleque, A. (2011). An overview of the effects of divorce on culture and society within Bangladesh. In R. E. Emery (Ed.), *Cultural sociology of divorce: An encyclopedia.* SAGE Publications.

Kharel, D. (2016). From *lahures* to global cooks: Network migration from the western hills of Nepal to Japan. *Social Science Japan Journal, 19*(2), 173–192.

Khondker, H. H. (2008). Bengali-speaking families in Singapore: Home, nation and the world. *International Migration, 46*(4), 177–198.

Kibria, N. (2009). "Marry into a good family": Transnational reproduction and intergenerational relations in Bangladeshi American families. In N. Foner (Ed.), *Across generations: Immigrant families in America* (pp. 98–113). New York University Press.

Kibria, N. (2011, August 9). *Working hard for the money: Bangladesh faces challenges of large-scale labor migration.* Migration Policy Institute. https://www.migrationpolicy.org/article/working-hard-money-bangladesh-faces-challenges-large-scale-labor-migration.

King, R., Castaldo, A., & Vullnetari, J. (2011). Gendered relations and filial duties along the Greek-Albanian remittance corridor. *Economic Geography, 87*(4), 393–419.

King, R., Mata-Codesal, D., & Vullnetari, J. (2013). Migration, development, gender and the "black box" of remittances: Comparative findings from Albania and Ecuador. *Comparative Migration Studies, 1,* 69-96.

King, R., & Vullnetari, J. (2009). The intersections of gender and generation in Albanian migration, remittances and transnational care. *Geografiska Annaler: Series B, Human Geography, 91*(1), 19–38.

Knights, M. (1996). Bangladeshi immigrants in Italy: From geopolitics to micropolitics. *Transactions of the Institute of British Geographers, 21*(1), 105–123.

Konseiga, A. (2007). Household migration decision as survival strategy: The case of Burkina Faso. *Journal of African Economies, 16*(2), 198–223.

Korteweg, A. C. (2017). The failures of "immigrant integration": The gendered racialized production of non-belonging. *Migration Studies, 5*(3), 428–444.

Kossoudji, S. A., & Cobb-Clark, D. A. (2002). Coming out of the shadows: Learning about legal status and wages from the legalized population. *Journal of Labor Economics, 20,* 598–628.

Kunz, R., Maisenbacher, J., & Paudel, L. N. (2020). The financialization of remittances: Governing through emotions. *Review of International Political Economy, 28*(6), 1607–1631.

La Barbera, M. C. (2015). Identity and migration: An introduction. In *Identity and migration in Europe: Multidisciplinary perspectives* (pp. 1–13). Springer.

Lacroix, T. (2013). Collective remittances and integration: North African and North Indian comparative perspectives. *Journal of Ethnic and Migration Studies, 39*(6), 1019–1035.

Lacroix, T. (2014). Conceptualizing transnational engagements: A structure and agency perspective on (hometown) transnationalism. *The International Migration Review, 48*(3), 643–679.

Landolt, P. (2001). Salvadoran economic transnationalism: Embedded strategies for household maintenance, immigrant incorporation, and entrepreneurial expansion. *Global Networks, 1*(3), 217–242.

Lee, J., & Zhou, M. (2014). From unassimilable to exceptional: The rise of Asian Americans and "stereotype promise." *New Diversities, 16*(1), 7–22.

Lee, J., & Zhou, M. (2017). Why class matters less for Asian-American academic achievement. *Journal of Ethnic and Migration Studies, 43*(14), 2316–2330.

Levitt, P. (2001). *The transnational villagers.* University of California Press.

Levitt, P. (2004, October 1). *Transnational migrants: When "home" means more than one country.* Migration Policy Institute. https://www.migrationpolicy.org/article/transnational-migrants-when-home-means-more-one-country.

Lindley, A. (2009). The early-morning phonecall: Remittances from a refugee diaspora perspective. *Journal of Ethnic and Migration Studies, 35*(8), 1315–1334.

Lipski, J. (2014). Roderick's and Peregrine's protean identities. In *Quest of the Self: Masquerade and Travel in the Eighteenth-Century Novel* (pp. 105–133). Brill.

Liu-Farrer, G. (2009). Educationally channeled international labor mobility: Contemporary student migration from China to Japan. *International Migration Review, 43*(1), 178–204.

Liu-Farrer, G. (2011). *Labour migration from China to Japan: International students, transnational migrants.* Nissan Institute, Routledge Japanese Studies, Book 77.

Logan, J. R., Alba, R. D., & Zhang, W. (2002). Immigrant enclaves and ethnic communities in New York and Los Angeles. *American Sociological Review, 67*(2), 299–322.

Love, E. (2017). *Islamophobia and Racism in America.* New York University Press.

Lucas, R.E.B., & O. Stark. (1985). Motivations to remit: Evidence from Botswana. *The Journal of Political Economy, 93*(5), 901–918.

Mahmood, R. A. (1994). Adaptation to a new world: Experience of Bangladeshis in Japan. *International Migration, 32*(4), 513–532.

Mahmood, R. A. (1995). Data on migration from Bangladesh. *Asian and Pacific Migration Journal, 4*(4), 531–541.

Mahmud, H. (2013). Enemy or ally: Migrants, intermediaries and the state in Bangladeshi migration to Japan and the United States. *Migration and Development, 2*(1), 1–15.

Mahmud, H. (2014). "It's my money": Social class and the perception of remittances among Bangladeshi migrants in Japan. *Current Sociology, 62*(3), 412–430.

Mahmud, H. (2016). Impact of the destination state on migrants' remittances: A study of remitting among Bangladeshi migrants in the USA, the UAE and Japan. *Migration and Development, 5*(1), 79–98.

Mahmud, H. (2017). Social determinants of remitting practices among Bangladeshi migrants in Japan. *Sociological Perspectives, 60*(1), 95–112.

Mahmud, H. (2020). From individual motivations to social determinants: Towards a sociology of migrants' remittances. *International Social Science Journal, 70*(237–238), 175–188.

Mahmud, H. (2021). Beyond economics: The family, belonging and remittances among the Bangladeshi migrants in Los Angeles. *International Migration, 59*(5), 134–148.

Makina, D., & Masenge, A. (2015). The time pattern of remittances and the decay hypothesis: Evidence from migrants in South Africa. *Migration Letters, 12*(1), 79–90.

Manzenreiter, W. (2017). Living under more than one sun: The Nikkei diaspora in the Americas. *Contemporary Japan, 29*(2), 193–213.

Mapril, José. (2011). The patron and the madman: Migration, success and the (in)visibility of failure among Bangladeshis in Portugal. *Social Anthropology, 19*, 288–296.

Mapril, José. (2014). The dreams of middle class: Consumption, life-course and migration between Bangladesh and Portugal. *Modern Asian Studies, 48*, 693–719.

Markova, E., & Reilly, B. (2007). Bulgarian migrant remittances and legal status: Some micro level evidence from Madrid. *South-Eastern Europe Journal of Economics, 5*, 55–69.

Massey, D. S. (1987). Understanding Mexican migration to the United States. *The American Journal of Sociology, 92*(60), 1372–1403.

Massey D. S., Arango, J., Hugo, G., Kouaouci, A., Pellegrino, A., & Taylor, J. E. (1993). Theories of international migration: A review and appraisal. *Population and Development Review, 19*(3), 431–466.

Massey, D. S., Arango, J., Hugo, G., Kouaouci, A., Pellegrino, A., & Taylor, J. E. (1994). An evaluation of international migration theory: The North American case. *Population and Development Review, 20*(4), 699–751.

Mazzucato, V. (2008). The double engagement: Transnationalism and integration. Ghanaian migrants' lives between Ghana and The Netherlands. *Journal of Ethnic and Migration Studies, 34*(2), 199–216.

Mazzucato, V. (2011). Reverse remittances in the migration–development nexus: Two-way flows between Ghana and the Netherlands. *Population, Space and Place, 17*(5), 454–468.

McKenzie, S., & Menjívar, C. (2011). The meanings of migration, remittances and gifts: Views of Honduran women who stay. *Global Networks, 11*(1), 63–81.

Meyer, S. (2020)." Home is where I spend my money": Testing the remittance decay hypothesis with ethnographic data from an Austrian-Turkish community. *Social Inclusion, 8*(1), 275–284.

Montes, V. (2013). The role of emotions in the construction of masculinity: Guatemalan migrant men, transnational migration, and family relations. *Gender and Society, 27*(4), 469–490.

Morad, M., & Puppa, F. D. (2019). Bangladeshi migrant associations in Italy: Transnational engagement, community formation and regional unity. *Ethnic and Racial Studies, 42*, 1788–1807.

Morshed, M. M. (2018). *Parenting, identity and culture in an era of migration and globalization: How Bangladeshi parents navigate and negotiate child-rearing practices in the USA.* Doctoral dissertation, University of Massachusetts Amherst.

Moskal, M. (2015). "When I think home I think family here and there": Translocal and social ideas of home in narratives of migrant children and young people. *Geoforum, 58*, 143–152.

Munck, R. (2008). Globalisation, governance and migration: An introduction. *Third World Quarterly, 29*, 1227–1246.

Myers, D., & Lee, S. W. (1998). Temporal analysis of residential assimilation. *International Migration Review, 32*(3), 593–625.

Neumayer, E. (2006). Unequal access to foreign spaces: How states use visa restrictions to regulate mobility in a globalized world. *Transactions of the Institute of British Geographers, 31*, 72–84.

Nugent, J. (1985). The old-age security motive for fertility. *Population and Development Review, 11*(1), 75–97.

Obinna, D. N. (2014). The challenges of American legal permanent residency for family- and employment-based petitioners. *Migration and Development, 3*(2), 272–284.

Oishi, N. (2005). *Women in motion: Globalization, state policies, and labor migration in Asia.* Stanford University Press.

Oishi, N. (2012). The limits of immigration policies: The challenges of highly skilled migration in Japan. *American Behavioral Scientist, 56*(8), 1080–1100.

Okabe, M. (2011). The "outside in"—An overview of Japanese immigration policy from the perspective of international relations. In E. Guild & S. Mantu (Eds.), *Constructing and imagining labour migration: Perspectives of control from five continents* (pp. 189–204). Ashgate.

Onasch, E. A. (2017). Lessons on the boundaries of belonging: Racialization and symbolic boundary drawing in the French civic integration program. *Social Problems, 64*(4), 577–593.

Ossipow, L., Counilh, A., & Chimienti, M. (2019). Racialization in Switzerland: Experiences of children of refugees from Kurdish, Tamil and Vietnamese backgrounds. *Comparative Migration Studies, 7*(19), 1–19.

Paerregaard, K. (2015). *Return to sender: The moral Economy of Peru's migrant remittances.* University of California Press.

Painter, G., Yang, L. H., & Yu, Z. (2003). Heterogeneity in Asian American homeownership: The impact of household endowments and immigrant status. *Urban Studies, 40*(3), 505–530.

Pande, A. (2017). Mobile masculinities: Migrant Bangladeshi men in South Africa. *Gender and Society, 31*(3), 383–406.

Park, R., & Burgess, E. (1921). *Introduction to the science of sociology.* University of Chicago Press.

Park, R. E. (1950). *Race and culture.* Free Press.

Parreñas, R. S. (2001). *Servants of globalization: Migration and domestic work.* Stanford University Press.

Parreñas, R. S. (2010). Homeward bound: the circular migration of entertainers between Japan and the Philippines. *Global Networks, 10*(3), 301–323.

Patel, V. V., Rajpathak, S., & Karasz, A. (2012). Bangladeshi immigrants in New York City: A community-based health needs assessment of a hard to reach population. *Journal of Immigrant and Minority Health, 14*(5), 767–773.

Paul, A. M. (2015). Negotiating migration, performing gender. *Social Forces, 94*(1), 271–293.

Paul, A. M. (2017). *Multinational maids: Stepwise migration in a global labor market.* Cambridge University Press.

Pesando, L. M., Rotondi, V., Stranges, M., Kashyap, R., & Billari, F. C. (2020). The internetization of international migration. *Population and Development Review, 47*(1), 70–111.

Peter, K. B. (2010). Transnational family ties, remittance motives, and social death among Congolese migrants: A socio-anthropological analysis. *Journal of Comparative Family Studies, 41*(2), 225–243.

Pinger, P. (2010). Come back or stay? Spend here or there? Return and remittances: The case of Moldova. *International Migration, 48*(5), 142–173.

Piper, N. (2003). Wife or worker? Worker or wife? Marriage and cross-border migration in contemporary Japan. *Population, Space and Place, 9*(6), 457–469.

Piper, N., & Roces, M. (2003). *Wife or worker: Asian women and migration.* Rowman & Littlefield.

Portes, A., & Rumbaut, R. (1996). *Immigrant America: A portrait.* University of California Press.

Portes, A., & Zhou, M. (1993). The new second generation: Segmented assimilation and its variants. *Annals of the American Academy of Political and Social Sciences, 530*, 74–96.

Puppa, F. D., & King, R. (2019). The new "twice migrants": Motivations, experiences and disillusionments of Italian-Bangladeshis relocating to London. *Journal of Ethnic and Migration Studies, 45*(11), 1936–1952.

Qayum, N. (2017, October 5). *Chasing the Dubai dream in Italy: Bangladeshi migration to Europe.* Migration Policy Institute. https://www.migrationpolicy.org/article /chasing-dubai-dream-italy-bangladeshi-migration-europe.

Rahman, M. M., Giedraitis, V. R., & Akhtar, T. M. (2013). The social sanction of divorce: Who ultimately pays the social costs of its adverse effects? *Sociology and Anthropology, 1*(1), 26–33.

Rahman, M. M., & Yeoh, B. S. (2008). The social organization of Hundi: Channelling migrant remittances from East and South-East Asia to Bangladesh. *Asian Population Studies, 4*(1), 5–29.

Ran, G. J., & Liu, L. S. (2023). Re-constructing reverse family remittances: The case of new Chinese immigrant families in New Zealand. *Journal of Ethnic and Migration Studies, 49*(1), 313–331.

Rashid, S. R. (2016). *Uncertain tomorrows: Livelihoods, capital and risk in labour migration from Bangladesh.* University Press Limited.

Redstone Akresh, I. R. (2006). Occupational mobility among legal immigrants to the United states. *International Migration Review, 40*(4), 854–884.

Riessman, C. K. (1993). *Narrative analysis.* Vol. 30 of SAGE Qualitative Research Methods Series. SAGE Publications.

Rindfuss, R. R., Piotrowski, M., Entwisle, B., Edmeades, J., & Faust, K. (2012). Migrant remittances and the web of family obligations: Ongoing support among spatially extended kin in North-East Thailand, 1984–94. *Population Studies: A Journal of Demography, 66*(1): 87–104.

Rodriguez, C. E. (2018). *America, as seen on TV: How television shapes immigrant expectations around the globe.* New York University Press.

Rodriguez, R. M. (2010). *Migrants for export: How the Philippine state brokers labor to the world.* University of Minnesota Press.

Rodrik, D. (2011). *The globalization paradox: Democracy and the future of the world economy.* W. W. Norton & Co.

Rozario, S. (2007). Outside the moral economy? Single female migrants and the changing Bangladeshi family. *The Australian Journal of Anthropology, 18*(2), 154–171.

Rubinstein, R. L., & Madeiros, K. D. (2005). Home, self and identity. In G. Rowles & H. Chaudhury (Eds.), *Home and identity in late life: International perspectives* (pp. 47–62). Springer Publishing.

Rumbaut, R. G., & Portes, A. (2001). *Ethnicities: Children of immigrants in America.* University of California Press.

Sabharwal, M., Becerra, A., & Oh, S. (2022). From the Chinese Exclusion Act to the COVID-19 Pandemic: A historical analysis of "otherness" experienced by Asian Americans in the United States. *Public Integrity, 24*(6), 535–549.

Salami, B., & Nelson, S. (2014). The downward occupational mobility of internationally educated nurses to domestic workers. *Nursing Enquiry, 21*(2), 153–161.

Sana, M. (2005). Buying membership in the transnational community: Migrant remittances, social status, and assimilation. *Population Research and Policy Review, 24*, 231–261.

Sana, M., and Massey, D. S. (2005). Household composition, family migration, and community context: Migrant remittances in four countries. *Social Science quarterly, 86*(2), 509–528.

Sasaki, K. (2013). To return or not to return: The changing meaning of mobility among Japanese Brazilians, 1908–2010. In B. Xiang, B.S.A. Yeoh, and M. Toyota (Eds.), *Return: Nationalizing transnational mobility in Asia* (pp. 21–38). Duke University Press.

Savage, M., Bagnall, G., & Longhurst, B. (2005). *Globalization and belonging.* SAGE Publications.

Sawada, Y., Mahmud, M., & Kitano, N. (2018). *Economic and social development of Bangladesh.* Springer International Publishing.

Schiller, N. G., Basch, L., & Blanc, C. S. (1995). From immigrant to transmigrant: Theorizing transnational migration. *Anthropological Quarterly, 68*(1), 48–63.

Scott, J. C. (1976). *The moral economy of the peasant: Subsistence and rebellion in Southeast Asia.* Yale University Press.

Scott, S., & Cartledge, K. H. (2009). Migrant assimilation in Europe: A transnational family affair. *International Migration Review, 43*(1), 60–89.

Sen, A. (2016). Food, place, and memory: Bangladeshi fish stores on Devon Avenue, Chicago. *Food and Foodways, 24*(1–2), 67–88.

Seol, D.-H., & Skrentny, J. D. (2009). Why is there so little migrant settlement in East Asia? *International Migration Review, 43*, 578–620.

Sharma, D. (2006). Historical traces of *hundi*, sociocultural understanding, and criminal abuses of *hawala*. *International Criminal Justice Review, 16*(2), 99–121.

Shen, Y. (2016). Filial daughters? Agency and subjectivity of rural migrant women in Shanghai. *The China Quarterly, 226*, 519–537.

Shipper, A. W. (2002). The political construction of foreign workers in Japan. *Critical Asian Studies, 34*(1), 41–68.

Siddiqiu, T. (2003, June 22–24). *Migration as a livelihood strategy of the poor: The Bangladesh case* [Paper presentation]. Regional Conference on Migration, Development & Pro-Poor Policy Choices in Asia 2003, Dhaka, Bangladesh.

Sikder, M.J.U., & Higgins, V. (2017). Remittances and social resilience of migrant households in rural Bangladesh. *Migration and Development, 6*(2), 253–275.

Sikder, M.J.U., Higgins, V., & Ballis, P. H. (2017). *Remittance income and social resilience among migrant households in rural Bangladesh.* Palgrave Macmillan.

Singh, S. (2006). Towards a sociology of money and family in the Indian diaspora. *Contributions to Indian Sociology, 40*(4), 376–98.

Singh, S., Cabraal, A., & Robertson, S. (2010). Remittances as a medium of relationship and belonging. In A. Babacan & S. Singh (Eds.), *Migration, belonging and the nation state* (pp. 85–103). Cambridge Scholar Publishing.

Singh, S., Robertson, S., & Cabraal, A. (2012). Transnational family money: Remittances, gifts and inheritance. *Journal of Intercultural Studies, 33*(5), 475–492.

Smith, M. P., & Guarnizo, L. (1998). *Transnationalism from below.* University of California Press.

Smith, R. (2006). *Mexican New York: Transnational lives of new immigrants.* University of California Press.

Soehl, T., & Waldinger, R. (2012). Inheriting the homeland? Intergenerational transmission of cross-border ties in migrant families. *American Journal of Sociology, 118*(3), 778–813.

Soysal, Y. N. (1994). *Limits of citizenship: Migrants and postnational membership in Europe.* University of Chicago Press.

Spaan, E. (1994). *Taikongs* and *calos*: The role of middlemen and brokers in Javanese international migration. *International Migration Review, 28*(1), 93–113.

Spener, D. (2009). *Clandestine crossings: Migrants and coyotes on the Texas–Mexico Border.* Cornell University Press.

Steinhardt, M. F., & Wedemeier, J. (2012). The labor market performance of naturalized immigrants in Switzerland—New findings from the Swiss labor force survey. *Journal of International Migration and Integration, 13*, 223–242.

Stevanovic-Fenn, N. (2012). *Remittances and the moral economies of Bangladeshi New York immigrants in light of the economic crisis.* Doctoral Dissertation, Columbia University.

Stodolska, M., and Santos, C. A. (2006). You must think of *familia*: The everyday lives of Mexican migrants in destination communities. *Social and Cultural Geographer, 7*(4), 627–647.

Strasser, E., Kraler, A., Bonjour, S., & Bilger, V. (2009). Doing family. *The History of the Family, 14*(2), 165–176.

Taylor, E. J. (1999). The new economics of labour migration and the role of remittances in the migration process. *International Migration, 37*(1), 63–88.

Thai, H. C. (2006). Money and masculinity among Vietnamese low wage immigrants in transnational families. *International Journal of Sociology of the Family, 32*(2), 247–271.

Thai, H. C. (2014). *Insufficient funds: The culture of money in low-wage transnational families.* Stanford University Press.

Thompson, E. P. (1991). *The making of the English working class.* Penguin Books.

Thompson, E. P. (1971). The moral economy of the English crowd in the eighteenth century. *Past & present, 50*(1), 76–136.

Thränhardt, D. (1999). Closed doors, back doors, side doors: Japan's nonimmigration policy in comparative perspective. *Journal of Comparative Policy Analysis: Research and Practice, 1*(2), 203–223.

Toruńczyk-Ruiz, S., & Brunarska, Z. (2020). Through attachment to settlement: Social and psychological determinants of migrants' intentions to stay. *Journal of Ethnic and Migration Studies, 46*(15), 3191–3209.

Tseng, Y., & Wang, H. (2011). Governing migrant workers at a distance: Managing the temporary status of guestworkers in Taiwan. *International Migration, 51*(4), 1–19.

Tsuda, T. (2003). *Strangers in the ethnic homeland: Japanese Brazilian return migration in transnational perspective.* Columbia University Press.

Tsuda, T. (2010). Ethnic return migration and the nation-state: Encouraging the diaspora to return "home." *Nations and Nationalism, 16*(4), 616–636.

Vanwey, L. K. (2004). Altruistic and contractual remittances between male and female migrants and households in rural Thailand. *Demography, 41*(4), 739–756.

Vaughan, J. M., & Huennekens, P. (2018, January 11). *Bangladesh: A case study in chain migration.* Center for Immigration Studies. https://cis.org/Report/Bangladesh-Case-Study-Chain-Migration.

Vera-Sanso, P. (2005). "They don't need it, and I can't give it": Filial support in South India. In P. Kreager & E. Schröder-Butterfill (Eds.), *Ageing without children: European and Asian perspectives on elderly access to support networks* (pp. 77–105). Berghahn Books.

Vora, N. (2013). *Impossible citizens: Dubai's Indian diaspora.* Duke University Press.

Vora, N., & Koch, N. (2015). Everyday inclusions: Rethinking ethnocracy, *kafala,* and belonging in the Arabian Peninsula. *Studies in Ethnicity and Nationalism, 15*(3), 540–552.

Waite, L., & Cook, J. (2011). Belonging among diasporic African communities in the UK: Plurilocal homes and simultaneity of place attachments. *Emotion, Space and Society, 4*(4), 238–248.

Wakefield, J. C. (1993). Is altruism part of human nature? Toward a theoretical foundation for the helping professions. *Social Service Review, 67*(3), 406–458.

Waldinger, R. (1994). The making of an immigrant niche. *International Migration Review, 28*(1), 3–30.

Waldinger, R. (2015). *The cross-border connection: Immigrants, emigrants, and their homelands.* Harvard University Press.

Wall, K., & Gouveia, R. (2014). Changing meanings of family in personal relationships. *Current Sociology, 62*(3), 352–373.

Walton, G. M., & Cohen, G. L. (2007). A question of belonging: Race, social fit, and achievement. *Journal of Personality and Social Psychology, 92*(1), 82.

Walzer, M. (1983). *Spheres of justice: A defense of pluralism and equality.* Basic Books.

Werbner, P. S. (1990). *The migration process: Capital, gifts and offerings among British Pakistanis.* Berg.

Wherry, F. F. (2017). How relational accounting matters. In N. Bandelj, F. F. Wherry, & V. A. Zelizer (Eds.), *Money talks: Explaining how money really works* (pp. 57–69). Princeton University Press.

Wise, J. M. (2000). Home: Territory and identity. *Cultural Studies, 14*(2), 295–310.

Wong, M. (2006). The gendered politics of remittance in Ghanaian transnational families. *Economic Geography, 82*(4), 355–381.

Wood, C. H. (1981). Structural changes and household strategies: A conceptual framework for the study of rural migration. *Human Organization, 40*(4), 338–344.

World Bank. (1981). *Labor migration from Bangladesh to the Middle East*. World Bank Staff Working Paper No. 454. https://documents1.worldbank.org/curated/en /750081468768650896/pdf/multi-page.pdf\.

Yeoh, B.S.A., Leng, C. H., Dung, V.T.K., & Cheng, Y.-E. (2013). Between two families: The social meaning of remittances for Vietnamese marriage migrants in Singapore. *Global Networks, 13*(4), 441–458.

Zeitlyn, B. (2012). The Sylheti bari and the Londoni flat. *Space and Culture, 15*(4), 317–329.

Zelizer, V. A. (1994). *The social meaning of money*. Basic Books.

Zelizer, V. A. (1996). Payments and social ties. *Sociological Forum, 11*, 481–495.

Zelizer, V. A. (2000). The purchase of intimacy. *Law & Social Inquiry, 25*, 817–48.

Zelizer, V. A. (2010). *Economic lives: How culture shapes the economy*. Princeton University Press.

Zhao, Y. (2002). Causes and consequences of return migration: Recent evidence from China. *Journal of Comparative Economics, 30*(2), 376–394.

Zhou, M. (1997). Growing up American: The challenge confronting immigrant children and children of immigrants. *Annual Review of Sociology, 23*, 63–95.

Zhou, M. (2007). Conflict, coping, and reconciliation: Intergenerational relations in Chinese immigrant families. In N. Foner (Ed.), *Across generations: Immigrant families in America* (pp. 21–46). New York University Press.

Zhou, M. (2009). How neighborhoods matter for immigrant children: The formation of educational resources in Chinatown, Koreatown and Pico Union, Los Angeles. *Journal of Ethnic and Migration Studies, 35*(7), 1153–1179.

Zhou, M., & Li, R. (2018). Remittances for collective consumption and social status compensation: Variations on transnational practices among Chinese international migrants. *International Migration Review, 52*(1), 4–42.

Zolberg, A. (1999). Matters of state: Theorizing immigration policy. In C. Hirschman, P. Kasinitz, & J. Dewind (Eds.), *The handbook of international migration: The American experience* (pp. 71–93). Russell Sage Foundation.

Index

About the Author

HASAN MAHMUD is an assistant professor of sociology at Northwestern University in Qatar. He is a coeditor, with Min Zhou, of *Beyond Economic Migration: Social, Historical, and Political Factors in US Immigration*.